THE GLOBAL SUITCASE

THE GLOBAL SUITCASE

Inspiring stories of adventure
from 25 intrepid travel writers

MARY J DINAN

NEW
HOLLAND

First published in 2014 by
New Holland Publishers
London • Sydney • Cape Town • Auckland
www.newhollandpublishers.com • www.newholland.com.au

The Chandlery Unit 114 50 Westminster Bridge Road London SE1 7QY
1/66 Gibbes Street Chatswood NSW 2067 Australia
Wembley Square First Floor Solan Road Gardens Cape Town 8001 South Africa
218 Lake Road Northcote Auckland New Zealand

A catalogue record of this book is available at the British Library and at the National
Library of Australia

ISBN: 9781780094571

10 9 8 7 6 5 4 3 2 1

Publisher: Alan Whiticker
Project editor: Simona Hill
Designer: Keisha Galbraith
Cover design: Kim Pearce
Production director: Olga Dementiev
Printer: Toppan Leefung Printing Limited

Follow New Holland Publishers on
Facebook: www.facebook.com/NewHollandPublishers

25 percent from royalties from the sale of this book will benefit The BBC Children in Need
Appeal, a company limited by guarantee (charity number 802052 in England & Wales and
SC039557 in Scotland).

CONTENTS

INTRODUCTION

by Mary J Dinan

Don't think you've found salvation or that the day is won,
When you reach your destination, the journey's just begun,
Lyrics by Kieran Goss singer/songwriter

I have always loved travel and travel literature. At times, in bookshops, I've found it hard to decide what to choose. I often wanted all the books written about exotic and not so exotic places. One afternoon as I was perusing the travel department in my local bookshop, I had an idea to interview and meet the people behind these wonderful stories. If these authors can all sit on the shelves together, so to speak, then why not put them all in the same book?

While continuing my day job at a special education school, I secretly hatched a plan. I wanted to write a treasury of interviews with people who had made and experienced their own fascinating journeys. I decided to contact as many travel writers as I could and broadened my category to include singers, actors and other people with a record of extraordinary travel. Monday morning blues were a thing of the past. There was no going back. The response I got from the travel writers and songwriters I contacted encouraged me enormously. I had entered a new world. Taking full advantage of my long school holidays, travel was now on my agenda. I was planning to read the books of my travel heroes then cross the sea to meet them. Many were in London but I also looked forward to a trip to Paris.

There is a saying that 'travel broadens the mind' and I was determined to get into the psyche of these people, study their characters and hear about their life-changing experiences either during their adventures or as a result of them. I wanted to meet people who have helped make the physical world a better place.

Many participants in this project showed great mental strength during their incredible or dangerous journeys, displaying courage beyond understanding. In particular, I think of Jonathan Dimbleby's trip to Russia. He went there feeling burdened with grief and despair, and returned with a sense of hope and recovery. Another story that stands out, in my mind, is that of Rosie Swayle Pope, MBE, who courageously sailed in an open boat to Australia from Gibraltar and later took a solo trip across the *Atlantic*. She travelled through unspeakable dangers, intent on bringing attention to a cause. Like Rosie Swayle Pope, Marianne Du Toit also travelled for the purpose of helping others. She rode a horse from Argentina to New York on a mission to raise funds to provide therapeutic riding to needy people, not thinking about the dangers she would encounter. Ken Doyle, singer with Irish band Bagatelle, tackled Route 66 on a Harley Davidson to help sick children.

Author Zoë Sallis set off on a quest to interview Fidel Castro in Cuba but her travels took her to Nelson Mandela's home in South Africa instead. She said her book 'wouldn't be complete' without that interview though it had taken five years to secure her meeting with Nelson Mandela. Christopher P Baker, the American travel writer, rode a 1,000cc BMW Paris-Dakar motorbike through Cuba back in the 1990s as part of his 7,000-mile (11,265 km) odyssey and luckier than Zoe, he did catch up with Fidel Castro for a brief meeting. Chris explored the country he fell in love with, taking a close look at Cuban society and history. He documented all in his book; *Mi Moto Fidel: Motorcycling through Cuba.*

I was intrigued by the Irish journalist Garry Finnegan who packed his bag and moved to Beijing, grappling with strange customs along the way, as much as with award-winning UK travel writer Geoff Hill, who rode from Chile to Alaska, then Belfast to Delhi, later taking in the Pan-American Highway, and ultimately around the world from Adelaide, all on a motorbike.

After the initial excitement of getting my project underway, panic set in. I had never written a book before, only articles for my local paper. I originally came from a radio and television presenting background but had changed direction in my career. Like my travel heroes, I battled against the odds on many occasions to follow my dream.

A HEALING ADVENTURE IN RUSSIA

Jonathan Dimbleby

Jonathan Dimbleby has had a varied career as a current affairs and political commentator in television and radio. In 1994 he compiled and presented a documentary about the Prince of Wales called *Charles, the Private Man – the Public Role*. He wrote a biography too, entitled *The Prince of Wales*. It proved to be a controversial study of the heir to the British throne, and was compiled after being granted unfettered access to the future king, and involved hours spent in deep and honest conversations with him, as well as time with the Prince's personal staff and close friends.

In July 1997, the territory of Hong Kong, a colony of the British Empire, reverted to the People's Republic of China. In the same year, Jonathan recorded a series about the final five years of British rule in Hong Kong called *The Last Governor*. Chris Patten, a former MP, Chairman of the Conservative Party and close friend, had been appointed the last governor of Hong Kong in 1992. As a result Jonathan had privileged access to the Governor and his documentary provided an insight into relations between Britain and China.

Jonathan has written and presented programmes about natural and political tragedies as far afield as Ethiopia and Kosovo. His writing extended to a biography about his father Richard Dimbleby, as well as a book entitled, *The Palestinians*. His television documentaries include *The Eagle and the Bear* and *The Cold War Game*, and he presented flagship political programmes for ITV for many years. He is well known for his presentation of BBC Radio 4's *Any Questions?*

Jonathan first visited Russia during the Cold War in the 1980s and thereafter developed a strong desire to discover the real Russia, to scratch beyond the surface of common perceptions and investigate the country that we don't usually see or hear about. Many years later the opportunity came his way and, Jonathan returned to Russia with a film crew and a vocabulary of no more than a half a dozen Russian words. The mammoth journey was to take him 10,000 miles (16,000 km) into rural Russia, via St. Petersburg and Moscow, taking in a Madonna concert *en route*. He travelled through the war-torn Caucasus to the Caspian Sea and the mouth of the Volga River, passing many cities to cross the Ural Mountains, Siberia and reach Vladivostok. The contrasting land of rich oligarchs and of peasants drew Jonathan. He wanted to see the disparity and diverse lifestyles.

In preparation, he researched the iconic people, events, wars and invasions that have shaped Russia, from the Vikings to the modern day, including Ivan the Terrible, the Invasion of the Mongols, Peter the Great, the Bolshevik Revolution 1917, the murder of Tsar Nicholas, communism under Lenin and Stalin, and contemporary Russia under Gorbachev, Yeltsin and Putin. His incredible journey crossed nine time zones and was traversed by boat, train and on foot. Dimbleby describes his travels as, 'a once in a life-time experience', which gave him the freedom to explore the past, present and future of the largest country in the world.

He undertook his journey at a time of personal despair: Susan Chilcott, the English soprano with whom he lived died a premature death caused by cancer. The bereavement left him devastated and with no inclination to carry on living. He recalls that he could barely get of bed. Planning the Russian journey hung in the balance. This was to be a physically demanding trip and his heart wasn't in it; he was too emotionally drained and in a frail psychological state.

Yet, rejuvenation and healing followed his journey, proving that the physical endurance of epic travel can be therapeutic. Russian landscape, history and personal journey melded, eventually becoming a five-hour documentary for BBC television called *Russia – a Journey with Jonathan Dimbleby*.

THE INTERVIEW

I met Jonathan in London on an unseasonably warm day. He greeted me with a warm smile and ushered me into his homely but elegant living room. I found him an easy person to converse with. Bearing in mind his busy schedule, I assured him I would only keep him for a short while, 'That is, unless I decide to do to you, what you did to Gorbachev,' I joked. In Jonathan's book *Russia*, he explains how he was allocated a five-minute interview with Gorbachev but ignoring all signals to stop, he managed to keep the President talking for almost half an hour.

So how did you feel about interviewing Gorbachev?

'Well, I was extremely tense because there was the pressure of only having a few minutes with the President... I thought, here I am, the first British television journalist to interview the President of the Soviet Union. It could all come to naught because I had to wait day after day. The butterflies were permanently at work and they never stopped flying and then when he came for the interview it was very interesting.

From the beginning, I felt sympathy for him; I felt he was a sad man. He was not a contentious person; nor was he arrogant. He was undoubtedly strong and he could be ruthless and tough and he was gifted with intelligence. Whatever else one may think or not think about Margaret Thatcher, she saw those qualities when she said, "Here is a man I can do business with," and I felt the same. I thought, here is someone that belongs to the human race. For me, it was a feather in my cap, but more importantly, I felt I had engaged directly with someone who ostensibly came from a different planet politically and diplomatically. I was able to have a proper conversation with him and that was a very powerful experience that I have never forgotten. I've met him maybe three times since but nothing matches that first meeting.'

Did Jonathan consider Gorbachev to be the most inspirational person he had met on his travels?

'I'm not given to hero worship but there are two people I feel, as it were, to be inspiring. One is Gorbachev, and the other is President Nyerere of Tanzania. He was the first leader of Tanzania and handed over peacefully to his successor who was, as it happened, a socialist. Socialism failed in Tanzania as it has elsewhere. He had a wisdom and decency so rare in political leaders. You meet smartness; you meet toughness and an ability to see short term. You see the spin. You see the reprehensible qualities in both Gorbachev and Nyerere and their transcending qualities.

They were in power in very different circumstances and coped with great strains and stresses with wisdom. There's a quality of wisdom about Obama. People don't necessarily define it in lesser terms but that's what makes Obama attractive. It isn't because he's smart with words.'

Jonathan has travelled extensively which must have provided plenty of time to think. I ask if this thinking time has contributed to his state of mind.

'Well I don't know because I'm naturally, I fear, not an un-troubled soul. I think the really important eye-opening quality of travel is the realisation that you or your country doesn't have a solution to everything. You are very blessed if you live in the United Kingdom and obviously Ireland and the British Isles. You are blessed by the environment, by the relative prosperity, by heritage, which has been very painful in places. In other parts of the world individuals long for that relative liberty and prosperity. It is humbling to witness people who are experiencing danger or poverty, or both. They have a quality of resilience. It's that quality and humanity that transcends, and that for me is inspiring.'

I probe for some nostalgic memories.

'Well, because I was born in the 1940s, even though our family was quite well off, I've a memory, which is inscribed into me still of myself in Hope Cove, Devon, near where I live now. My brother David is on film taken by my father, Richard, with an old cine camera. David is shown wading across the sand like a policeman. A tiny little creature [me] is crawling and then the camera pans up and shows this little creature crawling toward the large waves. I suspect my brother was either diverted to other things or my father and mother picked me up, and removed me. That's one of the first memories. Another is of going away from home for the first time in the summer. I must have been eleven years old. I went with David to the Lake District, where my father's company made one of the first series of holiday television programmes for the BBC. The family went to six different places. It was interesting and historically it was quite important. It was the mid-1950s when people started to think about taking holidays for the first time, particularly in Europe. It was only a decade after the end of the war. David was seventeen at the time and had a 1926 Austen Seven. Most of the time while I was there I was water-skiing, and for the purposes of the film, it was required that I fall over after a little bit, which for an eleven year old was humiliating. I dutifully fell over, having run and clowned my way into falling. As a child at boarding school, we were occasionally allowed to watch television. In those days, in the gap in between programmes, they would run little bits of film. They didn't have voice-overs or trailers for other programmes and what kept coming up was me water-skiing, clowning around, falling off, and all the children around me saying mockingly, "Jonathan can't water-ski".

Another memory is having ham and eggs in a bed and breakfast place. That was the extent of it. You see the memories aren't very dramatic, except in terms of the intensity of the memory of a child.'

I ask Jonathan if he thinks his father influenced his choice of career and, maybe, served as an inspiration. (His father had been a war correspondent with the BBC and travelled a great deal).

'Well Mary, that's a really good question, I think I was absolutely determined to do anything but be a reporter. I didn't like leaving home. I didn't want to travel. Although on the surface, I was ebullient and cheekily confident, I was actually quite insecure and shy. I would only go to parties under coercion and bribery. However, I tried everything and kept coming back to, "What's the one thing I can do?" I got very involved in politics at University College London and then became interested in journalism. I was offered a job, largely because of my brother David who was already in the business – my father died when I was twenty-one. I was given a chance. I was lucky I suppose.'

So what drew Jonathan to Russia?

'I had originally gone there during the Cold War. It dominated my professional and personal life in the 1970s and '80s. I was in a position to make documentaries. I went into the satellite countries in the late 1970s and then in the early 1980s to the Soviet Union. I tried to understand what Russia was like and what the Russian people were like. It was exceptionally difficult in those days. Then, fast forward, to the glorious liberation of Eastern Europe and the collapse of the Soviet Union. I went back again.'

What changes did you notice in Russia since the Cold War era?

'Well, the dramatic shift in the cities in terms of consumer goods, trading, large office blocks, raw capitalism. It had been a very controlled socialist economy and, of course, as someone who is brought up with Western consumerism, it's actually quite reassuring that people have access to what I've always had. The other change was a different kind. The people were very open with me, and that was very important. It meant that I could have proper conversations and be absolutely frank.

I felt that I could say what I wanted once I'd had a vodka or two or three or four. Therefore, you can genuinely get beneath and reach the other person in a way that was quite impossible before that.'

I ask Jonathan if it was his idea to make the documentary *Charles, the Private Man – The Public Role*.
'It was a joint decision. I was approached by a producer and I am quite certain, although I was never able to establish, I'm quite confident my name came up for discussion between him and what was then, St James's Palace. I think they must have thought, because I wasn't associated with royalty in any way, but had a certain, I don't know, credibility as a journalist/reporter that it would make sense from their point of view. I was quite cautious because there had been royal documentaries in the past, which had a pretty dire impact on the presenter. I was sympathetic to Prince Charles, his general demeanour and his outlook on issues such as the environment and I liked what I'd seen of him. I had met him a couple of times and I thought he had a terrific sense of humour about him. I like his sort of Goonish quality. We discussed the project and I said I would do it and the book, and that the Palace would have the right to see it but not the right to edit it or censor it.'

I ask how long the documentary took to make.
'I wasn't there every day, but travelling back and forth over a year. It was quite a hectic time as I was also writing a book about the change of government in Hong Kong. I was there for the changeover and there was a moment of tension and a real fear that if miscalculation were made the Chinese might militarily move in and there would be nothing the British could do. As it happens, it went off very smoothly. I went with the Prince of Wales and Chris Patten, Governor of Hong Kong on the last journey of the *Yacht Britannia* and we sailed out with the whole British fleet as an escort. That was quite an experience with all the big ships roaring by on each side of aircraft carriers. It was in the South China Seas, so it was a way of saying to the Chinese we are going but we still exist. And of course there were fireworks.'

Where does Jonathan travel when he's not working?
'I tend to stay at home. I live in South Devon; Dartmoor is not far away. It's close to the loveliest beaches. I've got two little children and if I'm forced to – like so many people of my generation, I go to France. France is near and can be easily reached by boat and Eurotunnel so no need for the hassle of airports and the

journey time is short.'

What about your fear of flying?

Jonathan revealed that he has a been afflicted with a fear of flying throughout his life. Travelling by plane is always a challenge for him and he is filled with terror before and on every journey, so much so that his stomach churns. He never relaxes until he reaches his destination. So far nothing has helped except for a Bloody Mary or two.

How are you dealing with your phobia?

'A very nice executive at the BBC says she knows a wonderful hypnotist and that she'll give me their details since the "cure worked for somebody else". I don't know whether I'll follow it up, but it's a real problem. If I can, I go by train or car.'
Or by vodka? I suggest jokingly.
He laughs. 'Yes, I fly by vodka-vodka airlines'.

I move on to the subject of food. Has Jonathan eaten anything weird or wonderful on his travels?

'Raw meat from the flank of a newly killed cow. I won't go into detail, but it gave me a tape worm.' Squirming at the thought, I steer Jonathan back to Russia, reminding him of the moment in the book when he 'rediscovered happiness and felt that Russia had been like metaphorical cushion of healing'.

'I'm glad you picked up on that. I felt that I'd tested myself psychologically as well as professionally with the discovery that I'd come out of the other side relatively unscathed, with the wound healed.' Jonathan mentions in his book *Russia* that he was broken by a grief that was more dreadful than he had ever imagined possible at the outset of his journey so it was extraordinary that he came home rejuvenated. He says it was nothing short of miraculous. 'It was a great thing and a very cathartic experience. I felt I had to tell the truth as I experienced it. It would be dishonest to conceal it and it was an extraordinary adventure. It was very gruelling and I'm very glad that I did it for a lot of reasons.'

Jonathan points to the pictures on the wall. He introduces me to the entire family through a pictorial journey and proudly shows me a picture sketched by Nelson Mandela while in captivity. It's time to leave as Jonathan has a dinner to attend. I pack up my bag while Jonathan brings in three neck ties. Looking into a large mirror, he holds them up to his shirt asking, 'Which one do you think would look best?'

I advise him to be a rebel and 'mix spots with stripes'. He seems pleased with my advice and says, 'Yes I like this one, why not?'

A full two hours after the start of the interview we were still chatting. I reminded Jonathan that I had done a 'Gorbachev' on him, and he laughed good-heartedly.

RUN FOR LOVE, TRAVEL FOR A CAUSE

Rosie Swayle Pope, MBE

osie Swale Pope, MBE makes Bear Grylls look like a pussy cat. She is an incredible woman with amazing stamina and unspeakable courage. Who on earth would think of sailing in a catamaran to Australia from Gibraltar? With her first husband she sailed a mammoth 30,000 miles (48,300 km) across the Atlantic Ocean, eventually crossing the Pacific Ocean, stopping at the Galapagos Islands and eventually around Cape Horn before reaching Australia, then back around Cape Horn and on to Britain, giving birth to her son James on board in the process. Another time, in the early '80s she made a journey across the Atlantic from Pembroke in Wales to New York, a single handed transatlantic voyage. She arrived at Staten Island, New York, after completing her record-breaking 4,800 miles (7,720 km), sailing in a 17ft-long (5.2 m) plywood boat. This voyage took seventy days and she encountered rough storms, risking her life.

Then, in 2003, she completed a 10,000 miles (17,000 km) trek from one end of Nepal to the other in aid of The Nepal Trust. The Nepal Trust is a charitable organisation that carries out development work in the remote rural areas of northwest Nepal in a region referred to as the Hidden Himalayas. They work with the community and governments for the development and conservation of infrastructure and especially for basic health care. They also support income generating projects, encouraging self-sufficiency for the people, reducing poverty and improving quality of life. Everything Rosie does is for the good of humankind.

Rosie was born in Switzerland, but shortly after her birth her mother contracted tuberculosis and was sent to a sanatorium for isolation, a practice that was usual in those days. Her mother requested that Rosie be with her. Rosie was two when her mother died and she moved to live with her grandmother in the southwest of Ireland. Incapacitated with osteoarthritis Rosie nursed her grandmother, missing out on much of her education while doing so. She has no regrets though and the legacy of that special relationship remains to this day.

I first heard about Rosie Swale Pope through a newspaper article and then read her story, *Just A Little Run Around The World*. I was awestruck. In her narrative, she recounts how she left her cottage in Tenby, Wales, for five years, to travel 20,000 miles (32,100 km) on foot and in the process wear out 53 pairs of training shoes. The idea for the trip came about after she lost her beloved husband Clive to cancer and it seemed an appropriate way to raise awareness of how an early diagnosis of that illness can save lives. Her journey was one of meaning. She set off on the adventure of a lifetime alone. Departing on her 57th birthday and operating on a modest budget, she had only a cart that she called Icebird for company. This was a three-wheeled cart, which was designed to hold her essentials. She bought her food en route to avoid carrying it.

Her journey encompassed Russia and Siberia, then Holland, Germany, Poland, and Moscow and then on to the Trans-Siberian route, across the Bering Sea, Alaska, America, Canada, Greenland, Iceland, Ireland, England, Scotland and back home to Wales.

Along the way, Rosie endured Siberian winds gusting at 50 miles (83 km) per hour, sub-zero temperatures, storm blizzards, snow drifts, sore feet and holes in her shoes. But she was undeterred. She was even confronted by a naked gunman; followed by a pack of wolves; and pursued by two knife-wielding men. At one point she shared her tent with a snake. In Alaska she nearly froze to death and almost lost her toe to frostbite. At times circumstances became so brutal that Rosie was afraid to sleep in case she didn't wake up. At other times, food was scarce. Rosie had fallen ill near Lake Baikal in Russia and wandered into the path of a bus. She was knocked unconscious and taken to hospital. The accident was a 'blessing'; while in hospital recuperating it was discovered that Rosie had double pneumonia, which could have killed her if not treated in time. At one point, she was helped by two men, only to find later that they were murderers on the run.

Rosie has a mission. Often she is running or travelling for a reason. Rosie tells me. 'It's important for me to run for charity when possible, to give something back to say thanks for life.' For example, she ran from one end of Nepal to the other for The Nepal Trust, a distance of 1,060 miles (1,700 km) and established a world-record time, completing the run in 68 days. Her mission raised 8,000 US dollars to support a health camp at the district headquarters of Simikot (a mountainous town [elevation 9,500 ft/2,910 m] in the Himalayas of northwest Nepal).

She supports the Siberian Railway Cancer Hospital in Omsk, and The Kitezh Children's Community for Orphans in Russia, and The Prostate Cancer Charity receive advertising and funding as a result of her self-imposed challenges.

THE INTERVIEW

I have never met anyone quite like Rosie. She is highly inspirational. As she tells me about the challenges she has set herself, all 101 of them, there is an infectious, child-like excitement in her tone. First, she talks about her experience in the freezing sea for charity. Each year in Tenby, Wales, the place where she used to live, there is a winter swim in support of local charities. Six hundred swimmers brave the icy seas watched by hundreds of spectators. A roaring bonfire greets the swimmers when they return.

Of the next challenge she has lined up, she says, 'I'm learning how to fly, but I have to do it bit by bit as I haven't got the money to do it all at once. I have to do a minimum of 50 hours flying to obtain the licence and I can only afford the lessons in batches of seven. There's a lot of work involved. It's fun; every minute is fun.

I thought it would be fun. I thought the instructor would let me hold the controls and gently fly around, but he turned the airplane upside down and asked me if I'd like to do the same. I did it, then made the plane stand up on its tail and roll over backwards, pointing towards the ground, then come up again and fly level. That was amazing. I had a feel for it and my instructor couldn't believe I hadn't done it before. When I flew upside down I was hanging from the harness with my hair hanging down. It was marvellous.' The aerobatics and the possibility of the experience leading to a new challenge drew her.

Rosie dreams of being qualified with a full pilot's licence by 2015, then to fly around the world solo to raise funds in memory of her late husband and to provide some financial support to a cancer charity.

What about other journey challenges, I ask?

'I've been doing another challenge known as Icebird. I was running from beach to beach on our coastline here in Pembrokeshire and I was going to pull Icebird, my cart, (the one on the front of my book).'

For this challenge she visited 26 cities and towns as part of her 681-mile (1,096 km) challenge, running the marathon routes at each location and raising money for Tye Hafan children's hospice in Cardiff and Helen & Douglas House in Oxford. The runs were challenging.

'At times it was difficult to go on. It was dark, but then something would happen to distract me. For instance I was settled for the evening by the shore, looking out and the waves were pounding. It sounded so beautiful. I was curled up in my sleeping bag, with a hot water bottle on my stomach and a cup of tea on the little stove. It was fantastic. It made the difficult times worthwhile.'

During all of this she wrote her book, *A Little Run Around the World*. 'My book was written from the heart and I spent several hours a day working on it. I'd take it to the supermarket with me and read excerpts. People would cross the street to get away from me. I'm working on a lot of projects. They do take over. I work very hard and I love my work. I don't think I have a single talent in the world, neither am I in any particular hurry to do anything. My grandmother used to say, "It's not good looks or natural gifts that really count... it's wanting to do things".'

I am staggered at her courage, how does she do it?

'I don't have particular courage. I've just been blessed to have extraordinary and amazing things happen to me. I have found the positive in any bad things that have happened to me. I've got 99 challenges to go. Some of them are going to be small-scale, caring kinds of challenges. I might go out and hand out tea or do a soup run for some of those organisations that take people in at Christmas. It might be nice to do something other than sitting around eating turkey. I might do that. There are all sorts of things up for grabs.'

What fascinates me about Rosie is how she turns tragedies into something positive. When her husband Clive was diagnosed with cancer and eventually died, she was determined to pick up the pieces and help others. Her little 'run around the world' for five years is a testament to this. She did it to create awareness that cancer may be healed if caught in time. Another time, on a voyage with her first husband she fell into the Caribbean Sea 900 miles (1,450 km) from the shore. As a result she needed emergency medical treatment in hospital, but never gave up in the face of adversity, kept positive and kept going, completing the voyage. On another occasion the whole family suffered arsenic poisoning from a meal of un-soaked beans.

'Well you know, I think you have to do this every day. ...Every time something is awkward, I say, 'How do we get over this? How do we survive it? And then try to turn it into something positive. I'm not really that special. Many people do a lot more than I do. I believe life is about this glory and if I ever get bored, I think of the two beautiful horses I rode on through Chile, with their dappled hair and their manes. Then I think of the smell of the ocean years ago when I went sailing through the Pacific; the Galapagos Islands; the giant turtles. Everyone is a time traveller in their head. You can think back to all the wonderful things that have happened and the fabulous times.'

She recalls some special memories.

'I was at Dromoland Castle in Ireland to see a friend of mine. It was so beautiful. We went out into the woods there and met a very nice man with falcons. Moments like these will stay in my head forever. Then there are memories of the school children who ran with me when I was running my 27 marathons in 27 days.' Her 707 mile (1,137km) route took her from Bristol to London and from Tunbridge Wells to Bury St Edmunds and back to Tenby, Wales.

'There are all the people I met in America and all around the world, including the Russian people. It seems to go on forever: every day something lovely happened. When I'm busy I tend to go out at about six in the morning. You could call it multi-tasking. I get some exercise.'

I laugh. What? More exercise after running around the world for five years?

She tells me, 'I go out in my Siberian coat, looking up at the stars and I love being out in the open. I run around for miles and miles, then I come back and lie down on a bit of parkland overlooking the sea and it really doesn't matter if the grass is crackling like cornflakes. Nobody is there at this time of the year. Nobody can see me making an idiot of myself doing my stretching exercises.

Many people learn hard facts when they become ill or something happens. I'm lucky. That's never happened to me. There are two basic principles in life: that you can keep going when you think you can; and when it seems that you are 90 per cent finished, you can go on longer that you ever dreamed. The other thing is, if you do keep going, something good may happen. And surprisingly when you believe something good is going to happen it probably will. I think you should never give up, and I believe it with all my heart. There is no such thing as an ordinary person. Everyone is special. You can do all you think you can. It's much more painful to give up. There's no point in being miserable and moaning because that's terribly painful to one's self. It's a fundamental truth of life. If you think that good will happen, you will feel so much better. My daughter is a therapist and she teaches people. The main thing is to be positive.'

Rosie took a voyage in an open boat to Australia, setting off from Pembroke in Wales, yet she doesn't seem to think it was anything special. I was bowled over to think she travelled for thousands of miles in an open boat and in all sorts of conditions.

'It's hardly worth talking about,' she says. 'That was years ago. I discovered I had a half-sister I didn't know about who had died in an air crash and left me some money, just enough to buy a house and the boat in which I sailed around Cape Horn. It was a very good voyage.

I wrote and had three books published before I was 27 and they were translated into several languages. *Children of Cape Horn* was written about a voyage to Australia with two children aboard, documenting the joys, the disasters and the overcoming of trials in a positive way. In her book *Return to Cape Horn* she swapped the boat for horses and rode from north to south Chile.

It was a happy experience but it was so long ago. It's like another age. My parting from my first husband was quite a difficult time. After that I decided to sail the Atlantic Ocean by myself in a boat which I bought for 500 pounds (sterling). I sailed from Wales to New York. It was a fairly bad boat. It took 70 days. I went on short voyages because I loved my home life and family life.'

Did you log your journeys?

'I've got notebooks. They're sort of scribbled books. It's more important to write down facts, like where you are, mileage, and things that strike you in word pictures in your mind. To write a regular journal is dull and I'd never have time for it because my journeys are very hard.'

What about your early travel experience?

'My grandmother couldn't really entertain me in the early days because she couldn't walk and she was in a lot of pain, so I used to not come home until I had something to write about; like the adventures I had.'

How did the marathon journeys begin?

'I ran in Iceland and then in Kosovo after the War of Terror. I wanted to make some money to buy school books, so I started running. I decided to do a marathon in Switzerland where I was born and when I was there I met my foster mother. She was nearly 100 years old then. I started to run across different countries. I ran from Rosslare in Ireland to the Giant's Causeway in Northern Ireland. I did a marathon each day for 27 days. Now I'm doing various talks for charities and things like that.'

Have you met any inspirational people?

'There are so many inspirational people. I've travelled so many routes. I have to tell you, there are not people that you'd even remember. They're not people you'd remember, not well-known people like Michael Palin, although he's a lovely and very charming man. I think the most ordinary people are the real heroes and hero-ines; homeless people, like Gary Young, people who struggle to get to university, the blind adventurer Miles Hilton Barber. He was in the airforce. He was young and healthy and then went to the opticians and was told he would go blind in a few years because of a hereditary condition. His brother lost his sight and I think he sailed across the Pacific. This guy is absolutely amazing. He's very humble; not one of those grand people. To me, he's one of the most inspirational. I've time for grand people, the likes of Chris Bonnington, but Miles Hilton Barber in my hum-ble opinion knocks spots off him. I've met a lot of mountaineers, explorers, sailors and all types of people, but he's one of the best. In the last ten years he's climbed mountains and he's done a 13,000-mile (21,000 km) micro-light flight. He's sledged across Antarctica. He's driven a racing car and travelled in the polar region. He's living a very full life, turning his condition into something positive. I keep meeting people who humble me so much.'

Is it difficult to adapt to home life after returning from your journeys?

'I'm sure I'm partly feral. Spaghetti and marmite will see me through the day. I can eat anything together: honey, cheese, spaghetti. I can sleep anywhere. I'd prefer to sleep on the floor rather than a bed. I'm a great one for being outdoors. I've learned many tricks while working the 24-hour clock. I can get up at three in the morning and go to bed at eight. The whole purpose of being an adventurer is to be ready to tackle anything. I'm so used to the wild forest. It trains you to deal with things and helps you to help other people. And when you go home there's a bath – my goodness, how exciting! You can turn the light on and off as much as you like. You can talk on the phone without worrying about battery power. It's exciting to fill the kettle from a tap. I had a day off when I broke two bones in my hips. When I got back, I wasn't able to think about that. I had to start writing. I was absolutely out on a limb working, really under pressure, much as I was when crossing the frozen wasteland of Siberia.'

Is it a lonely existence? Being away from your family must be tough.

'Yes, I can feel lonely. Loneliness is just as much of a problem for people in the city. You can be so desperately lonely for the people you love. That's a universal problem. On a journey or voyage, or anything in life, you've got to stay focused, going one step at a time, to keep at it and think of nice and good things to cheer you up. When I was out in the forests in Russia and was feeling bad, I'd never say, "I can do this because I am strong". I could do it because I had people who loved me and I'd name the stars after my friends and family and that's the way to go really. It's all very "beam me up Scotty". It's a tremendous sacrifice to be away from your family for a while. On the other hand, you are always with people who are focused and of the same mind.'

Do you find it amusing that parts of Europe grind to a halt with 3 inches (7.5 cm) of snow and minus three degrees?

'I just feel sorry. It's hard. People are not used to the cold and England is not equipped for it like Russia. The cold is always nasty but that's why I chose to go on my fourth swim. I'm used to the cold. I cover myself with olive oil so I smell like a salad,' she laughs. 'I had a bikini on. I had tinsel on my bikini and olive oil. Not very romantic is it?'

What was the highlight of the round-the-world trip?

'That's totally, ridiculously impossible. I suppose you could say there were many highlights: like when the wolf stuck his head in my tent; when I was alone in the frozen waste of the Yukon River in winter; meeting the children in the orphanage; meeting the survivors of the Gulags; running around Ireland; The Giant's Causeway in the storm.'

Is your family in awe of you?

'No. They are quite used to it. They are absolutely wonderful. I love them dearly. There's Gerald and Kay, my brother and his wife, well, my half-brother (but I call him my brother), and my other brother Nicolas. He's an artist and a composer and lives in Limerick, and my wonderful French step-mother Marianne. I can't remember how old she is, about 90 at least. She's still teaching French. She works really hard and drives a nice car like a racing driver. She's a wonderful woman.'

What about Wales?

'I like Wales, mostly because Clive my husband was there. I love anywhere. Ireland is closest to me at anytime.'

What have your journeys taught you?

'Do you know something I've learnt in my life? I don't know if you've tried this in yours, but you have to make plans and have a structure. Catch it whole in your imagination and your dreams, and the rest of it is work and preparation. But you must also obey gut instinct and reach out and grab chances. Some of the best things that have happened to me are when I have just woken up in bed and thought, 'Wow, this is the way to go. Nothing is impossible.'

THE JOURNEY WITHIN AND WITHOUT

Zoë Sallis

After five years spent writing and researching her book, *Ten Eternal Questions*, Zoë Sallis was to reap the rewards when it became an international bestseller. This book took Zoë on a spiritual journey and exposed her to the beauty of the world. The book asks thought-provoking questions about life and its meaning. For it, she interviewed influential and well-know people including Nelson Mandela, Bono, Jack Nicholson and Sophia Loren and to conduct her interviews she travelled to Hollywood, Paris, Los Angeles, Venice, Cuba, and South Africa, among others.

When Zoë talks about inspiration for the book, she mentions how her son Danny asked her what she liked to do and she replied that she liked to write. He suggested that she should write a book. That night she wrote ten questions that she would like to ask of people. 'The more people I got to agree to an interview the more people wanted to join. I couldn't believe these people would give me the time of day because I'd never written anything and, anyway, who the hell was I?' she recalls. Numerous publishers initially rejected the book but the joy of finally being signed up and seeing her book on the shelves brought indescribable joy.

For another book, *Our Stories, Our Visions*. Zoë conducted 40 interviews with some of the world's most influential women. In it Judi Dench, Jane Fonda, Yoko Ono, and former Irish President Mary McAleese, to name a few, shared their insight and wisdom. She asked what inspires each woman and if the upbringing and experiences of each influenced the direction their lives took. She asked what provoked them to anger and whether they believed in forgiveness. She asked them about their greatest fears and if they ever thought there would be equality in humankind and an end to poverty and injustice. The people she interviewed were trying to make the world a better place, using their voices to fight for change. One such person, Dame Judy Dench, is battling with macular disease and is helping others in the area. Among others, she interviewed Professor Wangari Maathai, the first African female to win a Nobel Peace Prize in 2004. She is internationally recognized for her persistent struggle for democracy, human rights and environmental conservation. She was instrumental in planting 20 million trees to improve the environment and the lives of others.

Each person she interviewed had worked hard in their chosen field to improve quality of life. She heard of struggles against the odds and met the women who make a difference to the world we live in both by their actions and example.

As for Zoë, she seeks peace, which helps explain the deeply spiritual themes in her books. She is interested in meditation and nature. Born in India at a time of great religious unrest, then educated at Cheltenham Ladies College, England, she went on to win a scholarship to the Webber Douglas Academy of Dramatic Arts, London. Then in the early '60s she met film director John Huston, her great love and soul mate. They moved to Italy for a while, a country Zoë loves. Travelling has always been a part of Zoë's life.

THE INTERVIEW

When I first contacted Zoë to ask her for an interview, she said, 'I can't think what I have to say about travel'. I was to find out Zoë has a lot to say about travel. When I met her she exuded warmth, just as she had in her emails to me, and seemed genuinely interested in other people. We spoke about her meeting with Nelson Mandela and how it came about. She recalled the emotion she felt as she drove to his house and as she viewed the prison on Robben Island in the distance where Nelson Mandela, Nobel Peace Prize winner and leading anti-apartheid campaigner, had been imprisoned for 27 years.

The division of colonial India into two separate states during the 1940s brought great conflict among the Muslims and Hindus. The Muslim League's leader,

Mohammed Ali Jinnah, began a public campaign in favour of a separate Muslim state, while Jawaharlal Nehru, a Hindu, of the Indian National Congress (INC) called for a unified India. Hindus formed the majority, and would have been in control of any democratic form of government. The partition was brewing and, when it finally happened, ten million desperate people migrated fleeing north or south, depending upon their faith, in what became the largest migration in history. Hindus and Sikhs fled to India, and Muslims to Pakistan. Independence came at a cost in 1947, the year that brought an end to British rule; British India was divided into two states, India and Pakistan. The Punjab and Bengal regions were split between the two new countries.

In 1948, Zoë and her family fled India but, despite it being a difficult time, she holds cherished memories of that time. 'One of my fondest memories was leaving India in a flying boat during the partition, in 1948. It was one of the last of its kind. I particularly remember the plane landing on the Nile in Egypt and sleeping that night on a river boat, which was a hotel. The trip took days by this kind of plane. *La Paloma* has been one of my favourite tunes ever since, as it was playing when we landed and always evokes romance, mystery, nostalgia and a longing for some intangible dream.'

I ask what kind of places she visited as a child and where she spent her childhood.

'I was born in India during the time of the Raj, which brings back some colourful memories. I can recall the birthday parties in our garden in India, with bears dancing and monkeys doing tricks, dressing up in costumes and performing in pantomimes. We also used to go hunting for tigers while riding on elephants – which I don't approve of, but was the norm in those times – as well as trips to beautiful palaces. My uncle was a Raja, a king. Although the system of rulers has passed in India, their successors are still known as Rajas and Maharajas, like an exotic fairytale, a time in the past. India has an innate spirituality that allows for self-discovery and broadens the mind. I have been back to India several times. The country has unique qualities.

I think the state of Rajasthan is a great place to visit. I love Jaipur, the capital of Rajasthan. It's known as the Pink City of India. Rajasthan is positioned in the north-western side of India and is rich in culture. The Aravallis mountain range is always in view and ideal for people who appreciate scenic beauty. There are spectacular sand-dunes and trails for wildlife and wetlands.'

She says, while in India, 'I met a teacher there. It's extremely rare to encounter such a personification of love and wisdom.'

I'd detected that Zoë's spiritual side was very much to the fore. So her talk of going to an Indian place of pilgrimage, where the joys are spiritual rather than physical, didn't surprise me. Having written a spiritual book *Ten Eternal Questions* and experienced all kinds of places and interviewed people from all walks of life, she knew she was searching for a deeper meaning to life. Leaving the comforts and familiarity of home, she went in search of a place of meditation and spirituality.

What was the most peaceful place for her?

'It has to be an Ashram in India; getting away from the everyday world. No hustle and bustle. I felt I was in contact with what really mattered and my soul found its tranquillity and peace.' I asked Zoe to tell me more, 'It is something that has to be experienced and felt in an individual way. It does not matter if one is there a month or a day in Ashram, it resonates to each person in a unique and special way depending on where they are in their own spiritual evolution.'

I refer to Zoë's book *Ten Eternal Questions*, in which she travelled far and wide to meet and interview many influential people. I ask her, of all the places she visited, which was her favourite and why?

'I think meeting Paulo Coelho in the Pyrenees was very special.'

Paulo Coelho is one of the most widely read and influential authors. He is known for his pilgrimage to Saint James of Compostela and his accompanying book, *The Pilgrimage*. He also adapted *The Gift* (Henry Drummond) and *Love letters of a Prophet* by Kahlil Gibran. Paulo Coelho has sold one hundred million copies. He is also Messenger of Peace for the United Nations.

Zoë told me, 'I interviewed Paulo in a forest. There was a stone bench and table where we sat, beneath huge tall trees, and talked of life and death. It was the most stimulating conversation. After the interview he and his wife took me to a beautiful church; there was a service taking place and we prayed and listened to hymns.'

What was your most exciting trip?

'I have to say Cuba. It was so completely different from anywhere I had ever been. I went to interview Fidel Castro, which became an impossible venture, but I wanted to feel I had tried. Walking around the old town of Havana was like walking into the past; all the stories I'd heard about the Revolution and the times before with Hemingway and the stars of Hollywood. The feeling of déjà vu. It's a place full of warmth, character and a certain sadness as well as laughter, song and dance. Even though the people didn't have a lot of material wealth, they seemed to make the best of their situation and were very reverent towards Fidel Castro. I felt I was re-living history. I went to Che Guevara's wife's house. She was very warm and hospitable. We had tea together. There were pictures of Che Guevara all over the house and his son who looks exactly like him was there. The whole thing felt unreal: the Revolution, Cuba, Castro and Che Guevara. It was something that happened somewhere else and to be so close and so involved was very exhilarating, moving and fired one's imagination.'

She refers to the famous pictures of Che Guevara on t-shirts and says, 'You see all those familiar pictures, but when you're there and see the actual photographs around you and are with his family... it was something I had never dreamt of. I also had dinner with Fidel Castro's daughter. I tried to get hold of Fidel himself... and I know I would have interviewed him if I'd stayed longer. I met the Ambassador of France who was a good friend of his. He was going to help me meet up with him but I had to leave for many reasons.'

Do you regret not having waited?

'Well, I would have liked to meet him. I could have gone on and on and on and included others but I had to stop somewhere and I thought, 'The minute I interview Mandela, that will be the moment I stop.' It was like something organic. It just grew and grew.'

She also went to Israel and interviewed Shimon Peres, the ninth and current President of Israel.

'I made a trip to Jerusalem to see the grave of Jesus and the garden where he was betrayed. It was a moving experience.'

I know Zoë's journey to interview people took her far and wide including the Pyrenees and the Hollywood Hills. What good memories do you have of this?

'As I mentioned, my encounter in the Pyrenees was special, and Cuba. Apart from this, it would be my meetings with the 'greats' of the silver screen: Marlon Brando, Jack Nicholson and David Lynch. One respects them for their extraordinary talent. Also, my trip on the Eurostar to Paris to meet the last Empress of Persia, a gracious lady whose painful past touched me.'

What was the most outstanding interview you had? The most unexpected and amazing?

'My last interview with Nelson Mandela in South Africa. Waiting for him in his sitting room and hearing his voice in another room; that was surreal. I had waited five years for my meeting with Nelson Mandela and felt I couldn't finish my book without him as it would seem incomplete. I was beginning to despair, but by some incredible stroke of luck, fate, karma, or whatever you wish to call it, Chief Mangosuthu Buthelezi, who I was interviewing, graciously organised the meeting. It took one telephone call after five years of agonising. The next day I was sitting in Nelson Mandela's house in Cape Town. I couldn't believe that this meeting had become a reality. I was actually interviewing Nelson Mandela, a truly iconic human being.

As I looked into his eyes I thought of all the years of suffering he had endured. I marvelled at his courage and dignity and how nothing broke his spirit. What strength in the infinite possibility of hope. He was the most gracious gentleman and answered my questions with warmth, truth, humanity, humour, and a twinkle in his eye from time to time. I can only say that was one of the most extraordinary moments of my life, which I shall always treasure. Now my book was complete. I had interviewed some very worthy people, who had openly shared their deep feeling and beliefs with me. I only hope that their answers inspire and encourage all to believe in themselves, no matter what curves life may throw.'

What lessons in life have you learnt from travelling?

'I am not a good traveller; the whole process is very unsettling to me. Once I get where I'm going I enjoy everything, but the whole process of deciding what to pack, getting to the airport, the worry about missing the boarding call, which means checking the departure board a million times, has me full of anxiety for days. I suppose it's some form of insecurity. I put it down to leaving India during the partition, as there was so much unrest. Maybe it all stems from there. However, the world is an endlessly fascinating place, and to be able to travel is a great privilege. I am grateful to have the opportunity. I like arriving and the stimulating experience of discovering different places; and understanding diverse cultures. I find it enriching.'

Zoë has travelled to many diverse places. I ask her what country she would most like to visit in the future.

'I would love to visit Burma and Thailand.'

Zoë strikes me as being quite an independent lady. How does she feel about travelling alone?

'I have travelled alone a lot, but I prefer not to. I enjoy travelling most with my son, and John when he was alive' (John Huston, film director and Zoë's soul mate).

I reflect on all the people Zoë has met on her travels and I'm curious to know if she made many friends as a result.

'Not really, I always go for a specific reason, and to see whoever I am interviewing or visiting and then I leave. Naturally, there are people I would love to see again but distance and busy lives always make this difficult.'

Where can you best relax?

'Rome. Italy is such a happy place, with friendly people. I smile, I am flattered, the sun shines, the aroma of the food is delicious, the warm colour of the buildings and the spectacular architecture. There is a visual delight on every corner; the atmosphere is altogether heart-warming.'

I understand she has a deep love for Italy and she stayed there for many years. What did she like about the country?

'I felt at home from the moment I arrived and wanted to bring up my son in a place where children are loved. Italians are warm and friendly and I understood their mentality and sense of humour. I never remember feeling sad in all the time I was there. It was such a happy and joyful atmosphere. You can't help but smile from the moment you get up. Every little corner of Rome has a special beauty; a fountain, a fresco, the eye feasts on extraordinary works of art by great artists everywhere. Not to mention the food and, to me, the small trattorias had the most delicious homemade dishes, the simpler the better. I am a vegetarian, so most Italian food is good for me; pasta and mozzarella and tomato. ...Oh to be with my son and grandchild in a villa in Tuscany, or anywhere in Italy, and have lots of time to enjoy it,' she says wistfully.

What part of Italy inspires you most?

'Rome. I lived there for 20 years. Positano and all along the Amalfi coast is worth a visit, it really is pure magic; the main part of Positano sits in an enclave in the hills leading down to the coast. John Steinbeck wrote an essay there and said, 'Positano bites deep; it's a dream place that isn't quiet real when you are there and becomes beckoningly real after you've gone. Italy is in my heart and I will always remember those years with a great nostalgia, and although one can never go back as everything changes, my memories will stay, to relive whenever the heart strings pull me in that direction and the soul yearns to remember. I think different places and people inspire at different times of one's life. I have mentioned Italy and India, both places inspire, but in such different ways. You ask me which people have inspired me. I think people who inspire me are those who think out of the box and have original thoughts. I find inspiration in those who have the courage to be true to themselves no matter what, and don't conform just for the sake of it. The nobility of the soul is always inspiring. John Huston was one such person. He was a larger-than-life personality, big and grandiose and charismatic, but with a deep sensitivity, which came out in his films, paintings or writing. His understanding of human nature, his innate wisdom was very inspiring. John O' Donohue said, "One of the deepest longings of the human soul is to be seen. John Huston saw my soul and, to me, there will never be another man like him".'

I ask if they travelled together or met through travel.

'I met him through working on films and then I gave it all up. Falling deeply in love with him and spending time with him, rather than being separated as one is when in the film business, was far more important to me. We travelled all over the world wherever his filming would take him – Rome, Tuscany, Sicily, New York, Los Angeles, Mexico and, of course, his house in Ireland.'

I ask what their favourite place was.

'I thought Mexico was a very special place. I think it was more special because of that particular moment in time. Danny was only one year old when we arrived in Puerto Vallarta. I was also very young. It was so simple and unspoilt; women washed clothes in the river. Mariachi bands serenaded whenever you went out. I am an incurable romantic at heart. John was filming *Night of the Iguana*, which is why we were there and I have an article in which he describes the place: "Puerto Vallarta has hardly changed for centuries and is isolated by bad roads with access only possible by sea or air." Little can the locals have realised that after Hollywood came to town in 1963, their isolation would rapidly come to an end. Almost overnight the patronage of Burton and Taylor and their acquisition of a villa in town, helped put Puerto Vallarta on the map. Today it boasts more than 100 hotels and has become a major cruise port.

Egypt was also a very extraordinary place. We were filming *The Bible* and I was playing the part of Hagar in the story of Abraham. We were filming in the desert, which felt so vast and foreboding, and then the magnificent Sphinx, full of mystery and wonder'. Egyptian pyramids were built as stairs for kings to climb after their death. A sphinx was erected to guard the pyramids. Many of their treasured possessions were kept in the tomb in preparation for the afterlife. It was believed in ancient Egypt that death was the beginning of a journey bringing the person into the next life, therefore they went prepared and that meant bringing with them whatever was necessary and they were taking no chances.

We also filmed in Rome and Sicily. I came to discover Rome through the making of the film. In the '60s Rome ...was more like a big village. It had that lovely laidback feeling. No hurry, no stress, pure bliss. I loved the fact that everything closed in the middle of the day. And siesta. It gave one time to enjoy the day and unhurried lunches sitting in piazzas looking at beautiful fountains such as the Piazza Navona, where one had the added spectacle of looking at the famous Fountain of the Four Rivers by Baroque sculptor Bernini. The Vatican is a treasure trove of masterpieces; The Pietà by Michelangelo is breathtaking, as is the spectacular and magnificent Sistine Chapel.

We also went to Marrakesh when John was making his film *The Man Who Would Be King*. Marrakesh is stunning and colourful', she says. She recalls the film *Casablanca* and tells me it's her favourite. 'Marrakesh is an interesting place steeped in history. It has the largest Berber market, the souq, which was a fascinating experience, is not to be missed. I would have liked to explore Morocco more, maybe some other time.'

Is there anyone else that you would like to meet?

She tells me Aung San Suu Kyi, who was held under house arrest in Burma for almost fifteen years until she was released in 2010.

'I tried and tried to meet her many times... but I didn't go to Burma as it could have been dangerous. I did make contact with those who were close to her... but it was not to be, unfortunately.'

Zoë tells me she sometimes looks back at all those people she met and wonders how she did it all and made all those journeys.

A FIERCE APPETITE FOR TRAVEL

Simon Majumdar

'When you travel around the world you travel around yourself.'
Simon Majumdar

I met Simon Majumdar during the Travellers' Tales Festival in the Green Room Cafe, Kensington, London. The son of a Bengali surgeon, he appeared oriental with his dark sallow skin and twinkling brown eyes. He invited me to his book reading, promising me a copy of his book, *Eat My Globe* (The Free Press, 2009). The first chapter called 'I Hate My Job' captured my attention. How desperate must things be to pack in a steady job in publishing and to risk his life savings on a romantic dream?

Being at such a low ebb must surely have spurred him into urgent action since a new life of travel beckoned. Life would never be the same again. Shortly after quitting his job he journeyed from Britain to Ireland, Sydney, Japan, Hong Kong, China, Mongolia, Russia and Finland, and all over the United States of America for his food travelogue book *Eat My Globe* and his quest to 'go everywhere and eat everything'. He was driven by a strong desire to travel and to meet people who share his passion for food and new experiences. This meant travelling to the locations where wonderful dishes originated and the more unusual, the better. He planned to eat everything from traditional dishes to the types of food many people would squirm at. His motto was to 'Go everywhere and eat everything so you don't have to'. Sharing food with the people who made it would add to the thrill of the journey and would be an education. Getting into the heart of a culture was high on his motivational list.

After quitting his publishing job to travel, his next adventure would take him to the United States (several times), Mexico, Argentina, Brazil, Scotland, Germany and Iceland. The second leg of the journey would take him to Thailand, Malaysia, Vietnam, the Philippines and India. Finally, he intended to travel to South Africa, Mozambique, Senegal, Morocco, Spain, Turkey and Italy. His quest to try food from other cultures had begun and he was prepared to travel extensively in order to try as much as he could. He was even prepared to go to China to endure his 'Top Ten Worst Eats' one of which is stir-fried rat. He says, 'Food is not just what I eat, it's what I am and what I do.' On his journey, he ate in fancy restaurants as well as from roadside stalls.

Simon used to write a food blog known as *Dos Hermanos*, which became popular in Britain. When it came to the attention of *GQ* men's magazine, it was deemed to be one of the hundred best things in the world. While blogging on the online site he received hundreds of invitations from people he had never met before. He decided he would take up as many offers as he could. One invitation was for a week at a Scotch Whiskey distillery. Included too was the offer of a guided tour around Mexico, a Thanksgiving meal in the US, a barbecue in Texas and a week's accommodation in Melbourne. With a travel itinerary in the planning stages, the invites would dictate his life for the next year or so. In that time he would take more than one hundred flights and sleep in as many different beds, but the best thing of all was that it brought him into contact with the things he loves most – people, food and travel.

Majumdar worked on a programme called *Market Kitchen* on the Good Food Channel. He now writes for numerous US and UK magazines and websites including askMen.com and the Food Network.

His other publication *Eating for Britain* recounts a journey through the United Kingdom, looking at the British diet and its link with people's identity. It revealed some surprises. To his amazement he found that many of the traditional foods he thought originated in Britain didn't necessarily, for example fish and chips and clotted cream. He was a regular on the Lifestyle channel (In the UK) and is well known in America where he became a judge on the Food Network's *The Next Iron Chef*, also *Iron Chef America* and *Extreme Chef*.

He has written articles for magazines as well as for *The Guardian* newspaper. He was nominated by *The London Evening Standard* as one of the 1000 most influential people in London in 2008. At the time I spoke to him he was due to embark on a US road trip to Seattle, Portland, Boise, Cheynne, Montana, Bismark, Sioux Falls, Omaha, and Kansas City.

THE INTERVIEW

What was the final straw that made you quit your job?

'It was a number of things. My mother died. I'd turned 40 the same year. I'd done one of those self-improvement courses and made a list of goals. I'd written the words, 'go everywhere and eat everything'. I'd been in my publishing job for ten years. I liked the people I was working with but the job had become frustrating. One day I sent 42 emails to my friends saying, 'I hate my job,' and then thought, 'well that's a sign'. I went home and while my lentil dahl was cooking on the hob, I started making a list of what I should do if I actually did go everywhere and eat everything. The next morning I handed in my notice. It was like a huge weight being lifted. People think I'm being melodramatic but if I hadn't done that or made this journey I wouldn't have been sitting here now. I was in a terrible state. I was having a total breakdown.'

How did he cope with his mother's death? Did travel help to dull the pain?

'I treated myself to the first holiday in 15 years and used some of the money my mother had left me. I went to New Zealand and that planted the seed. I went back-packing and had to organise my own way. I got the bug for it.'

Were friends supportive?

'Some were supportive and remain supportive. Some thought I was nuts and some got a little bit angry because they thought I was being irresponsible. If you do things that other people would love to do but don't have the courage to do, they get a bit cross. The friends who supported me when I set out on the journey are the people who are my friends now. They are beginning to see there are benefits. My journey was to "go around the world and to eat everything so you don't have to".' If that meant trying out fermented mare's milk in Mongolia, braised dog in China (he regrets that one) and camel meat in Casablanca, then that is where he would travel. He wanted to satisfy his own curiosity about foods he had read about but wanted to sample in their true birthplace. He loves people and wanted to meet the faces behind these dishes.

Quite simply he adores food and loves people who share his passion about growing food, discovering new flavours and talking about cuisine. He wanted to connect with people all over the globe who shared his passion for food; the people that would open their lives and hearts to him. This journey would satisfy his curiosity and was the basis of his book *Eat My Globe* (One year to go everywhere and eat everything). He considers it a privilege.

'I was just very lucky that the story of a middle-aged man seemed to connect with the people who like the book. Not everyone could do what I did. People have family commitments and all sorts of things but I think if it shows anything, it shows that if you've got a real passion for something, there are ways of fitting it into your life so that you can really improve your wellbeing and enjoyment of life. You should go out and seek whatever makes you happy.'

Did his parents expose him to new cultures and the love of food?

'Both of them cooked amazingly well. My mother learned to cook very good Bengali food when she moved to Calcutta. My father was intuitively a good cook and passed that love onto us. We were open to foods from other cultures. I lived in Yorkshire in the '60s, '70s and early '80s, then moved to London. That city was about to explode from a dire, post-war food era, to something more interesting. I was lucky to be around at that time. British food is most entirely predicated on immigration. In my book *Eating for Britain* I discovered that there were very few dishes in Britain that don't have some relationship to immigration. Fish and chips were created by Portuguese Jewish refugees; fried fish came from Portugal and fried potatoes from Belgium. They met in London. Irish stew, Welsh cawl and Lancashire hotpot all come from Scandinavia, chicken tikka masala was created by a Pakistani man in Glasgow. I met him. He's running a restaurant in Glasgow called The Shish Mahal.

The book was phenomenal fun to research. I was on the road for a year. I went from the north-east of Scotland to the west of England and the apple orchards in Kent. I'd been all over the world but knew very little about the food in my own country. We've no need to be apologetic about our food because when it's done right, it's superb.'

Simon asked people on the internet to decide what he should eat and where he should go. Can he recall some of the most memorable suggestions?

'First I looked at the invitations I had and would get by using my blog and then I made a list of those dishes that I knew existed and which I'd be really cross if I didn't try; you know if I didn't try taco in Mexico, if I didn't try a hot dog in New York or whatever, so I made a list and then I looked at all the invitations I had. "If you're ever in X come and join us." "Come and hunt in Finland." Here an invite to Santa Cruz for Thanksgiving and there a "Come and join us while we ride on the Trans-Siberian Express". It was a real mixture from the world's biggest barbecue in Kansas, to the sherry fair in Spain. I got invitations as I travelled.'

On the Trans-Siberian express, a 4,735 mile (7,621 km) journey he chose to travel via Mongolia. What was the journey like?

'There's a lot of red tape and paperwork, particularly with cross borders, so I did that journey with a small group and a guide. I travelled from Beijing to Ulaanbaatar, the capital of Mongolia, picking up the train journey there. I broke my journey in Lake Baikal, Russia, and then went back to Moscow. I thought the journey would be tough but it turned out to be a special moment; I had a lot of down time just staring out of the window. It was really relaxing. You're on the train for nearly seven days. I was in a carriage with four people playing cards, drinking beer and watching DVDs and people's computers.'

Majumdar travelled up the Yangtze River, one of the longest in the world and certainly the longest in Asia, measuring 6,211 miles (3,859 km). China relies on the river economically. It's a source of prosperity and highly populated. What was that like?

'It's described as a luxury tour cruise. I'd hate to see a non-luxury tour cruise. It's an interesting thing because the Chinese are beginning to discover the notion of holidays. Travelling in China is challenging and it's worth making the effort.'

The Gobi Desert is a place of great historic interest. It was a part of the great Mongol Empire and contains many notable cities of the Silk Road. It takes in Northern China and Southern Mongolia. It's one of the largest deserts in the world, measuring 1,000 miles (1,600km) from south-west to north-east and 500 miles (800 km) from north to south. Much of it consists of bare rock, not sand. What was the experience like?

'Well you wake at three o'clock in the morning and realise that you are coughing and spluttering. The whole train is filled with dust and by the time you get out of it you are caked in dust, which stays with you.'

Did you like Mongolia?

'I liked the people. They're very hospitable. Ulaanbaatar is ugly and Soviet. Once you leave the city you go out into a Soviet wilderness, which is beautiful, rugged and green.'

As well as travel to the other continents, Simon has returned to Germany on a road trip each year and will visit even in the middle of winter. Why do you love Germany so much?

Simon reckons that Munich has the highest standard of living in the whole of Germany. He loves the architecture, which has been preserved for centuries and he believes there is nowhere better to drink beer, where he says, 'the joy of beer and meat come together in perfect harmony'.

'I love Germany, the people and the food. I used to go to the Frankfurt Book Fair, when I worked for a publishing house, and to Munich for my book publishing work. That's one of the most beautiful and under-rated cities. It has great quality of life, terrific food and one of the best bar scenes in Europe. Germany's food reputation is similar to Britain's but there are some terrific dishes there. Bavaria is very meat heavy though some regions can be quite the opposite.' They make wonderful sausages, cured meats and cheeses. He reckons that sausage from the Weisswurst to the Dunkel Bier is almost a religion in Bavaria. 'It might not be the most sophisticated cuisine on earth but there's lots of delicious food.'

What were the most inspirational places?

'Mexico, the Philippines and Senegal – I fell in love with them. In Mexico City I found myself in one of the big markets watching a man with a rather rickety old motorized taco (tortilla) roller. He threw flour in at one end and made tortillas at the other. He waved me in and for the next 20 minutes, we made tortillas. In the Philippines and Senegal it was the same. It's very hospitable in the Philippines. My favourite country in the world is Spain. The Spanish have a passion for life.'

Has travel changed the way he looks at food?

'Oh entirely, I was very hedonistic before. I liked dining out, and I think, now more than ever, I look at the context in which the food is served. A chef with an ugly spirit never serves good food. You will always be able to taste the bitterness and cynicism in the food. If food is made with real passion and care, the chef will care about how it is cooked and give you the best. And that means everyone from someone making fish and chips to a chef making a three-star meal.'

We talk about the blessings that travel has brought, especially meeting his beautiful wife.

'She lives in Los Angeles. Her family is from the Philippines but I met her in Brazil at a street party in Salvador De Bahia. I had a very tough time in Brazil suffering attempted muggings and sunstroke. I was with a group of people. My future wife heard us talking in English and because she hadn't spoken to anyone in English for three weeks, gravitated towards us. She came to visit me after I finished the journey and we travelled around Spain together.

My journey has really been magical and has moulded into a career, which was totally unexpected but wonderful. I'm asked to lecture about my journey from a number of different angles and from a motivational point of view. I'm really grateful for the 5,000 emails I have received from throughout the world. Contact with people means more to me than anything else. One of the things I talk about when I'm doing my motivational talks is that travel is an investment in yourself. The money I spent in the last three or four years might be a very high percentage of my income, but I'll continue to do this. Every trip is special. There is always something new to see. I'm going to Korea and I'm as excited about going there as I have been about going anywhere.'

What did you discover by doing these journeys?

'I discovered a great many things about me; such as my ability to do things I thought I'd never be able to do. When you travel around the world, you travel around yourself. The highs and lows help you find out about yourself. People may disagree, but I've come back from my journey a better person than the one who left; a more tolerant, caring and open person; a person who surprised himself. It's physically very arduous, you know – a hundred flights. At points it was rather hellish because of the sheer energy needed. I was happy with my achievements. I'd definitely climbed a mountain, even if that mountain was only sleeping in a hostel or wherever. There's an element of travel I find a bit disheartening, for instance the travel snobs, who say, "If you don't rough it as you go, you're not proper travellers." Two of the most incredible people I met while on my journey were Bill and Betty, a couple in their seventies from Southern Australia. They came on the Trans-Siberian Express. We gave them a hand but they were really tough as old boots. I really liked them. They were travellers, yet if people looked at them they would say, "Oh they're just tourists". I think people should go out there and explore. The natives of the country you visit will guide you in the right direction.'

Any urge to travel again?

'I remember coming back to London in 2008. I had written the book and achieved much of what I had wanted, but when I returned I felt like a stranger in a strange land. I'd been back in London a week but it still didn't feel right. I had a displaced sort of feeling. I didn't know where home was but that's not a bad thing. It just means that I like to be on the road. God willing with health and everything we can travel well into the next decade. We have a small apartment, drive a cheap car and we don't buy expensive clothes. We are comfortably well off, but would rather spend our money on food and travel. It's a choice you make. I can't understand people who don't see food as an integral part of travel.'

For the foreseeable future food is going to be an integral part of Simon's travel. His new book *Fed White and Blue: Breaking Bread with America* is due for publication. He tells me that he will be spending the next year travelling around the US learning what it means to become an American citizen through that country's food experiences. He enthusiastically tells me he is looking forward to making his own whisky in Tennessee, brewing his own beer in Seattle and hunting in North Carolina.

Simon asked the public to help him to discover America by inviting him to be part of their food experiences. He put out a plea asking, 'If you are a brewer, winemaker or distiller, I want to come and help you make your wine, beer and spirits. If you are a farmer, I want to come and help you harvest your crops and sell them at farmers' markets. If you are a restaurant owner or run a food truck, I will come and help in your kitchens, serve customers and even bus tables. If you are a fisherman, I want to head out into the rough waters with you as you catch some of the finest fish and seafood in the world, and if you are a cheese maker, I want to join you getting elbow deep in curds.'

He knows that America is a land of opportunities, so asking if people had food experiences that he simply mustn't miss was essential to his planning. He specifically requested contact with America's vibrant ethnic communities, such as Vietnamese, Indian, Filipino, Greek, German, Italian and dozens more. He was even prepared to go to family celebrations, learn about their cuisine and show the world just how much they all contribute to the tapestry of that country's cuisine. He was especially interested in food festivals and asked if anyone would be organizing a food festival, or a celebration of an ingredient, for which their part of the country is renowned. He looked for suggestions for the best things to eat as he travelled around the country and requested that the people he met would break bread with him. He isn't a food snob. As he says himself, 'I'm just as happy discovering a great burger in the humblest of surroundings as I am enjoying a multi-course-tasting menu from an internationally famous chef.' As well as all the food invitations, he has sought places to stay while on his great adventure.

When organising his adventure he said he was prepared to sleep on couches, floors, and in cars or trucks. Heck, he was even prepared to spend a night under canvas if it meant there was a great food experience to be had. He was reminded about that famous backpack companion; the first rucksack he bought after quitting his job and deciding he was going to travel. It would be packed and ever ready for the next journey, telling of his determination to 'see, do and eat it all'. With an agenda like this he can't fail in this next incredible journey of a lifetime. From the day he tried on his rucksack, his bag has been packed ready for the next journey.

ENVIRONMENTAL WONDER

Simon Reeve

British author, adventurer and BBC TV presenter Simon Reeve has seen some strange and wonderful sights through his travel. In Mozambique he discovered giant rats specially trained to detect landmines, in order that farmers can work the land. These giant Gambian pouched rats are known for their sharp sense of smell and are excellent for sniffing out explosives.

Travel has brought him into the strangest of cultures and he throws himself in wholeheartedly to experience the life of the locals, even if it means eating dried caterpillars and sheep's eyes. One of the most bizarre experiences was hunting with a legendary tribe of former cannibals in Borneo. He has been invited by royalty to eat penis soup from the zebu (a species of cattle that is native to the jungles of South Asia).

He's faced dangers and awesome wonders all in the line of duty of film and travel. One of his more terrifying moments was being surrounded by a pack of hungry cheetahs in the Namibian countryside. Simon had a close shave, while attempting to feed them. The fact he was covered in bits of bloody meat didn't help matters. He had joined a French conservationist nicknamed 'Catman', who kept a watchful eye on the hungry cats and had to fend them off at one point; all five of them.

Some of the more gentle sights included bathing with the elephants in the Satpura National Park, India, and discovering a large colony of flamingos at Lake Nakuru located 102 miles (165 km) from Nairobi in Kenya and again in the Andes mountains known as Andean Flamingos.

He has kite-surfed in the Western Sahara, searched for wild honey in the forests of northern Argentina and taken a train across Arabia. He has had some challenging moments, especially when he was tracked by terrorists and had to evade the Moroccan secret police in Western Sahara. Simon attempted to meet and interview activists from a rebel opposition group in Western Sahara, who were wanted by police. If they had been able to follow Simon towards the activists then he would also have been in trouble.

Not only have Simon's journeys been extraordinary, but his career progression has been remarkable. For somebody to go from post boy at a newspaper to best-selling international author and BBC TV presenter, travel explorer and BBC terror correspondent without ever having set foot in a college or university, shows extraordinary acumen and a sense of adventure. It's something that has taken a lot of hard work and ingenuity.

Growing up in West London, Simon was unsure what to do when he left school. After spending some time on the dole, he took numerous jobs including working in a supermarket, a jewellery shop and a charity shop, before landing a job as a post boy for *The Sunday Times* in 1990. It was while he was there that he started researching and writing in his spare time. His talent was noticed by the newspaper when he began investigating two foreign terrorists on the run in Great Britain. Following this he was invited to conduct further investigations into terrorism, crime, smuggling and arms dealing. From this time on golden opportunities came his way and he continued to learn his craft and take on new challenges.

After the attacks of 9/11, he began making travel documentaries for the BBC in little known and troubled parts of the world. Since then his whole life has been encompassed by investigative travel in one form or another. The World Trade Center bombing had captured his interest and he studied the events with great interest and insight, writing a book on the subject; *The New Jackals: Ramzi Yousef, Osama bin Laden and the Future of Terrorism* which became a *New York Times* bestseller.

Over time, Simon interviewed Afghan Arabs as well as supporters of Osama bin Laden. He spent many hours in a series of meetings with senior FBI, CIA and intelligence officers. He interviewed spies and militants in cafes, fast food outlets and even car parks. There was always an element of danger as he was followed by secret agents.

His successfully investigated a former Lebanese arms smuggler, in the process travelling across three continents and uncovering the intentions of one of the most dangerous terrorist organisations. Discovery about the world and its people were the motivating factors. If he could get into the lives of people and find out the truth about their worlds, then he could convey this to the wider world to give a better understanding about the countries and its people.

The purpose of his trips was to look at the issues affecting our world and a vital part of it, is mingling with the ordinary people as well as government officials, and blending travel with current affairs. Simon goes the extra mile and risks his own life to get right to the heart of the story. This is evident in so many of his BBC documentaries.

In the BBC's *House of Saud: Saudi: The Family in Crisis* documentary, he entered and gave a rare glimpse of one of the most conservative countries in the world, looking at what life is like there. He examined the culture and religion and the lifestyles of the women. The journey took him across Saudi Arabia, from the cities of Jeddah and Riyadh, to the vast Empty Quarter desert. He met people from all walks of life to get a broader picture of what it is like to live in such a country, meeting a liberal student who became a radical Wahhabi Muslim and had a rare encounter with a senior Saudi doctor. Included among those he met were Saudi princes, Islamic militants and Osama bin Laden's former best friend Jamal Khaleefa, who was running a fish restaurant at the time.

The Tropic of Capricorn (BBC 6 part documentary) in 2008 took him 23,000 miles (37,000 km) around the globe. The point of the journey was to navigate the Tropic of Capricorn, travelling off the beaten track to remote places untouched by foreigners. He describes the Tropic of Capricorn as one of the most interesting and important regions in the world. He traversed the most spectacular landmarks of Southern Africa, Madagascar, Australia and South America. Witnessing strange rituals, diverse ethnic groups and exotic wildlife, he encountered the desperate Zimbabweans frantically climbing razor wire to cross the border into South Africa. Simon recalls the journey as, 'frightening, uplifting, upsetting, challenging and shocking'. It was a journey in which he ate foods and saw sights that he will remember all his life. Around the Kruger National Park he listened to controversial proposals to cull the exploding elephant population; in Madagascar, he drove through one of the poorest, and in his view, one of the most beautiful regions in the world. Its coral beaches, lagoons, steep sea cliffs and the contrasting volcanic crater lakes proved unforgettable natural wonders.

His trip following the line of the Equator exposed him to some of the most dangerous places in the world, including the Democratic Republic of the Congo and Columbia, as well as to the unrecognised places on which he based his BBC documentary series *Places That Don't Exist*. His project in 2005 was to visit breaka-way states that are not recognised by the rest of the world. There are more than 200 such countries and he set out to find out how they operate and how the peo-ple who live there cope under a regime without structure and order. His mission was to make known places such as Somaliland, Transnistria, Aiwan, Georgia, and Nagorno-Karabakh, southwest Azerbaijan. He uncovered corruption and yet, at the same time, he revealed the radiant beauty of the earth.

The Tropic of Cancer 2010 (known as the Northern tropic, is the circle of lati-tude on the earth that marks the most northerly position, again a 23,000 mile (37,000 km) journey, which gave Simon the opportunity to expose world issues such as climate change, poverty, and industrial pollution.

In the BBC series *Explore* in 2009, he looked at many different issues from forced farming to the fashion Goliaths, World Heritage rice terraces to dwindling honey industries, and extreme hunger to extreme football.

Going on these journeys is a way of way of educating the wider world about what goes on in areas we might not know about and more importantly gives a voice to the marginalised people of the earth.

In one of his most recent exotic and extreme adventures yet Simon travelled 6,000 miles (9,600 km) around the edge of the beautiful Indian Ocean for a new TV series, aptly named *Indian Ocean* (2012). As Simon explored the area, from Mogadishu and the Maldives to everywhere in between, he uncovered its beauty but also its history, tensions and many conservation issues.

In 2012, Simon received the 2012 Ness Award from the Royal Geographical So-ciety. Approved each year by Her Majesty the Queen, this royal medal is one of the highest honours in the world for the development and promotion of geography. Simon is particularly proud of his One World Broadcasting Trust Award for an outstanding contribution to greater world understanding.

He has traveled across Australia for a new BBC series *Australia*. He planned to visit the South of the country and on to Perth in the west. He travelled north to one of the remotest parts and on to the Great Barrier Reef and then to Sydney and Melbourne.

THE INTERVIEW

I have arranged to meet Simon at the Royal Geographical Society in Kensington, London. It's a high ceilinged, elegant building and as I wait I notice a familiar face peering down at me from the wall; it's a portrait of Michael Palin, President of The

Royal Geographical Society. When Simon arrives, he is taller than I imagine and he is a wearing a broad and welcoming smile. We wasted no time in getting the conversation started about his early travel memories.

'My earliest memories are going to Tenby in Wales with my family, where my brother James scoffed sand. He was just stuffing his face. Such activity wasn't quite as harmful to health then as it would be today, because the beaches weren't as polluted, so nobody tried to stop him. I knew it was the wrong thing to do and I was in some way responsible. I have a very happy memory of this... a reminder of his daftness now he's a sensible adult. We also went to an idyllic place in Dorset until I became a rebellious teenager. There's a place called Studland Bay, a proper old, wide, sandy beach. We stayed in Wareham in a tiny market town, in a little house there. My dad was a teacher and didn't have sacks of cash lying around. It was a cheap and wonderful holiday.'

What inspired you to visit the places that aren't acknowledged as existing?

'I've always been fascinated by those parts of the world. We don't hear much about them because people don't go there. Plonk yourself down anywhere in the world and there will always be people with stories, tales, problems, issues, joys and delights. A friend was working in Somaliland. I'd heard of Somalia, which I knew was in a completely anarchic collapsed state, but not Somaliland the democratic, stable, unrecognised country in the North of the Horn of Africa. I discovered that more than 250 million people in the world live in unrecognised countries; they are described as unrepresented people. These countries are neither members of the United Nations, or have international recognition. They have a sense of their own identity. That was the genesis of the project *Places That Don't Exist* in 2005.'

What has travel taught you?

'Travel has educated me about humanity. It has taught me a lot about our species, what we are like and our achievements. We are a spectacular creation, the most extraordinary thing that has been created. The fact that you can see us all around this amazing planet is testament to that. There are many positives. Travel has shown me some of the negatives about our species including our ability to get to the edge of the cliff and sometimes not step back, fall off or jump. This is what concerns me about major issues of the future, such as climate change and our ability to deal with it.'

Are you a brave person?

'No, it doesn't take a lot of courage. I've been to Mogadishu, one of the most danger-ous places on the planet, which would suggest I'm not obsessive about safety. I'm prepared to take a degree of risk. When filming, I get into a mindset where I think I'm protected by the BBC force field. I know other people have said they experience this as well. When you are filming, you are focused on doing, so you don't entirely notice the people standing around with guns or the threat they pose to you. Well, when I'm filming they can't do anything can they? Well, of course, they can. A BBC producer and I were in Saudi Arabia just before Simon Cumbers and Frank Gard-ner were attacked. Sadly Simon Cumbers was killed. We try to eliminate those risks and we take precautions.'

Simon was locked up by the KGB during his travels. I ask is it true that he managed to get out by saying he was related to royalty?

'I didn't, but somebody did. I was detained in Transnistria; a breakaway state be-tween Moldova and Ukraine. They have proper old style KGB there. Transnistria has stuck to the old style communism and has statues of Lenin. We were creeping through bushes towards a great Russian military base. We couldn't say much in our defence, like, "We're just filming the flora and fauna".'

So is it true that you are related to Sir Christopher Wren?

'It's what my mum claims. When we were arrested and our guide turned up and said, "What are you doing? You cannot arrest this man, he's related to the Queen of England. It will bring shame on Transnistria." In the middle of the night the KGB came down to the holding cell. We were released with much shaking of hands and apologies. They gave us KGB badges.'

Was it scary?

'I was nervous. There wasn't a British Embassy we could turn to, as Transnistria didn't have diplomatic relations with Britain. Transnistria is said to be one of the main centres for illegal arms manufacturing. It's got that sort of edgy feeling to it. I was concerned but very relieved when we were released. I was scared that some-thing would go horribly wrong. Who would have thought that my mentioning Sir Christopher Wren would result in someone turning up and declaring I was British aristocracy, and that it would get me released? That's something I've joked about with Will with whom I was incarcerated.'

While travelling to Moldova, Simon encountered 32 desperate men who sold their kidneys. One man sold one of his kidneys in exchange for a cow. Were you humbled by what you saw?

'It's one of those situations where you don't know how desperate somebody is and how they can go to such extraordinary lengths, then you remind yourself how lucky you are not to have to do this.

What stands out from my tropical journeys was when I visited refugee camps; those on the Kenya-Somalia border housing Somalian refugees who'd fled the fighting. Kenyan authorities wouldn't allow them to travel any further than into Kenya. They couldn't go to Somalia. I met a young woman called Fatima who'd been there for 17 years. She arrived as a small child and had grown up in this camp. She'd been educated by aid workers and spoke very good English. She understood the world so she had a sense of her place in it. She was only allowed to travel 2½ miles (4 km). That was her world, and there was I, dropping in with my British passport and hopping on a plane to continue on my journey. I can't help thinking about the thousands of people like her who exist around our world, living their lives, unable to travel far, sometimes by choice, but generally through poverty and a lack of employment. The reasons for her not being able to leave was purely political but poverty is also a factor. Thinking of them helps me realise how lucky I am to have a passport, an income and the ability to travel. Never in history have ordinary people like me had such ease of opportunity to travel. It is an extraordinary privilege.

Every journey has a memory where I've been moved, often to tears. Maybe I'm too sensitive, but I'm constantly moved and upset by what I see. In *Tropic of Cancer*, one very emotional moment was when we arrived in a village of the ethnic Chin people in western Burma. The Chin people are found mainly in the western part of Myanmar (the Chin State). We travelled from India to Burma, trekking for hours, and sneaking across the enemy lines to see these people who have an appalling time, living under a rampaging, military occupied country. They live in an extraordinarily beautiful part of the world, and are subject to endless human rights abuses. I find it jarring because a human rights organisation had met us, yet as the Chin people explained to us, they were suffering from torture, arbitrary arrest and executions, and the women were regularly abused by Burmese soldiers. I arrived under a lot of pressure and facing the threat of discovery by the Burmese military. It feels raw to think about it. They still live under threat. It gave me a sense of what it must have been like to live under military occupation in occupied France during the Second World War. It was a terrifying and scary experience, upsetting for everyone.'

Was it difficult to adapt to normal life when you returned home?

'Yes, I think what's really jarring for me is the relatively banal level of political debate at home. Having spent time in countries in the world that are poorly run, where there is extreme poverty and a lot of suffering and to come back to our little island, with people up in arms about relatively parochial matters regarding the state of such and such is upsetting. I think people don't realise just how fortunate they are. I realise I am a visitor when I go to these places. I have come from my homeland and I will return there. Normality for me is being here rather than being there.'

Did you find more contentment among the poor?

'I think that's true generally, but we're on slightly risky ground. I think often there's a risk of romanticising poverty. My ears start to prick up when I hear things like that. People say the way to be happy is to be wealthy in a poor area. I think when you're living in a poor community from South America or Central Asia or Africa and people don't have much then they are bonded together and their expectations are perhaps lower but their appreciation of what they have may be greater. I can imagine that. When you get to cities where you are thrown up against people of great wealth, I think you don't find that contentment in the urban population. In a slum, they say, people are more remote and cut off but they are more aware of the possibilities of what they can get from a job, you know, selling a few mobile phones, hustling to make some money. They are hustling because they want more. Maybe there's a slight distinction there but, yes, I would generally agree.'

Any cultural difficulties?

'One of the places I struggled to connect with people was Australia and meeting Aborigines. That came as a shock. My normal tactics for communicating tend to work. I've been to 90 countries or so and I've found that human interaction wherever you go is often similar. What people want to see is your eyes, smile and genuine warmth. It was unnerving because I was in a country defined as a First World nation and yet there is a section of the population that don't enjoy the contact. They have just cut themselves off from the rest of Australia, largely as a result of the extraordinary suffering inflicted on them.'

Did you encounter any strange customs?

'Early on in my journeys, I tended to adventure-travel. It was all fresh and new. While working on *Meet the Stans*, we came across this local game played with the corpse of a headless goat; the concept struck me as very odd. I had a go at it, having to heave this corpse onto my horse. The only thing I could find to hold on to was his balls. That's the most revolting and one of the most bizarre.'

Simon married Anya while working on *Tropic of Capricorn*. How did they both meet?

'We met at a book launch. It was a proper 'eyes across the room' experience; well it was for me anyway. She thought I was a bit too young but then she found out I was a bit older than she expected. Anya worked on wildlife documentaries as a film camerawoman and had her own camera kit so it was a very nice, happy partnership. I was able to persuade her to come with me. I couldn't do the journeys without my wife's involvement. Being away for eight months last year would not otherwise be conducive to a happy family. It's all worked out well. She has proved herself, travelling across North Africa or Saudi wearing a black abaya in temperatures of 50°C (122°F) or leading the intelligence agencies a merry dance using a diversionary tactic, while my colleagues and I sneaked into Burma. She distracted the agents who came to look for us. They weren't the brightest berries in the bowl and were told that we were asleep. They didn't notice that our doors were locked on the outside with padlocks.'

Do you travel with the same team each time?

'Yes, the journeys are tough. We tend to be in the same place for a few nights. We all muck in. Two or three hundred kilos of camera equipment is shunted around. They're exhausting journeys, wonderful as well. I'm not trying to make you feel like, "Oh Simon, yes, you must have all our sympathy, poor thing". The Tropic of Cancer journey was by far the biggest project. Travelling for six months was a huge undertaking.'

Simon had a health scare that almost cost him his life. He had travelled to Gabon in West Africa and had forgotten to take his anti-malaria pills. He was struck down suddenly with aches pains and convulsions and needed to be admitted to an African hospital for emergency treatment where he was diagnosed with malaria. and successfully treated. It's a particularly nasty illness caused by a parasite and transmitted by a mosquito bite, which rapidly infects the red blood cells. The World Health Organisation discovered that in 2012 there were 99 countries and territories with malaria.

Did your health scare make you fearful of future travels?

'Yes, at the start of my tropical journeys, I was struck down with malaria. I had a really tough time. My temperature rocketed and I was vomiting blood. It was horrible. I felt so ill. It was upsetting and frightening. I was lucky to get treatment. Malaria is the greatest enemy of the species. It has killed half the humans that have ever walked the earth so it's an extraordinary threat and almost entirely confined to the tropics. It was perversely fitting that I was to experience this threat at the start of my tropical journeys. I was diagnosed in West Africa and treated with medication. It worried me to have to head back to the same region to continue my journey. It also made me realise that I'm not invulnerable. I'm careful now. I mean, I felt the effects for at least six months. This general malaise and weakness hung over me. It progressively went away and my health and strength returned.'

What has inspired you on your travels?

'I met a Vietnamese American while travelling on the Tropic of Cancer journey. He'd done something very rare. He had left Vietnam as a child, went to live abroad and studied at an American university. He'd heard an appeal from the Vietnamese Government for foreign ex-patriots who had special skills to return and help the country. He uprooted his family and went back to Vietnam, moving back from the richest country in the world to work on conservation issues. He was a lovely, gentle conservationist, running a sanctuary project for bears that have been rescued or released from bear bile farms. Bears are held in appalling conditions and milked for their bile, which is used as a treatment in traditional Asian medicine, particularly China. They are kept in coffin-shaped cages. He'd given up his life to help the country he felt a bond with.'

One of the aspects of emigration is the effect it has on the country that the emigrants have left. There are more Ethiopian doctors in Chicago than in all of Ethiopia, for example. I think there are big issues surrounding that, which we don't think about. '

I put Simon on the spot and ask if a genie were to appear and grant him one wish to improve the world, what would he do? How would he put the world to rights?

'Blimey. What a responsibility Mary. I'm not going to say anything witty and funny. In my experience of travelling, what is needed most is a rule of law, a clear sense of what the law is and an independent judicial system. That's probably the most important thing for struggling nations. All other things come as a consequence, you know, democracy, a stable economy, healthcare and sanitation. If the law rules the country and rules people's behaviour, then it reduces corruption. It reduces political issues and keeps people on the straight and narrow.'

Where would you most like to return to?

'Madagascar was spectacular. It's been cut off for a long time. The flora and fauna have had to adapt and evolve in serious, mysterious and bizarre ways.

They've some really strange customs and rituals. Some are frightening, some are exciting and some are just plain old bizarre. We'd go over a hill and be confronted by an extraordinary new sight. But I also like to go to the same places, well, my missus and me. We go to Denmark regularly. My wife is half Danish and Denmark is one of my favourite countries. It's one of the most organised and happiest.'

Do you read travel literature?

'I am impressed by the author Rory Stewart. I love the way he just walks and walks. It's the best way of travelling. I like the way he travels simply. It's a way I would love to spend my time. You could go to some of those countries now or you may have been there years ago and life would not be different now, except maybe for a few western t-shirts.'

Has terrorism changed your thoughts about travel?

'It certainly influenced my take on the world and how I think about the world... I like to know what makes a country tick; the problems the people in these countries face. It can appear like I am looking for problems. I'm not, but I'm perhaps slightly too aware of them and some people say my account of the journeys is too negative. I'm more inclined to think we are trying to show the state of the world. It's a means of exploring and understanding the world.'

Where did you write the *Tropic of Capricorn* book?

'I wrote it during the journey. Initially I bought a dictaphone. My colleagues just cracked up laughing. I had to exchange it for a laptop. We were bouncing along, through the Kalahari Desert. I had to time my keystrokes between the bumps. It was so very difficult and I decided that I wouldn't do it again.'

I remind Simon when, with a look of glee, he sucked the eye out of a fish as if it was a piece of candy on the Tropic of Cancer. Did anything disgust him?

'The dangly bits' soup in Madagascar. Well, I didn't have to eat it. I'm open to trying anything and our guide was a member of the Madagascan royal family, obviously completely trustworthy and she ate this soup regularly, so I said I'd give it a go. It was disgusting. But things like sheep's eyes? They're actually pretty good, sheep's eyes, quite delicious.'

In the Kalahari Desert he found himself in darkness, encircled by wild animals. Maybe the animals were curious. It was hard to tell but one never takes chances with wild animals. He walloped the sand with a spade and they fled. I thought it was a clever thing to do. Simon doesn't agree.

'I was going to the loo. This was to bury my personal waste. It was then he realised he was being encircled. It was scary, and joking aside, it's funny when people go to those places where the landscape itself looks deeply unthreatening. There are lions out there for goodness sake. Be careful.'

Has travel restored your faith in humanity?

'Where my faith in humanity has been restored is in terms of our innate friendliness and how amazingly pleased people are in general to see strange foreigners arriving. It's a wonderful thing when you are met with a smile and a hug rather than with suspicion and threats. The world is generally a friendly place, and is surprisingly so. Often people try to paint their adventures or expeditions as being a journey into the heart of a "dark continent", whereas in reality the people may be the sunniest and lightest in spirit that you can meet in many ways.'

Where was the friendliest place?

'Somaliland, because there was such a genuine delight. The people were so happy to see us. It appeared as if they were carried away on a tide of happiness.'

As our meeting draws to a close, Simon admits to getting lost on the London Underground after returning home from his Tropic of Cancer journey. Even for the most seasoned of travellers, anything is possible, it seems.

TIPTOE THROUGH THE MEDITERRANEAN

Carol Drinkwater

Carol Drinkwater, actress and author, was born in London to Irish parents, and grew up in Ireland. During her acting career she worked in film, television and theatre, notably alongside Laurence Olivier at the National Theatre and also starring in a production of Stanley Kubrick's *A Clockwork Orange*. She is perhaps best known for her role in the BBC's television programme *All Creatures Great and Small* in which she played Helen Herriot, the wife of TV vet James back in the early 1980s. Her first children's novel, *The Haunted School*, was made into a mini-series, filmed in Australia and won the Chicago Film Festival Gold Award for children's films, She also acted in Wolfgang Bauer's play, 'Ghosts', at the Hampstead Theatre Club in Hampstead, London.

Carol had a strong desire to buy a property with a view; a place that would be her own personal paradise; where she could entertain friends and still be in a haven of peace and tranquillity; a place to escape to between busy assignments. She had a preference for a property with character and in need of renovation, which could be lovingly restored. Her desire to have some land for growing her own fruits and herbs made the Mediterranean the ideal choice, as did her love for eating *al fresco* on a terrace in the sunshine. When an opportunity came her way to buy an abandoned olive farm set on ten acres (4,500 sq m) of land, she seized it and immediately fell in love with it. Set on massive balustrade terraces and nestled among magnificent cedar trees the farm proved to be irresistible. With panoramic views overlooking the bay of Cannes, it had the potential that Carol and her fiancé Michel sought. This extraordinary haven was named 'Appassionata'. Living in the Mediterranean inspired Carol to write a number of travel books including *The Olive Farm*, *The Olive Season*, *The Olive Harvest*, *The Illustrated Olive Farm*, *The Olive Tree*, *The Olive Route* and *Return to the Olive Farm*. In total, more than a million copies have sold worldwide and two of them have inspired films.

In each of these narratives the author successfully evokes the feel, taste, touch and smell of the Mediterranean for the reader. Each title bursts with colour and adventure and there are vivid descriptions of the wildlife and the idyllic haven in which she lives. Life is not always plain sailing though. Farm work can be gruelling and Carol has battled with all kinds of trials, including an erratic water supply, an infestation of insects and inclement weather. Being self-sufficient has a high price, but the fact that Carol was willing to try, adds to the appeal of her writing. When Carol and Michel cleared the dense undergrowth on their land, they discovered that they had magnificent four hundred year old trees, which would produce a bountiful olive oil harvest in the years to come. The reality of owning olive trees fascinated Carol though she discovered that information about them, how to look after them and their history was limited. Carol went to UNESCO (The United Nations Educational, Scientific and Cultural Organization) for advice. Among the information she gleaned, she found that Greece was keen to establish an olive route, though it had proved difficult to determine where the route began or ended. Carol resolved that she would find the original route.

For her journey Carol travelled from the Middle East, along the eastern Mediterranean shores to North Africa, then across to Greece, Sicily, and into southern Europe, through Italy and north to southern France. In total, she travelled a distance of 2,200 miles (3,540 km) on a stunningly beautiful but dangerous route meeting Cretans, Phoenicians, Greeks and Romans on her journey. She recounts the anecdotes that were told to her in *The Olive Route* and other olive tree titles.

Recently she undertook a major American tour in which she gave talks and hosted a lecture in Ohio Northern University about the olive route.

THE INTERVIEW

Carol popped her head around the door and I recognised her immediately. She looked remarkable with her warm chestnut hair and twinkling hazel eyes. As she smiled warmly, I instantly felt at ease. I knew she had a gruelling schedule ahead with book tours and interviews, followed by travel plans for Australia, New Zealand and Tanzania, as well as a tour to the USA.

I ask Carol if she has any early travel memories.

'Yes, going to Devon on holidays with my parents, and wonderful warm summers.

I was educated in an Irish convent in England. My mother always brought me back here to Ireland, to County Laois to the family farm and I have very beautiful memories of that. I mean very, very, strong memories. The combination of the two, the holiday in Devon was to do with my parents being together, and the other in Ireland was about time with my mother and my mother's Irish family. My father didn't come over [to Ireland] for various reasons, so we'd get the ferry across from England to Dublin and get the bus down to County Laois. Someone would pick us up and we'd end up at the farm. I'm a Taurus and I've always loved things to do with the earth so I get my love of farming from somewhere.'

I turn to earthy things, to the land of James Herriot, her days on the _All Creatures Great and Small_ and ask her how she felt about the Yorkshire Dales, and was it a place she loved?

'I did like it very much and I loved the time I spent there. It was a bit cold for me, of course, in the winter. You know, we were right up on the moors and it was nippy up there. Much as I liked it, it isn't a place I could settle and I wouldn't necessarily go back. I don't want to haunt the _All Creatures_ steps as it were, but if I was to go on a book tour or an opportunity arose to go back, if I was invited, then I'd very quickly say yes. It would be a chance to reconnect to people I met there.'

Was it easy to adapt to the French culture when you moved to 'Apassionatta', your home in southern France?

'I didn't actually realise we were moving there. When we bought the place, it was originally going to be a holiday home, somewhere we could chill out and then, maybe, start writing there. I hadn't intended it to become my principal residence. It kind of crept up on us, the trees, the blossoms, Provence. I'm not comfortable if I'm too far away from the sea you know, I begin to feel nervous. I'm at peace when I can smell the sea or see it within my range.'

I ask what fascinates her most about the olive tree.

'In the beginning I didn't really know anything about it. When I was in my early twenties and went travelling around the Mediterranean – well not around the Mediterranean – but Greece, I spent time walking through and meditating in the olive groves, but it wasn't that I chose the olive groves – I just happened to be there.

It was only after we cleared the land two years after we bought our place in France that we realised that we had 68 olive trees, all 400 years old, that I began paying attention to them. I walked the land around the trees in every season, in every light, in all weathers and I began to get a sense of the beauty and the poetry of the trees. Then I started to ask about their history and where they came from, what does the olive tree mean and why is its culture so absolutely founded in the cornerstone of the Mediterranean?'

I move on to Carol's extensive journey – she spent sixteen months travelling from Gibraltar to Syria. Did the trip enrich her life?

'Well, I'd need to write another book to tell you,' she laughs. 'I found tremendous changes, there's no doubt about it. One of the fundamental messages I've understood is the damage that industrialised farming does – olive farming, for example, and the concern it causes about the way we look after the planet. There were always issues for me, but through travel, they became much more acute. *The Olive Tree* took me into the present and the future. *The Olive Route* took me back 2,000 years into the past. I found trees that are said to be 6,000 years old and are still fruiting. I found signs that take the culture of olive farming back at least that far. I ventured on a journey that took me more than 16 months to make. In time, it's taken me back 6,000 years in history and it's taken me into the future. For example, some sections of Andalucía will be desert in 20 years' time if Spain doesn't stop the way that it uses its land. The people will suffer desertification in some parts and that is a fact.'

What draws you to Lebanon apart from the Olive trees?

'I've been to Lebanon many times; in fact my Christmas present to my husband was to take him to Beirut to meet friends of mine, and to see the 6,000-year-old trees there.'

Carol has been to troubled regions on occasion and was caught up in Algeria at the time of the bombings. Does this put you off visiting these places?

'I try not to put myself in unnecessary danger. I won't go to countries where there is a risk. I wouldn't do anything ridiculous and go on my own without telling anybody where I was, or somewhere I might be knifed in the back. I'm not stupid. On the other hand, I'm not going to allow other people's judgements about what and where is dangerous to influence me. Americans say Algeria is dangerous, don't go there. You could say certain places in America are equally dangerous, don't go there. It's a perspective and a point of view. I've met some of the most wonderful and generous people in Algeria. I've wrote a piece for *The Observer* newspaper about it. I can't state strongly enough how wonderful the people are who live there, and, yes, there are terrorists, but there are terrorists in England, Belgium and other countries. When I used to go to Northern Ireland people would say to me, "My God, what are you doing in Belfast?" The whole of Northern Ireland suffered. The tourist industry suffered because everybody thought there was a war going on everywhere in Ireland, so I think one has to put it into perspective, not take unnecessary risks, know who to trust and always let people know where you are.'

I'm curious about how Carol started writing. Did you always want to write or did travel inspire you?

'I've always wanted to write, I've always written. I had my first piece published in a girls' magazine when I was nine. I've always written poetry. I used to have a big green book of words that I loved from about the age of six; you know unusual words in Shakespeare and the like. I knew I'd be an actress and I dreamed of being a writer. I've travelled on my own from about the age of twenty. My parents used to say that I should write about my travels, that I should start writing professionally and I'd say, "I've nothing to say". I think it was Michel who actually said, "It's really time you started to do this," and that's what really set me on my way.'

So what kind of travel literature do you like to read?

'At the moment I'm re-reading *In Patagonia* by Bruce Chatwin, who I think is a master, and another author I like is Jean Giono, who wrote fiction that was set in Provence. I don't read books specifically because the authors are travel writers. I read writers because of their use of language or because of their perspective, and you know, their take on the world inspires me.'

What travel plans do you have for the future?

'I'm planning a trip to South Africa, partially for work reasons and because there are some places I would like to see.

I went to New Zealand for a literary festival and visited other places while I was there, then went on to Australia and Tasmania. I loved it. I met my husband in Australia. Actually, I had a resident's visa. I would have stayed there if I hadn't met Michel. Ah, I'm so happy to be going back to these places. I'm really excited about that. I love Australia. I love Tasmania. There's always something new to discover. Going back to places is good; I mean, I know so many of those places. New Zealand, I'd only touched ground upon twice. Every place is so big and different each time. There are trips that I've got this year that I'm looking forward to; they are business trips but I always take time aside to discover something new.'

Now that you have traced the Olive Route have you any plans to trace your own heritage?

'Perhaps.... One of my cousins is currently doing that, and I'm fascinated with how he's getting on. I like having a place to visit here [in Ireland] because I've a concern about leaving my mother tongue; I mean a language is a living thing. When I was at school, I was in trouble for having an Irish accent and it was all but beaten out of me. I left England more than six years ago and now I'm based in Provence and don't miss England, though, as you can hear, I don't have an Irish accent. The Irish language has its own rhythm. Actually, that was one of the decisive factors about coming here [to Ireland]. I bought a place in Ireland near to where my mother was born, and she's over eighty now. It's important for me to spend a lot of time with her and to give her back some of her past. I love to visit Ireland. Every time I come I discover something new. I'm enchanted with Listowel. My mother who's from County Laois was with me last time I was there. I love Sligo too – I think it's such an underrated place. Kinsale and Dublin too, I mean, I just love so many places here. I feel as if I've come home when I come here.'

If you had to choose the ultimate journey, where would that be?

'Well, if I had to make one more journey, I'd go to my husband, wherever he was. I took him to Sicily for his birthday because I'd discovered that country when I was writing *The Olive Tree*, and I wanted him to discover it too. We only spent a few days there and only saw a little bit of it, but I am extremely fond of Sicily – I'm extremely fond of many places. They all offer something different, so it's very hard for me to choose just one. It also depends on my mood. I would prefer to be in a warm place because I'm a bit of a lizard, I think. I'm not very comfortable in cold and wet climates.'

Has your mother adopted a love of the Mediterranean culture and way of life?

'Well, I've been trying to persuade her to come and live with us but she doesn't speak French. I can't cart her around the world with me. In some ways she would love to come but she would be a bit cut off.'

Are you still processing olive oil?

'Yes, indeed we are and we are in the process of going organic. Certainly, olive oil is very much a part of my life. It's got many medicinal attributes. It has anti-cancer properties, is good for blood pressure, stress, heart diseases, and the skin, and Arab ladies use it against stretch marks.'

What have you learned through your travels?

'I'll tell you what I've learned; something that is fundamental to who I am and, perhaps, wasn't before I left. I've learned the depth of goodness of humanity, because you know, there were occasions when I was afraid. I was held at gun point in Israel; yes I saw this, that, and the other here, there and everywhere; but actually what I saw were people in war zones, the people who had nothing. I saw people who live without enough water or with access to water for only one hour a day, if they're lucky, and who have to shower and wash in a bucket.

I met people who didn't have enough food and they shared their meals with me. They're the things I remember. Currently I'm working with Devon County Council and Fair Trade organisations to help Palestinian farmers to get their olive oil out into the world so that they can earn some money and not have to live off Red Cross aid. If they asked me to go to Palestine and spend time doing something over there to promote this, I wouldn't think, "oh gosh, am I putting myself at risk?" The issue is more important to me.'

FROM ARGENTINA TO NEW YORK ON HORSEBACK

Marianne Du Toit

Born in South Africa, Marianne studied Political Science and Psychology at Stellenbosch Univeristy. After graduating wtih a BA degree in 1992, she travelled and worked extensively throughout Europe and in 1995 planned and embarked on a three-month cycling tour of that continent. The wanderlust still very much alive, she visited southwest Ireland and fell in love with that country, making it her adopted home. She took up numerous jobs including pulling pints and baking apple crumble and scones for tourists, before moving to work in a medical administrative position and then as a human resources officer. Throughout all this time, she was quietly planning an American challenge.

Marianne Du Toit is an inspiration to anyone who wants to follow their dream. Who else would undertake a 6,000 mile (9650 km) journey, over 21 months, travelling from Argentina to New York, with just two horses for company? Marianne, then 32 years old, was venturing into an unknown continent, had next to no equestrian experience, only one contact in the whole of Latin America and had no idea where she would sleep each night. Her 'dream' journey seemed almost insurmountable. However crazy, ambitious or nightmarish it may have seemed, it was the journey of a lifetime. Compelled to do it, she set off, armed with the bare essentials: two resilient Criollo horses; a pistol; a machete; two stuffed saddlebags; and perseverance, optimism and courage in spades. Trudging the rough terrain of South, Central and North America, she kept track of events in her diary. Heart-warming encounters with locals as well as hell-raising moments of sheer terror were recorded, and here notes were punctuated with her feelings of joy, hunger, loneliness and vulnerability. The journey showed her the immense physical beauty of the terrain through which she travelled but also brought intense frustration, with the odd snake, crocodile and cockroach added into the mix.

Marianne's journey was not just one of personal gain, but an opportunity to create awareness and raise funds for therapeutic riding in Ireland. Her love of animals is not confined to horses. Marianne is passionate about all animal welfare issues and campaigns against the production of foie gras, the use of animals in circuses, puppy farming and much more. She strives to increase awareness about responsible pet care as well as the overcrowded conditions and inhumane treatment of animals reared for human consumption.

Returning to Ireland, she set about rewriting her travel diaries which chronicle her epic adventure. *Crying with Cockroaches*, Marianne's first book, was the result. Described in turn by numerous reviewers as 'unputdownable', 'incredible', 'unique', 'enthralling', 'spellbinding', 'a real page turner'and 'deliciously unbelievable', it was undoubtedly well received.

THE INTERVIEW

The terrace was lit with a golden glow from the evening sun on a gloriously evening. With the calm Irish Sea as a backdrop, the *al fresco* café was the perfect setting to share Marianne's cherished travel memories. A warm and firm hand-shake cemented our introduction.

'I remember travelling eight hours by car, usually twice a year, to stay in my grandfather's house at a seaside resort in South Africa with my family. I remember my dad waking us up at 2 am, singing a song he made up with words to the effect of 'seaside, let's go to the seaside, there where the big waves roll like white horses...'. I remember waking up in a daze, tired but excited. My dad would put the last bit of packing into the car and we would all scramble in, trying to get a window seat before falling into dreamland again. Just after sunrise, we would stop at the side of the road and my mom would produce fresh sandwiches (first salty, then sweet), hard-boiled eggs and a flask of tea. The atmosphere was always electric with us kids bursting with excitement to get to the sea. We'd have a competition to see who could spot the ocean first. On the day we came back, we'd stop at the last beach accessible from the road and go down for a final 'feel' of sea and sand and fill up bottles with sea water for the people who worked on our farm and who used it as a remedy for all kinds of illnesses. Adventure always featured on these holidays. Our "annual thrills" included going at top speed in the car down a very steep hill near our holiday home with my dad, doing hand-break turns in a buggy on an isolated beach, and my dad urging us to surf the biggest waves.'

Marianne tells me about her regular visits to the family farm, with bushveld-like vegetation, thatched bungalows built by her dad, an outside 'long-drop' (toilet) and having to walk over rocks and rough terrain to wash in the river. With only candles and the occasional oil lamp, the evenings created a romantic atmosphere and they would cook over an open fire, tell stories and sing songs long after the wood had burned out.

'The highlight was when my dad would invite us to accompany him to the gate to lock it, about half a kilometre (1/3 mile) away in pitch darkness. We would be giddy with nervousness and anticipation to venture outside the stone walls of the "compound", clutching on to each other. About half way up, there would be an explosion of yelps and hysteria when the sound of a lone jackal would fill the quiet night air and the four of us kids would scatter in all directions. It was only when we were much older that we found out my mom "moonlighted" as a fox during those nightly escapades.'

I was moved by Marianne's book, *Crying with Cockroaches,* a 400-page account of her adventures on horseback. When did she get the idea to undertake this out-of-the-ordinary journey?

'The idea grabbed hold of me in the summer of 2001. At that stage I had been living a relatively settled life in Ireland for seven years. Looking back, it was clear that I was getting itchy feet again. I had just come out of a relationship, had no mortgage or kids, and not that many worldly belongings, apart from an old Nikon camera and a piano. So, in a way, it was a perfect time to "break loose", to dare and to explore. I've always admired women who could do adventurous things and often thought, "If they can do it, what is stopping me?" My journey took about seven to eight months to plan. Not everything was in place before I set off. I couldn't speak Spanish. I was green when it came to equestrian skills. I had only one contact in the whole of Latin America. People thought that I should have had every day planned and to know where I'd put my head down at night. That was just not possible. From a logistical viewpoint that would have been a nightmare to organise, given that the trip was over such an extended period, but also, it would have taken the element of surprise and adventure away from my journey. The not-knowing actually gave me more of a buzz and a sense of adventure rather than the security of knowing that somebody was waiting for me at the end of a day's ride.'

Why this route?

'In my mind, Latin and North America was going to be safer than Africa but more exciting and adventurous than Europe. It's the same route that Aimé Tschiffely, a Swiss school teacher, took in 1925 with his two Criollo horses [sturdy animals from the Argentine Pampas]. I read his book and it was as if it had been decided for me. Mind you, when he finished he did so in Washington DC, citing "crazy traffic" as a reason he couldn't finish in New York City.'

How did people at home react when you told them what you were planning?

'Awe, surprise, shock, fear, excitement, indifference. I have to say, though, that most people responded in a positive way, with close friends being very supportive and wanting to assist with the numerous preparations. Family members all reacted differently; my mom was worried but didn't want to hold me back, my dad commented on my lack of equestrian ability, my youngest brother felt I had more "guts than brains", my other brother wasn't sure what to make of this "mad idea" and my eldest sibling reckoned it was all a bit "far-fetched". Men especially worried about my safety and would warn me about the dangers, real or not.'

There were times during the trip when people didn't offer help. Was it out of suspicion and fear or was it just lack of thought?

'A bit of both. Mostly I think it was suspicion and fear but at times one got the impression from certain individuals that they simply didn't want to be bothered. They had their little routine of daily living worked out for themselves and were perhaps a little irritated to have an intruder disrupt the status quo. I had to understand that. For so many people I was a strange and unusual sight and, just because I wanted to explore the buzz of adventure travel and everything it entails, didn't mean everyone shared that enthusiasm. People had their own struggles and challenges. Combine that with the hardships of daily poverty and I'm not surprised that some individuals simply didn't care to engage. In isolated places such as the Bolivian Altiplano where Indians live their lives in an uncomplicated way as they have done for centuries, their demeanour was more aloof and distant. Not everybody understood what I was doing. Many of the countries in Latin America are still considered macho societies where the roles of males and females are clearly defined. A woman with two horses and a large machete strapped to the side of the saddle would not be an everyday occurrence and many people didn't know how they should respond. I was aware that as much as I had to trust people, they had to do the same. There were many though who couldn't contain their curiosity at the sight of this unusual travelling trio and their zest and earnestness made up for whatever apathy I might have experienced every now and then.'

Do you prefer to travel solo?

'I do. Especially in places where the cultures are so different to what I am used to and where connecting with local people often makes the trip worthwhile, giving it a unique perspective. There is a different dynamic when travelling alone – you often need people for various reasons. You are more open to making friendships and being curious about the lives of the locals. During my journey, I found that women especially, acted in a protective manner toward me, always making sure that I was okay. Many men were equally caring and assisted me in different ways, but it was always women I approached first when entering a small village. There was an almost unspoken code of sisterhood among the women, reaching out to a strange female gringa on her horse. Help had many different faces: a stranger offering something to drink; a local person going out of their way to show me the right road; somebody offering their bed; an email from a friend, family or loved one telling me they were thinking about me; a couple offering to collect a horse hundreds of miles away; somebody actually giving me the use of their horse, no strings attached; a woman dedicating her time and energy for weeks on end to making sure that the horses and I got to our next destination safe and sound. People helped in such diverse ways. Each one had a tremendous impact and warmed my heart in a way that I still have difficulty explaining.'

What were the scariest moments?

'There were many: when Tusa my horse got a fright from the rumbling sounds of a passing train and nearly got himself, me and Mise (pronounced 'Misha', my other horse who was on the leading rope) run over by a truck; in Nicaragua; when the horses were stolen during the night; somebody in El Salvador trying to enter my tent while I was sleeping; being held up by two young men (one with a machete, the other with a large silver revolver) in Guatemala; when Tusa was diagnosed with Equine Infectious Anaemia in Brazil; when Tufein, my other horse, tested positive for Piroplasmosis in Guatemala.'

I ask about the funnier incidents.

'There were daily funny moments. I remember one incident in particular, when I was wearing no knickers, when medics wanted me to remove my trousers to take X-rays after I was kicked on the hip by Tufein in Nicaragua. I travelled lightly and had only one pair of flesh-coloured knickers to wear underneath a pair of flimsy cream coloured three-quarter pants. The underwear was washed the night before and was still damp the following morning so I had to go without. It was a very funny (and embarrassing) moment when I had to ask my host to explain in Spanish to the medical staff that I needed privacy (and a sheet) before I could take off the trousers. My host apparently got a lot of mileage out of that story.

In another incident, two young boys, not older than eight or nine, were watching me intently as I was saddling up the horses in an isolated spot in Bolivia after a "lunch break". I enjoyed the audience and tried to impress them with my expertise and quickness. When I put my foot into the stirrup to mount Mise, the saddle, which wasn't fastened tightly enough slid to the side and I landed unceremoniously on my backside. They stared at me wide-eyed but didn't utter a word. Trying very hard to keep my composure I also kept quiet, walked over sheepishly to where they were standing, and red-faced simply handed them a coin each – I was sure they understood the unspoken deal that they would not repeat to anyone what they had just witnessed. I also remember a crazy looking man, dirty with wild hair and no shoes, come out of nowhere and chasing the horses and me down a street in Central America, shouting and cursing and throwing a plastic bottle at us. He gave me an awful fright but then I turned the tables and started to chase him while still sitting on Mise with Tufein in tow. He didn't expect it and tried to run away in the most frantic but comical way, probably scared out of his wits to have had his own lunacy reciprocated.'

What was the highlight of the journey?

'Experiencing nature and the beauty of the world in such a natural way, with only two horses for companions; surviving from day to day, not planning ahead, living in the moment. There was an attraction in that kind of simplicity of life that I still often long for, the times that I found fodder and a comfortable spot at the end of a day's ride for the horses and me, and not too many questions from the locals, would have to count as regular highlights too.'

What did you miss about home?

'There are a few things I missed, especially in the beginning when the basic living was still new and I had daydreams about warm baths by candlelight. I really missed my own bed, a lot. Of course, there was a longing for close family and special friends, yet I never felt lonely. I didn't pine for a travelling companion, apart from on a couple of blue days. To be alone didn't mean a lonely and solitary existence for me. No phones or intruding technology, no incessant talking; I saw that as a tremendous luxury.'

Did the trip turn out to be what you expected?

'I didn't quite know what to expect so in a way I had no pre-conceived ideas about what my journey would ultimately offer. I was realistic to know that it was going to be tough and challenging. It was. I had this strong belief that people would be helpful and friendly. Most were. I knew my body would be in agony from all the riding and roughing it. I just never thought it would hurt that much. Having expectations can be good or bad because if you have them, you're either going to be surprised or disappointed. I took each day as it came and because it was mostly day-to-day survival, there really wasn't much opportunity to dissect yesterday or contemplate tomorrow. Perhaps living in the moment was the best and most pragmatic way to have done it.'

What condition were you in when you returned?

'Physically I was in relatively good shape, quite thin but not as bad as while I was going through Bolivia and some other parts of Latin America. The horses and I were fed quite well for the three months we travelled through the United States. Most of the aches and pains I had throughout the 21 months began to subside. I looked less weather-beaten than expected. Mentally, I felt fine. I didn't analyse things too much. The journey coming to an end was a natural progression. Nothing lasts forever. Some things come to an end; some things should come to an end. I was looking forward to seeing friends and family. I was also excited about having some kind of normality again, especially having my own bed to crawl into every night.'

Was there a point in the journey when you felt like giving up?

'I could cope with the daily body soreness, the hunger, uncomfortable sleeping, difficult horses, heat and horseflies and more, but when Tusa was diagnosed with Equine Infectious Anaemia and I heard that he had to be put down, it was really the one point during the journey I thought I couldn't go on. I had tremendous guilt and I wondered if the trip was worth it. It was something that I wasn't prepared for and part of the journey that still evokes a lot of strong emotions when I think about it. I gave my best to the horses and their wellbeing was my main concern, but it wasn't possible to control everything.'

I ask Marianne if she is in touch with any of the people she met on the way.

'I have more regular contact with some of them than others. There are many people in Latin America I would like to see again or have contact with. The majority of them don't have email or telephone so once I said my goodbyes after staying with them that was it. The only way to meet again is to make the effort to visit them in person.'

Are you likely to plan another journey?

'I am, but nothing on the same scale. I would like to see many more places, especially the ones off the beaten track. I love challenges and to experience the world in an alternative way. Even though I might not have the luxury of time to plan another adventure, I can see myself involved with something, especially if the logistics and all of that are done by somebody else. I would like to visit some of the places in Latin America again, this time maybe in a camper van filled with copies of my book, which I'd like to give to people who helped me. I would also be very keen to see again a little Indian girl I met in a small Guatemalan village. She was mesmerised by my jodhpurs for some reason. She stole my heart and I find myself thinking about her quite often. She's already ten years older than when I last saw her. It's hard to explain it in words but I thought we had a "special connection". I would be interested to know what her life is like now.'

What did you learn about human nature?

'Most people, when given the opportunity to help, will reach out and do so. Some will do just what is required; others will walk the extra mile. Universally our needs are the same and quite basic: food, shelter, hope, friendship – the rest really is superfluous.'

Who inspired you on your journey?

'The horses were the true heroes and inspired me no end. I was attached to all of them but Mise and I did forge a special bond very early on. Through her demeanour and how she conducted herself, day in and day out, she truly taught me so much about perseverance, loyalty, consistency and forgiveness. When I visit her and look at her, I often wonder how she is really doing. She had experienced different landscapes, places and people for almost two years and suddenly, she's in a field in Co. Wicklow with not that much going on.... I often wonder if she remembers our journey, if she misses me, the daily camaraderie, the challenges, the joys and the tribulations that were part of a journey, rich in its imperfection but ultimately rewarding beyond description. Of course, there were people that I met on the way who made an impact and inspired me with their free spirit and strength, zest for life and positivity, their sense of humour, their selflessness and their generosity. And then those individuals, especially in Latin America, who had very little, not much to look forward to, surviving from day to day but who wouldn't hesitate to share their food, be quick with a smile, never complaining about the cards they were dealt.'

How did you adapt to normal life when you returned to Ireland?

'I didn't think it was going to be difficult until I found myself in a nine to five job not long after I returned. I felt imprisoned and like a bird with clipped wings. I found it hard to be answerable to others, to adhere to bureaucracy and not to have the freedom to work out my own schedule and routine. I resigned a few months later and started to work on my book. I relished the freedom and the ability to set my own timetable, working when it suited me and stopping when it didn't. I worked harder during the two years when I got my book ready, than any other time of my life, and felt alive and free.'

What is your preference for travel literature?

'My choices of travel literature might be considered unusual, given that they are edgy, somewhat dark and not mainstream. I liked Brian Keenan's *An Evil Cradling*, a book that was penned by the author, not choosing the road or the circumstances he found himself in, but rather having had them imposed on him. For me it's probably the most moving and memorable work I've ever read, because of its eloquence, rawness and honesty. I also will never forget *Into The Wild*, the true story of Chris McCandless who ventured into the wilderness of Alaska, highlighting some people's insatiable desire for risk and adventure, the mystery of his life and death and the choices we make. I don't believe he was foolish or ill-prepared for what he undertook. He simply had bad luck in the end, not realising the river would be in full flow when he wanted to return and then ultimately dying from having consumed a poisonous berry. *Into Thin Air* by the same author (Jan Krakauer) was another unforgettable account of an extraordinary undertaking climbing Mount Everest, drenched in excitement, danger, heroism and humanity.'

What's your favourite place to escape to in the world?

'The Blasket Islands in Ireland will always be a special place for me and I remember that road so well, rising from Dingle to Dunquin around Slea Head, a dramatic mountain and seascape route in County Kerry. It feels as if it is the edge of the world with a landscape that teases with offerings of freedom, wildness, restlessness and mystery. It is impossible to be untouched by the beauty and ruggedness. I spent two months on the island, running the little café, next to Peig Sayer's house, and at night slept in an attic, accessible by a steep ladder, with no electricity or running water. I'll never forget one weekend when everybody on the island had gone to see a play in Galway and I was there on my own for three days with only sheep for company, howling winds and little to eat.'

What valuable lessons in life have you learned from your travels?

'Never to burn your bridges; to leave any place you visit better than how you found it and to try and look for the humour in all situations. Oh yes, I have also learned that there is no place like home.'

GOOD SPORT TRAVEL

Tracy Piggott

Tracy is the daughter of legendary and much-admired champion jockey Lester Piggott. She is very practical and down to earth and says of herself, 'You won't see me appearing in a feather hat at the races, I do too much running around.'

Much of her life is spent travelling. Adventure travel doesn't hold any fears for her. She took a keen interest in Marianne Du Toit's mammoth 6,000 mile (9650 km) trip across the Americas on horseback and made a spur of the moment decision to visit her when she was in Bolivia. Marianne was taking a rest for a few weeks from her gruelling journey and she offered to show Tracy around the area in Bolivia. Travel and adventure seem to have been in her blood from early in her life. At the age of eighteen she moved to Kentucky and Florida to work in the race horse industry for three years. She then moved on to Los Angeles to work for some of the leading trainers. When she returned to Ireland she spent two years with respected horse trainer Tommy Stack, who helped her gain more in-depth knowledge of the horse-racing industry.

A new career was launched in 1988 when she competed in a race as a jockey and won the 'ladies race' at Leopardstown race course. She was interviewed and impressed the Sports Department so much that the head of RTE Sport asked her to audition for the job as racing presenter. She agreed and by June 1989 she was in full swing in this role, in time for Derby weekend at the Curragh race course in Kildare, Ireland. Tracy also had the privilege of anchoring the Olympics in Atlanta,

Sydney, Athens, Beijing and more recently London. She had a regular show in the RTÉ studio giving coverage as a presenter in all aspects of the Olympics.

She has shown great versatility presenting at show jumping, snooker and greyhound racing; acting as pitch-side reporter at rugby internationals and narrator on documentaries including *The Young Prince of Ballydoyle*, chronicling the life of the great Irish trainer, Aidan O'Brien. She was also involved in documentaries featuring Dermot Weld and Vincent O'Brien.

She spends her time giving tirelessly to others. If it means swimming the icy cold Galway sea, a distance of nine nautical miles across Galway Bay in 1998, taking a gruelling seven and a half hours in choppy, freezing cold waters and raising 171,000 Irish pounds for Leukaemia research, or cycling coast to coast in America to raise money for the blind, then she'll do it without a thought for herself, or the discomfort she may suffer. Currently she is involved with Playing for Life, a charity that works with impoverished rural communities in Tanzania, Kenya, Malawi and Ethiopia, assisting them to become self-sufficient. In 2000, her travel extended to a cycling expedition with Sean Kelly, the legendary Irish cyclist, a 2,875 (4620 km) mile journey. She travelled from Santiago to South Carolina with a large group of cyclists, journeying across eight states and taking in the Rockies to The Blue Mountains in their sights. It took five days to cross Texas, through every kind of terrain, and with temperature extremes ranging from freezing to baking. The journey was completed in twenty-five days. Proceeds went to the National Council for the Blind.

Tracy's approach to life is holistic. She is qualified to teach Pilates and Tibetan yoga and is skilled in holistic massage. She is passionate about food and just couldn't resist the opportunity for an invitation to cook for *The Restaurant*, a prestigious culinary programme in which participants are judged by a panel of experts.

Tracy helped to coach some of Ireland's politicians and business people with Carr Communications, a company with a long history of preparing people to handle media interest, especially challenging interviews on television or radio. It's not surprising that she gives motivational talks, an area that suits her natural humour, optimism and the good rapport she has with everyone she meets.

THE INTERVIEW

Tracey arrived home late the night before our interview after a hectic week presenting the Cheltenham races in the RTÉ studios. Always on the move, even during this meeting, I ask her where she travelled to as a child with her family?

'We travelled a lot as children. My dad was constantly riding during the winter months when the flat season (racing on flat land) was on in England. So my strongest memories are of Malaysia.We travelled to Malaysia on many occasions in the wintertime. Once the flat season was over we left the UK so my Dad could continue to ride in the winter months. He rode in both Kuala Lumpur and Singapore. I remember playing on the beach in Malaysia during the Christmas holidays. We used to stay in lovely hotels and I loved the food there and the wildlife.

I've also got good memories of times spent in Hong Kong and the Far East. I like the people and the food. We travelled to Caracas in Venezuela, Tobago and Trinidad and we spent one Christmas in Jamaica. Horse racing was popular everywhere. I would have been about five or six at the time. I was attracted to the vibrant colours of the women's clothing, the smells and the food.

I think when you're small you are much more adaptable to travel. For a start it's easier to sleep on a plane and you don't get so affected by jet lag. I remember my mother used to sleep on the floor of the plane, something you couldn't do these days. It was a very different way of travelling. Everything was provided for us so we were all very nice and comfortable. Later on in my life I travelled a lot on my own. When you are travelling solo you have to be a bit more self-sufficient. You meet more people when it's just you. If you travel with friends or family you limit yourself to your little group.'

Tracy tells me she went to live in the USA when she was eighteen.

'I was based in the outskirts of Los Angeles, at the foot of the Sierra Madre Mountains. You think of Los Angeles as being built up and urban but this was very rural and beautiful. I had the mountains right there in front of me; great for hiking and cycling. I'd start work around 4.15 am and finish about six hours later, free to do whatever I wanted for the rest of the day. From there I moved to Kentucky, New York and Florida, where I began riding and exercising race horses. It gave me an opportunity to see and explore the areas where I was based. I relished the expanse of space as far as the eye could see. It's interesting how every state in America is different; almost like a separate country with different cultures and people.

In 2000 I cycled through Texas. It was so gruelling and we rarely got the chance to stop and look,' she laughs. 'However, afterwards, I did visit a place where the staff worked with horses and autistic children and was fascinated by what they were doing. I spent a couple of nights on my own in Austin, a lovely city and very friendly. I felt completely safe.'

My ears pricked up when she mentioned her cycle through Texas. I asked her more about this massive coast-to-coast challenge.

'I travelled from San Diego to South Carolina and averaged 130 miles a day. I had a sore neck and back rather than a sore bottom. Going over the Rockies, the Smokey and the Blue Mountains meant there was a lot of different terrain as well as fluctuations in weather; the temperature went from -5°C (23°F) to 35°C (95°F) in a couple of days. I trained beforehand in Ireland, following a programme designed by famous Irish champion cyclist Sean Kelly who was the leader of the group. I had to cycle a few hundred miles every week to get fit enough for the challenge. I cycled all over Ireland including the Wicklow Mountains, which were stunning. It's only when you travel like this that you appreciate how truly beautiful Ireland is.'

Tracy recalls some of the difficulties she faced while cycling through America.

'I'd just finished presenting at the Sydney Olympic Games working the "graveyard shift" from midnight to 7 am every night for 16 nights. I flew out to America the day after the Olympics finished so you can imagine how my body clock was all over the place. I had to adjust to the eight-hour time difference and really felt "out of it" for the first week.

I remember a journey that was challenging and difficult throughout. The first week was particularly testing and I ached from head to toe. It took about seven days for my body to accept all that I was asking of it. The exercise created a build-up of lactic acid and the soreness it caused never really left me. Then my body clicked into a rhythm and the physical hardship began to subside, although psychologically it remained quite tough. It took five days to cycle through Texas and at times there was nothing to see. The group I travelled with were on the back roads, not the highway so it was just brown and dull with nothing to distract our attention. All we were left with were our thoughts. It was so cold that one of the cyclists got hypothermia.'

Tracy describes the strange effect of this kind of travel.

'Even though we were a group (24 of us in total), everybody functioned in an isolated way. We were all going through different experiences at different times. Some were suffering physically, others emotionally.'

I assume it must have been difficult to get back to a routine after returning from the trip. Tracy agrees.
'Very much so. A lot of people found that. We were advised that we should keep cycling because it would be bad for us to stop abruptly. I did carry on because I was really into it, though I knew there was going to be a feeling of anti-climax after we'd reached our goal. I just forced myself to start focussing on my life in Ireland, looking for the next thing to do.'

I ask her to recall the highlight of the trip.
'There were different highpoints along the way. I discovered different things about people and myself that I wouldn't have otherwise got to know. I had a strong feeling of achievement after the first week when I realised that I was able to meet the challenge. Deep down I never truly believed I could get through it. I thought I would be heading home and throwing in the towel.'

Tracy lost her friend John to leukaemia so she dealt with her grief by undertaking a long charity swim across Galway Bay.
'It was a seven and a half hour ordeal during a very bad summer in Ireland. After the first two hours it was pitch black and I almost got into a meditative state. I experienced a peace that I haven't had anywhere else. I really enjoyed it. The challenge started in County Clare at the Martello tower outside Kinvara, then headed directly across to Salthill just outside Galway. It was a mammoth task because of the very unpredictable currents in Galway Bay. It was more difficult psychologically than physically.'

After the swim Tracy felt exhilarated and didn't want to get out of the water, but the next morning she was reporting the Galway races.

'I literally got out of the water and went to do the races. There were no ill effects bar sore ankles.'

I know Tracy travels to Africa on a regular basis. Why so frequently?
'I set up my own charity in 2005 called Playing For Life and we work in different parts of Africa. I went to Ethiopia and it inspired me to want to help educate young people. We started in Malawi and branched out to Kenya and Tanzania. Then when I had my daughter five years ago I wasn't able to go as much. I was

shocked when I went there at first. I thought I was prepared but I wasn't. What really stood out for me was the incredible dignity of the people, the way they are so happy, positive and how they want to share their possessions, even though they have so little. It was a very humbling experience. It left me with very mixed emotions; wanting to fix things, but I've learned the hard way that everything cannot be fixed. The corruption and waste makes it very frustrating. It has made me accept that I can help. The charity concentrates mostly on Tanzania and it's been wonderful to be able to help the young people with their literacy and computer skills. Before we put in place a particular programme we ask the community what they want from us rather than give them random hand-outs.'

Tracy tells me travel has helped her to get over tough times. As soon as she gets on a plane she can step back from everyday life.
'I always find that when I've been away I can figure things out better when I come back. I think it's important to get out of your comfort zone.

I wanted to go on a safari and decided on Salon in Tanzania, a place about the size of England. I spent a few days there and visited a very small reserve as well as the game safari park. Only a fifteen minute flight from the Dodoma, capital of Tanzania is Zanzibar. I spent ten days there just exploring, chilling out on the beach, walking and reading; it's a stunning place.'

I ask her about her Bolivian trip to meet Marianne Du Toit who was in the middle of her 6,000-mile journey on horseback. Marianne rang Tracy to see if she would be willing to become a patron for the TATA Challenge, Therapeutic Riding for People with Disabilities. They met and kept in touch.
'Marianne and I became very friendly before she departed on her challenge and kept in touch during her adventure. I always said that if I could, I would try to go out and see her. She and the horses were taking a necessary break for a couple of weeks, having come through the isolated Altiplano. I had a love affair with South America at the time and I really wanted to see more of the continent. I arrived at the airport outside La Paz, a city more than 13,000 feet (3962 m) above sea level and the capital of Bolivia. The air was very thin and I had difficulty breathing: at night it felt like there was an elephant on my chest. Marianne gave me cocoa tea, renowned for assisting with altitude sickness. It worked a treat. We stayed with Chacho, a friend of Marianne's, in his lovely apartment in the heart of the city. I particularly remember his flair for cooking spectacular dishes full of flavour, herbs and spices.

In La Paz I was fascinated by the explosion of colour everywhere, in the markets and the clothes the women wore. It was a captivating city and I loved going up the narrow streets and looking in to these weird little shops with magic potions and lotions in them. It's the colours, smells and music I remember mostly.

While I was there we decided we'd go for two days to the jungle in Peru. In the middle of the night a guide took us by canoe to a little lodge on the Amazon River. We had no clue where we were. There was a huge full moon reflected in the water and there were wild otters swimming along the sides of the canoe. It was very hot and sticky and if I shone my torch I saw the camens (little alligators) swimming across the river, their eyes lit up under the light. We were staying in a wooden shed. I think I started to cry and Marianne said, "Come on it'll be fine". We paid about three dollars a night and I hinted about moving to the luxurious tourist lodge down river, but Marianne wouldn't hear of it and insisted we do it on a shoestring. Our beds consisted of just planks of wood with something on top that could hardly be described as a mattress. I remember the guide saying, "look", and shining the torch on a giant tarantula on a tree trunk just a few metres from where we were going to sleep. The guide was very impressed with how beautiful this creature was and that it was female. As if knowing that would have made us feel any better! We had mosquito nets over our beds and made sure every corner was tucked in so that nothing could get close to us. I don't think I slept during the four nights we were there. It was also really hot and humid. I was constantly aware of all the creepy crawlies and could swear imaginary giant spiders were creeping up my neck. We could hear the wild boars and the monkeys.

There was nowhere to wash or shower so we cleaned ourselves in the river where the piranhas swam. Apparently they won't eat you unless there's no food available. They have sharp little teeth and I couldn't get over the funny little human-like noises they made. The loo was an outside hole in the ground and I wouldn't go. I don't know how I managed.' Tracy insists that she wouldn't have wanted to miss this jungle experience for the world. She chuckles, remembering a funny incident. 'One afternoon, Marianne was having a nap. The door of our shed was open and I was sitting on a log, writing my dairy. There were chickens everywhere. The next moment one walked in nonchalantly squawked and climbed onto Marianne's stomach. She woke with a startle and screamed at the top of her lungs when she saw this really ugly chicken just a few centimetres from her face. I got a great laugh out of it.'

I ask Tracy if it was difficult leaving, knowing that Marianne would be alone for the rest of the journey.

'Oh yes, I was very sad and upset to leave her. We cried a lot when the time came to say goodbye. I wouldn't be seeing her for another year at least but we continued to stay in touch. It was extraordinary what she did and it was wonderful to share a little bit of the adventure, to get the opportunity to be in that part of the world.'

I mention individuals who have inspired her and ask Tracy about 'Chacho', Marianne's friend in La Paz.

'He was a unique individual, in his seventies, but with an incredible energy and zest for life. He regularly danced at carnivals in fancy costumes, wore a hat every day and had all his clothes tailor-made. Grabbing every day by the horns and living a full life, he was one of those people that stood out for all his positivity and warm nature.'

She also mentions Sean Kelly who supported everyone during the cycle, going back to stragglers and motivating them to keep going.

Tracy travelled to Switzerland recently where Thea, her daughter, learned to ski. Does Tracy have plans to travel futher afield with her daughter?

'I'm looking forward to travelling with Thea when she gets older. I took her to Zanzibar but that was a mistake. She got bitten by mosquitoes and the African kids gave her such a hard time because of her blond hair and blue eyes. They wouldn't leave her alone. Then she was ill after eating ice-cream that wasn't properly frozen and was violently sick for twelve hours. It's not a place for a young child.'

AROUND THE WORLD WITH PALIN

Nigel Meakin

If you've watched any of Michael Palin's travel series on television, you'll have heard him making references to cameraman Nigel Meakin. Nigel was nominated for television BAFTAs in 1990 for *Himalaya*, in 1998 for *Hemingway Adventure*, in 2000 for *Full Circle* and in 2005 for *Around the World in 80 Days*. He won a BAF-TA in 1993 for *Pole to Pole* and in 2003 for *Sahara*. With his work he has travelled extensively with Michael to far-flung destinations including Mount Everest, the Poles, and the Sahara Desert, as well as circumnavigating the Pacific.

MICHAEL PALIN

Michael Palin agreed to meet me after I met Nigel Meakin. He greeted me with a warm firm handshake. His chocolate brown eyes were friendly and engaging with a naughty twinkle about them. He towered above me, a ruggedly handsome man with a craggy interesting face. Presented in a softly woven dark brown jacket and a crisp white open-necked shirt, he looked fresh and fit. We browsed through some photos I brought along and he was particularly amused by a sneaky shot I took of Nigel in the kitchen, polishing his BAFTAS.

Michael's success grew especially with the emergence of *Monty Python's Fly-*

ing Circus and his many Monty Python films, including *The Missionary* and *A Private Function*. While still involved with screenwriting, a unique opportunity came his way when BBC television offered him the chance to travel the world with all expenses paid. It proved too tempting to turn down. Michael Palin and his cameraman Nigel Meakin began to travel together in 1988 while filming the series *Around the World in Eighty Days*. Michael confesses that he has fond memories of the first of his BBC journeys around the world. *Around the World in Eighty Days* had been turned down by three people, so it was providential that it should fall into Michael's lap. He was to leave the world of scriptwriting behind since, as he says, 'there was no script for this journey', which according to its title was to be a trip against the clock.

Michael had 80 days to circumnavigate the globe following in the footsteps of the fictional character Phileas Fogg after which the television series was named. The journey must be taken over land or sea but not in the air. He later wrote: 'Nigel Meakin has been closer to me on the journeys than any other member of the team. Apart from the second forty days in the Around the World in 80 Days series, he has been my cameraman throughout seven series. We once worked out how many meals we'd eaten together per series. For *Full Circle* alone it was about 870. In a way we are very similar, we have high standards and like to get on with our work with as little fuss and bother as possible. We have established a good rapport so that I know when Nigel wants me in shot and when he doesn't, and I know how important it is for him to have time on his own to photograph all the detail of a location, which provides the vital background and adds so much richness to our portrait of a country. Nigel has won more BAFTAS for his work on the series than anyone else and yet the only time I've ever seen his nerves show is when he has to get into black tie and go and collect them. He has a wonderful eye and I trust him completely.

Nigel's efforts to capture our work on film make him look like the one-man bands that used to entertain cinema queues. He balances precariously on a deck rail, a sheer drop into the sea behind him, with camera on one shoulder, tape recorder on the other, headphones over his ears, microphone between his knees and clapper-board in his teeth.'

Here is a man who has slept at the North Pole in temperatures of -40°C (40°F); he's been hoisted over the side of a ship without a survival suit to film icebergs; onto an ice floe occupied by a hungry polar bear; filmed at the South Pole with a wind chill dipping as low as -50°C (58°F); a man who endured tricky conditions at 18,000 feet (5,480 metres), climbing twelve miles (19 km) a day and losing a crew member to altitude sickness. He is described as having nerves of steel and doesn't suffer motion sickness, even on the choppiest of seas. He is known to have the constitution of an ox. Nothing fazes him. Yet he has a shy quality, a quietness and modesty about him. Facing people terrifies him. According to Michael Palin, on one occasion, 'He ran off the stage without making a speech after receiving his BAFTA'.

Nigel has worked on numerous high-profile programmes including BBC's *Horizon* and *Panorama* documentaries and investigations to *King Hussein of Jordan, Profile of a Very Special King* and *Secrets of the Ancient World*, all of which took him far and wide across the world.

Nigel travelled with an expedition led by the mountaineer Chris Bonnington for the programme *Search for the Yeti*. One of Nigel's favourite documentaries, *The Last African Flying Boat*, chronicles the journey of London journalist Alexander Frater who travelled from Cairo, Egypt to Mozambique in a Catalina flying boat, a vintage seaplane designed to carry passengers in luxurious comfort throughout the British colonies in Africa during the 1930s.

THE INTERVIEW

Without a doubt Nigel is a warm and friendly individual and when I met him I could see why Michael Palin loved working with him. I began by asking how Nigel came to be working on the Around the World in 80 Days series.

'I was thrilled when director Clem Vallance asked me to shoot the series. I had worked with Clem in 1979, making a film about the Marsh Arabs in Southern Iraq. It was on the strength of this film, and our ability to get on in tough conditions that persuaded him to ask for me. Director Roger Mills, who has an amazing track record in documentaries, was new to me but he had an excellent reputation.'

So, what sort of preparation was needed?

'We had to be sure of the reliability of the equipment. I was working for the BBC film department, then based at Ealing Studios. Because it was a relatively small department it offered fantastic support. It was decided that a second camera was essential because if the first camera failed there would be no time to wait for a replacement due to the pressure and timing of the schedule. It was important though to keep the number of travel cases to a minimum. Because we were shooting on film, the equipment was swollen by the sheer bulk of the film cans and the second camera.

My personal equipment consisted of a normal size suitcase; we knew that there would be time, in a few locations, to get some laundry done.'

Was Nigel overwhelmed by it?

'I was in no way daunted by the scale of the trip in 1988 because, by this time, I'd been filming as an assistant cameraman and cameraman for 21 years and had visited more than 50 countries. Living out of a suitcase and moving from hotel to hotel seemed normal.'

What were your fears?

'Mostly they focussed around the possibility of technical breakdown. There's always a concern about the equipment but also all the everyday problems of shooting on film; hairs in the gate, scratching, fogging, X-ray damage and potential processing issues, for example. I experienced a combination of excitement and apprehension knowing that most of the shooting required me to get it right first time, as invariably, there was no time for a second take.'

Surely it must be difficult being in confined spaces with the crew for long periods? Did you all get on as a team or were there minor irritations?

'I'd worked with the technical team; Julian Charrington, assistant cameraman, and Ron Brown, sound technician, on numerous occasions, so I knew we would get on. Clem and I had worked together before and Roger Mills lived up to his reputation. Michael Palin is a person who fits into any group. He is always jolly and great fun. I think the excitement and challenge of the series, combined with such a fine group of people, made it impossible not to get on. I know it doesn't make exciting reading but I don't recall anything irritating about any of the team.'

What was your best travel experience?

'Without any doubt it was the journey by dhow from Dubai to Bombay, lasting a full week. The crew were fantastic. They welcomed the five of us as if we were part of their team. I wish to this day that I could have understood what they were saying to each other about us. We must have seemed an odd bunch. The great thing is that any differences in religion or behaviour quickly became unimportant. It was an education to observe a group of Indian men doing such important work and leading such uncomplicated lives.

There were humorous moments every day because Michael has a natural ability to turn any situation into a comedy moment. The most hilarious focussed around the half-barrel toilet strapped to the side of the dhow. It was a precarious enough journey just to get there, fighting the roll of the vessel and navigating the uneven sacks of dates and then the individual concerned would just disappear into the barrel as if dropping overboard. Poor Michael had to use it constantly over a 24-hour period because he developed a stomach upset.'

Michael later wrote: 'Talking later to passpartou (the crew who went everywhere with him as assistants), it transpires that what we all fear, even more than sharks, pirates or a resumption of the Gulf War, is to miss our footing while clambering onto the loo in the middle of the night. What a way to go.'

'It's amazing how easily we were amused when confined to the dhow for seven days. With little to do on board, apart from lying in the sun, watching the sea slip by, and observing fabulous flying fish, I filmed virtually everything that happened. The original idea was to get about 15 cut minutes from this journey but because there was so much material our editor, Dave Thomas, created an extra episode for the series. It turned out to be one of the most memorable episodes of Michael's entire travels.'

Nigel finished his journey in Japan and had to hand over to the new passpartou. Did you find this difficult?

'I have never been so disappointed. Right from the outset the BBC decided it would be too arduous for a single crew to shoot the entire journey. When we reached Hong Kong the second crew, Nigel Walters, Simon Maggs and Dave Jewett were ready for the challenge. We had all got on so well and had become a very efficient team, understanding each other's wishes and rapidly shooting sequences when there was very little time. After handing over, they filmed in the bird market, which was followed by a black tie dinner. Then we all met up for a farewell dinner the following evening.'

Did you feel sad handing over to another crew on the *Around the World* trip?

'When the filming was over there was this rather empty feeling, as if someone had stolen my favourite toy the following morning, after passpartou number two had taken over. I remember lying in bed and really savouring the feeling that I could stay there for as long as I wished. Arriving back home there was a great feeling of achievement but I was disappointed not to have completed the journey with

Michael.'

I ask Nigel about his favourite locations.

'The first extraordinary place was the Corinth Canal, an awe-inspiring piece of en-
gineering. Our ship, the *Espresso Egitto*, squeezed through the canal with less than
2 metres (6½ ft) spare on each side. Exhilarating! Another favourite was Egypt,
with such wonderful people; such a huge contrast between the frantic main city
Cairo and the almost biblical pace and atmosphere of the countryside. I loved India
too; the vibrant colours, variety of smells, the proud people, the slow rickety rail-
ways and, of course, the food.'

You must have faced dangers. Did you ever feel your life was at risk?

'I never felt my life was in danger. However, there was one occasion when I was
apprehensive. We were on the dhow for the *Around the World* series and in the
middle of the night, I was woken by urgent whispered instructions between the
ship's crew. I noticed that all the navigation lights had been turned off and the
engine was idling at minimum revolutions. There were sounds of high-speed motorboats in the distance and it appeared as if we were edging silently between
two high rocky cliffs. The captain was acting nervously and the crew were alert
and attentive. There was an atmosphere of danger. The sound of the motorboats
stopped some time later. The navigation lights were switched back on and the engine regained speed. The danger, whatever it was, had passed. Pirates or smugglers
perhaps? I will never know, but certainly a moment of tension.

   More tension was to come in 1976. I was promoted to cameraman and was sent
on a *Tonight* tour of the Far East. The tour lasted about five weeks and ended in
Bangkok during an attempted coup. We were filming outside The Thammasat University among a huge crowd. There were gunshots and suddenly the crowd of
many thousands dropped to the ground. The only two remaining standing were
myself and my assistant. We realised that the guns had been turned on the crowd
and everyone had dived for cover. My assistant, John Adderley, an Australian,
said, "Right, we're out of here". We fled to the hotel. The sound recordist, Bill Searle,
had previously become detached from us. It was a good two hours later, when
John and I were sitting at the hotel bar, that Bill caught up with us. He was furious, assuming we had deserted him; he made sure that the entire hotel knew and
we heard about it in no uncertain words. We apologised, he calmed down and
we drank beer. We later heard that hundreds of students had been killed. The
next morning we had a telex from the film operations manager at the BBC saying,

"Assignment complete, return to base immediately", so we did.'

Was there a journey you would never forget?

'Thankfully Michael Palin dominated the next few years with Sahara, Himalaya and New Europe. I feel very privileged to have been part of Michael's team for so long. The crowning highlight from all these travel series was the journey from Cape Town to Antarctica. We had inquired about the possibility of going on an Antarctic survey vessel named MV SA Agulhas but it was booked. After travelling 6,800 miles (10,943 km) down the length of Africa we were confronted with a major problem. The only possible way to get to the South Pole was to abandon our goal of surface travel only and fly to Santiago, then down to Punta Arenas. We had several days waiting in Punta Arenas for the weather to be calm enough for us to fly to Patriot Hills in Antarctica. We eventually boarded an ancient Douglas DC 6 built in 1953. The flight time was eight and a half hours, flying over Drake Passage, then with increasing sightings of icebergs we flew over the Bellingshausen Sea. The landing was both spectacular and alarming as we touched down on the heavily rigged blue ice runway; no braking was allowed for fear that the aircraft would go into a spin. On the short walk from the plane to the camp most of us fell over on the incredibly slippery ice. The camp consisted of a collection of sleeping tents and one large kitchen/dining tent, all very cosy.

I've never experienced 24 hours of daylight before and it's quite odd to get up for a pee at three in the morning and find the sun shining just above the horizon. Once again we waited for the weather to be calm enough to fly the 600 miles (965 km) to the Pole. We took off in a single engine turbine Otter in –26°C (-15°F) and I felt so excited to be finally on the last leg of this wonderful journey. Our pilot, Dan, had never been to the Pole before but one always trusts the pilot. We landed at the Amundsen-Scott South Pole Station on a wide snow runway. The place was littered with snowploughs, oil drums, building materials and various vehicles. We filmed inside the USA base at the Pole, some 100 plus people dressed in T-shirts, munching on hamburgers, chilli dogs and all the classic American fast foods. It was quite bizarre. Outside we did our final piece of filming with Michael at the Pole in –50°C, (58°F) with added wind chill. Despite there being plenty of spare rooms in the cosy American research station, we were told we couldn't sleep there unless we had special permission from Washington, so we pitched our tents on the ice and I spent the coldest night of my life. We travelled nearly 23,000 miles (37,015 km) on Pole to Pole, an experience I will never forget.'

How did you manage to keep your spirits up during the low times on the *Around the World* series?

'There were frustrating moments but our spirits were never low. The momentum kept us going and if some transport connection failed; it just made the journey more exciting. As a team we all got on extremely well and I suppose the testament to that is that we went on for 20 years doing the same sort of documentaries. It was always fun, always hard work but always rewarding.'

Was there anything in particular you couldn't have travelled without?

'I took a small short-wave radio and it was wonderful to keep up with world news, especially when we were on the dhow. Apart from that and a couple of books, I tend to travel with very few accessories. I'm more than happy just to observe everything I see around me.'

Nigel's wife, Rhian, joins us for a chat and takes on the role of photographer. She is a warm, attractive lady with a distinctly Welsh accent. They met on the *Goodies* series where Rhian was working as a make-up artist. She tells me how she tried not to worry about Nigel while he was away, but nevertheless always did. One time she got a call to say he had an accident in Alaska.

They were filming a dog sled race and hit black ice. The entire crew were ejected through the windows of the crew van. Nigel ended up with a fractured spine, three cracked ribs and severe damage to his left shoulder.' Peter, their son, was with him. They had to be flown back. Amazingly Nigel made a full recovery, missing only eleven weeks of work and he insists, 'I have no problems now.'

Where is you favourite place to travel?

'I have visited 117 countries. Each has its own charm, atmosphere and culture. It's impossible to pick a favourite.'

Was it hard to adjust to home life after being away for so long?

'*Around the World* was such an unusual shoot. It's rare to be on a foreign assignment where the entire unit is constantly moving on. After I returned home it did take a while to adjust to normal life simply because the race against time, the excitement and the pace suddenly wasn't there anymore.'

What's your favourite in the Palin series?

'I've filmed all of Michael's seven journeys except for the second half of *Around the*

World in 80 Days. Each journey offered fantastic opportunities for photography and terrific experiences in so many different countries. I suppose if I had to choose a favourite it would be *Around the World* simply because it was fresh, new, spontaneous and extremely popular. It was a huge success and was a catalyst for the BBC to urge Michael to keep on travelling.

My other favourites would be *Sahara* and *Himalaya*, stunning scenery, fascinating people and great physical challenges. Even though I won a BAFTA for best photography for *Sahara*, I felt *Himalaya* was a better series.

Michael had the lovely idea of trying to trace the crew of the *Al Sharma*, the dhow we travelled in years earlier. In 2008 we set off for Dubai and India. We had departed from Dubai on the dhow 20 years earlier so it was a logical place to begin the search. We discovered it had sunk a couple of years previously with no loss of life, though it wasn't our crew who suffered the loss as the boat had been sold on. Our crew had retired and returned to their homes in the state of Gujarat, northwest India. I was very much looking forward to meeting them all again and wondering whether we would all recognise each other. When we finally met up there was no question as to who was who. Captain Hassan Suleyman had filled out a bit but his ever-smiling face was exactly the same. It was sad to discover that Kasim had died – he had been such fun when listening to Bruce Springsteen on Michael's Walkman (tape machine) rocking back and forth to the music, grinning from ear to ear. The cook, Deyji Ramji, had also died. He had made terrific food, freshly caught fish with all the great Indian flavours.'

Talking of food, Nigel must have eaten all kinds of everything?

'I've always been quite adventurous when trying different foods and I'm lucky to have a strong stomach. I will try anything that's put in front of me and I love strong, spicy flavours. In China, in 1982, the crew were invited to a classic Chinese banquet, a meal consisting of numerous courses. When the soup arrived I asked our interpreter to tell me what was in it and he said he would after I'd eaten it. It tasted OK and I finished the bowl. It turned out to be made with the ovaries of the snow frog.

When filming the Marsh Arabs in Iraq I soon learned that the height of politeness is to immediately offer the half goats head back to the host.'

What have you learned from travel?

'I've discovered that all cultures are fundamentally the same. We have the same needs and desires and treasure the love of a family. Most people are warm, friendly and very hospitable. I make an effort to respect the customs and practices of the local people and they respect me for that. If you are open, friendly and smiling, they will be the same. My travel tip is to remember that you and your country will be judged by the way you behave abroad. If you are rude or disrespectful, or shout or lose your temper, then you have damaged the reputation of your home country and have certainly done yourself no favours. Stay calm, stay quiet, stay polite.'

What's next?

'I'm working, at the moment, for the FIA Foundation – an independent charity that manages and supports an international programme of activities. It promotes road safety, environmental protection and sustainable mobility, and funds specialist motor sport safety research. It is running a ten-year road safety campaign aimed at reducing the horrendous number of people killed on the world's roads. We have filmed in Vietnam, South Africa, Malaysia, India, Costa Rica, Russia and in Europe. The aim is to convince governments to make fundamental changes regarding safety by introducing laws on crash helmets, seat belts and road design as well as educating drivers on all road safety matters. Over ten million people have been killed since the beginning of this decade. My work with the FIA continues with trips to Malaysia and South Africa.

I plan to continue travelling with my wife. We have visited India, China and Peru. There are many places I would like to visit as a tourist but you never quite get the same access as a film crew. My ideal holiday would be a week in the sun on some un-crowded beach, followed by a week of exploring ancient sites. My holiday from hell would be a coach tour anywhere. At least I can go back and visit many of my favourite places without all the camera equipment.

Being a documentary cameraman has to be the best job in the world and I have to thank the BBC for first-class training and for presenting me with so many fantastic opportunities.'

CHILE TO ALASKA, THEN BELFAST TO DELHI... ON A MOTORBIKE

Geoff Hill

was intrigued by Geoff Hill's book, *The Road to Gobblers Knob*, published in 2007 recounting an epic journey from Chile to Alaska by motorbike.

Here was a man who had reached his forties, still relatively young, but was suddenly faced with the loss of his job in journalism. No longer required to write the travel section that he loved, his world simply fell apart. Trapped in the grip of this crisis, he became depressed and overcome by feelings that he had made a failure of his life. Geoff had a dream of riding on the Pan-American Highway on a motorbike but couldn't find a book about it, so he decided he should write one. The route he chose was one of the most difficult and dangerous with rough terrain and all kinds of temperatures. In *The Road to Gobblers Knob*, he describes his 16,500-mile (26,550 km) journey on the longest road in the world. The decision to travel was to be a turning point and from here on his life would be transformed into one lasting and exciting adventure.

An award-winning feature and travel writer, Geoff hails from Tyrone, Northern Ireland. His first travel book, *Way to Go*, which details a journey from Delhi to Belfast, and Route 66 from Chicago to Los Angeles, was nominated as UK travel book of the year. He went on to tackle the Australian road equivalent, from Adelaide to Adelaide, writing an accompanying book as well as making a documentary, *Oz: Around Australia on a Triumph*.

Geoff has won or been shortlisted for the UK Travel Writer of the Year Award nine times. He is a former Mexican Government European Travel Writer of the Year, and in 2005 he was presented with a Golden Pen Award by the Croatian Tourist Board for the best worldwide feature on Zagreb. He has written travel articles for *The Daily Telegraph*, *The Sunday Telegraph*, *The Independent* and *The Independent on Sunday*. He was an editor for *Fodor's American Guide Book* series and has presented travel shows on independent radio. He has won numerous awards including two UK newspaper design awards, several UK and Northern Ireland feature writer of the year awards, and in 2007 was the NITB Northern Ireland Journalist of the Year. Geoff is a qualified pilot and at 6ft 7in (1.8 m) tall is a record-breaking former international volleyball player. He currently writes a motorbike column for the *The Sunday Times* and lives with his wife Cate in Belfast.

He is getting ready for another epic, around-the-world journey by motorbike. The journey was first undertaken more than 100 hundred years ago by American writer Carl Clancy Stearns. Geoff and his bike companion Gary Walker, a former road racer, are taking the boots that Clancy wore on the journey. They were donated to them and it has been requested that Geoff and Gary take them to a museum. It's going to be a gruelling three months on the road but it's the life Geoff dreams of. His publisher, Blackstaff Press, have commissioned him to write a book about the trip.

THE INTERVIEW

I was stunned when I met Geoff. I found myself wondering how he managed on a motorbike with his long legs. He towered above the book shelves, yet appeared surprisingly gentle and softly spoken with a lilting Northern Irish accent. His open expressive face was framed by his light red hair and dimples. Smartly dressed with a trendy rain coat and umbrella, he was natural and easy going.

I ask Geoff to tell me about his first treasured memory.

'It has to be when I had my head stuck in an aunt's gate in Larne when I was four. The feeling of freedom when the fire brigade arrived and got me unstuck was so overwhelming that I cancelled my plans to become a fighter pilot with the Mounties and decided there and then to be a travel writer if I ever grew up. Despite that never happening, I stuck to my promise. I remember heading off to air shows and days at the beach in my parents' first car, a black Ford Popular, with trafficators and red leatherette seats. At the end of a day in the sun, we returned covered in sand and eating the last of my mum's tomato sandwiches which were by now soggy and infused with the cerebos salt, leaving them even more delicious than they had been fresh. The air inside the car would have disturbed even the most masochistic Finnish saunaphile, and the seats had reached the temperature of molten steel. My grandfather, a butler who had spent the day on the beach in his only garments, a three-piece black suit, would climb inside, declare that it had been an excellent day, and fall happily asleep until we reached home.'

Where did you get your love of adventure travel?

'I remember it exactly. On a bright September morning in 1975, I walked down the road from my parents' home with a new rucksack over my shoulders, wearing a faded university rag t-shirt, matching jeans and a pair of Dunlop green flash shoes that had seen better days, and would see worse yet. As I stood at Victoria Station in London watching the clickety-clack board unfold its destinations, I felt, at that moment, that life was full of infinite possibilities, and all I had to do was step on a train to find them. Two mornings later, I sat on the platform of a little station in the south of France, eating an orange. Across the road, a girl with a swing in her hips and a baguette in her wicker basket walked past a white wall, bright with Bougainvillea. She looked over and smiled, and I was besotted. Not with her, but with that same sense of infinite possibilities. I took the next train north and for the next four weeks roamed through France, Switzerland, Austria, Germany, Holland, Belgium, Denmark, Norway, Sweden and Finland. I had no guidebook, only a Thomas Cook international timetable and a map of Europe on which the name of every country, every town and every village sang with romance. Every morning, I would haul out the map, decide where to go just because I liked the sound of it, and get on a train with no other aim than to find out what lay over the horizon.'

Any intriguing experiences?

'On a freezing winter's day in December 1979, I set out from Belfast clutching in my fevered grasp a ticket to a Leonard Cohen concert the following night in Manchester. I'd been a fan of the intensely beautiful poetry of his lyrics for years and, being an equally gloomy bastard, felt a deep empathy with him, but this was my first chance to see him live. By midnight, after taking the ferry from Larne to Stranraer then hitching south, I'd got as far as Carlisle, at which point I decided it would be a good idea to walk to the motorway. By four in the morning, I came to a phone booth in the middle of nowhere. I crawled in, settled down in the corner and nodded off. The next day, I hitched a ride up the motorway, and asked to be dropped off at a café. When I walked into that building there was Leonard Cohen sitting eating a box of maltesers.

If I don't go over and say hello to him, I thought, I'll always regret it, so I walked over and said, "Excuse me, I'm sorry to bother you, but are you Leonard Cohen?"

"You're not bothering me at all. Sit down and have lunch," he said.

For the next hour, we shared the box of maltesers and talked about life, the universe and everything, although the truth is that I don't remember much of the detail of the conversation, since I was too busy sitting there being amazed at how decent, pleasant and down to earth he was.

Finally he looked at his watch and said, "Well, I'd better be heading up the road to Glasgow. Can I give you a lift?"

He did, and after he dropped me at the turn off for Stranraer, I stood there for a good five minutes after he'd disappeared from sight, not really believing what had happened.'

How has travel changed your life?

'As a journalist, my travel was limited to holidays, but it was still the finest feeling in the world to close the office door, leave the everyday world behind for a while, and just go. In 1990, I had a stroke of luck: Geoff Martin, the editor of the daily paper I worked for, asked me if I fancied becoming features editor. I said I'll do it if he'd let me travel as well. He thought about it for a moment and conceded that I could have 25 days a year. He said it with a calmness, which belied the fact that I had got my own way. For the next 14 years, every six weeks or so I had that feeling of euphoria which the passage of time never diminished. In my head was the knowledge of an adult, in my heart was the joy of a child seeing the world for the first time. And in my soul, it always felt like Christmas morning. Anticipating the feeling of going somewhere new and then actually travelling there was thrilling.'

Any favourite locations?

'I could pick individual countries, such as Canada for its people and the glory of the Rockies, or Italy for the sheer joy of life, or Japan for the exquisite attention to beauty and the feeling that if you lived there for 1000 years, you would never get to the bottom of all the layers of ritual, manners and intrigue. The truth is that every day when you are travelling is a day when you wake up with that same sense of infinite possibilities that we all lose as we get older. As we age we become burdened with the tyranny of possessions so much so that we forget the simplicity that we had as children, of leaping out of bed in the summer holidays, jumping on our bike and going off to have an adventure. That's one of the reasons why I love travelling by bike: because you can take very few possessions with you; it shows you just how little you need to survive. There can be few finer feelings in the world, as I found when riding from Chicago to LA on Route 66 on a Harley, than waking up in the morning, packing your stuff into the panniers of a motorbike, checking out of a little motel and riding off down the open road with no idea what the day will bring.'

I wonder if Geoff, looking back now, would say losing his job in journalism when he was 48 was a blessing in disguise?
'I fell into a depression in which I wondered if happiness would ever be possible again. Yet again, travel, in this case riding a motorbike the length of the Pan-American Highway from Chile to Alaska, proved that it was.'

What was the most outstanding place on the Pan American highway?
'Ecuador and Guatemala were both beautiful, but probably Colombia, because everyone, from the Foreign Office to the British Embassy in Bogota to Ron Ayres, a professional motorcycle adventurer specialising in South America, had told us that if we tried to ride through Colombia we would almost certainly be kidnapped and shot. In fact, the Colombians turned out to be friendly and helpful. Indeed, when they heard I was from Belfast, several of them asked: "Wow. Isn't that a bit dangerous?"'

Any low points?
'Funnily enough, that was Colombia as well – when I crashed. I stood up with most of the skin gone from my left forearm and bruises and scratches all over me, the bike was down the road, lying on its side in a ditch with a trail of wreckage behind it. I thought that two years' planning and the trip of a lifetime had been ruined in a moment's loss of concentration. Fortunately, I was rescued, yet again by the Colombians. They got me and my bike into a truck heading north to Cali, where friends of my travelling companion Clifford nursed me and the bike back to health, so that we could continue a week later.'

What were the highlights?

'Probably crossing the border from Mexico into the USA and feeling that the most difficult part of the trip was behind us. I remember, too, spending a Saturday afternoon talking to other bikers at Alice's Restaurant in California, then riding down through the pines and across the Golden Gate Bridge in glorious sunshine. After I'd finished the trip and crossed the Arctic Circle on the way to Gobblers Knob, I rode south again the next morning down the fearsome gravel switchbacks of the Dalton Highway in the rain, (these are a part of a mountainous highway with sharp hairpin bends,) then reached tarmac just as the sun came out. I was overcome with an incredible sense of achievement.'

Were there any difficulties?

'Every single border crossing in South and Central America. You arrive and are immediately mobbed by every kid in town who wants to mind the bikes for a dollar; their mothers, who want to sell you everything from lizards to puppies; and their fathers, who want to be your special best friend to ease your way through the endless process of border crossing. Once you've either made a deal or managed to fend them off as politely as possible, one of your party watches the bikes while the other joins various rugby scrums for the passport office, the customs office, the health office and several other offices. Then you switch places. That gets you out of one country. Then you go 100 yards (90 m) down the road and repeat the process to get into the next country. In Central America, they added an extra twist by demanding photocopies of your passport stamps, including the one you'd just got. Naturally, the photocopy had to be made at the photocopy shop half a mile (0.8 km) down the road owned by a man who looked very like the head of the customs office. The whole process usually took three to four hours in searing heat and humidity. One day, crossing into Honduras, we did two in a day, and then had to go and lie in a darkened room for a while.'

Did anything hilarious happen on the journey?

'I spent a month travelling around eastern Canada for a series of tales that included *Painless Parker the Dentist* and the *Famous Frog of Fredericton*, both stories in a series in the *News Letters* he wrote. As well as writing, I was taking photographs, and decided only to take one film roll of 36 shots, but to make sure every single one was a masterpiece. At the end of the trip, I got to the airport, opened the camera to take out the film and found no film. I took this as a sign that I wasn't destined to become the Ansel Adams of the late 20th century and since then have stuck to writing.'

Geoff was joined on the Gobblers Knob journey by a Scots man called Clifford Patterson, a former Isle of Man TT winner who had become a businessman then changed to run one of the 100 Camphill worldwide communities, which produce opportunities for people with disabilities, especially in the area of finding work. He had telephoned Geoff because he had read Geoff's travel book *Way to Go* and it struck a chord with him. They arranged a meeting and that was the start of a great friendship and life on the road together.

Did you plan to go alone on the Chile to Alaska journey before you met Clifford (who joined him on the trip). Was he a good companion?

'It [the trip] was almost impossible as it was, but would have been completely impossible without him. Even simple things like border crossings or going to the loo were so much easier with someone to mind the bikes, and Clifford was brilliant at dealing with emergencies, of which there were many. Quite apart from that, it was much less lonely than on my own, and the book was so much better with the dialogue and banter between the two of us, rather than me going quietly mad on my own for three months. Clifford also had another hobby; taking photos of the lovely ladies he met with the intention of producing a book on the Pan American beauties. It is not yet published but I still have all the photos on file if he ever wants to.'

Geoff describes him as 'one of the weirdest and most wonderful people I was ever to meet'

What have you learned through your travels?

'Three things: With enough determination, you can overcome most obstacles. People are essentially good all over the world, especially if you travel with a good heart and keep smiling. That falling off a motorbike hurts.'

What helps in tough times?

'Writing, which expresses the same feeling of childlike joy at the wonder of the world, combined with an adult wisdom in explaining that wonder. Being funny helps as well, since there's no rule that says writing can't entertain at the same time as it's educating.'

Have you any favourite travel writers?

'Bruce Chatwin, Robert Byron, Bill Bryson, Redmond O'Hanlon and the early Eric Newby.'

And your own books. Do you have a favourite?

'My favourite is all of them: the first, *Way to Go* because it started out as a newspaper series, and it was very rewarding to see it turned into a book that did so well; *Gobblers Knob* because it represented such an epic journey; and the latest, *Anyway, Where Was I?*, my alternative A–Z of the world, for the same reason as *Way to Go* – that it was a series of individual newspaper pieces that deserved a wider audience.'

Did travel cure the mid-life crisis or do you think it's something that may surface again?

'Are you mad? It's just made it worse. I've been having a permanent mid-life crisis since I was 30, and plan to keep on having one until I'm 90.'

Geoff's other epic journey took him around the periphery of Australia, starting and ending in Adelaide, on a Triumph motorbike. He covered 15,000 miles (24,140 km) in three months along with his travelling companion and co-author of the book; *Oz: Around Australia on a Triumph*. Colin O'Carroll grew up in Melbourne, Australia and has a passion for motorbikes. Like Geoff, he has worked as a newspaper and radio journalist. Colin is Deputy News Editor with *The Belfast Telegraph*, so they had a lot in common before they started, as well as sharing a great sense of humour. His book, *Oz: Around Australia on a Triumph* is based on this trip.

I ask him to describe a typical day on this Adelaide to Adelaide trip.

'As we swept down the road in the golden sun of late afternoon, the shadow in the trees at the side of the road suddenly stood up and hopped towards the verge. It was, in fact, a large kangaroo, followed half a mile later by a dead one providing afternoon tea for two wedge-tailed eagles, a herd of wild goats scampering across the road, an emu lolloping through the grass with a baffled look, and a cow lying on the hard shoulder in a state that suggested it wouldn't be going any further. Yes, it was just another day riding through the Australian Outback.'

What was the strangest journey?

'I've ridden from Delhi to Belfast on an Enfield and from Chile to Alaska on a Triumph, but riding around Australia was the strangest adventure of all: three months and 15,000 miles (24,140 km) to end up back in Adelaide, exactly where we'd started. Still, if the fact that it was one country, with one language and no border crossings, visa hassles or *carnet de passage* documents made it easier logistically, there was the whole new challenge of writing a newspaper series, blog and book on the trip, as well as filming for the planned DVD and TV documentary.'

What were the highlights?
'There were two. Firstly, the Great Ocean Road on the south coast: 150 miles (241 km) of motorcycle heaven, with countless bends and vistas where you swoop down through an alpine landscape then come over a rise to see the ocean, before dipping through hills and dales straight out of Middle Earth and rising into the forest. Breathtaking! Then there was the Queensland coast, a sub-tropical paradise of beaches, parrots, banana plantations and scenery so lush you want to get off the bike and eat it.'

What was your favourite spot on the journey?
'The bucolic woods, vineyards and meadows of the southwest; such a delight after riding down through the vast nothingness of the Great Sandy Desert of Western Australia that I rode along grinning in my helmet and saying: "corners, fields, streams, cows".'

Was it difficult to get back to normal after the freedom of the road?
'It sure was. Once you start doing this kind of stuff, it's hard to be at home for long without looking at the horizon and wondering what lies beyond it.'

Did anything shock you?
'I was shocked by the poverty in places such as Nicaragua and El Salvador, where I'd see families living in shacks made of black plastic stretched over a few sticks. However, their washing was still hanging out to dry on the bushes and a little girl would be out the front sweeping the dust away with a branch. You often find that people like these, who have next to nothing, are the most generous you will ever meet.'

Which of your travel books had the strongest impact on your life?
'It was probably *Gobblers Knob* because it took two years of planning through some very difficult personal times and because it was such an epic undertaking, not least because it meant abandoning my wife for three months.'

What kind of food do you like to eat when abroad?
'Whatever's local, since food is part of the experience. On the Chile to Alaska trip, we had everything from guinea pig, the national dish of Ecuador, to fried grass-

hoppers in Mexico, although it's hard to see the point, since it takes 4,000 of them to make up a square meal. My favourite dish, though, is anything my wife Cate cooks. Her mother was a chef, and she's a natural-born cook. I look in the fridge and see nothing but air and an onion, and yet out of the same fridge half an hour later she's produced ambrosia of the gods.'

What's your ideal holiday?

'Italy because of the sheer joy of life there, and in terms of activities, my favourite type of holiday is probably still a road trip. I just love that feeling of getting up and setting off every morning.'

What has travel taught you?

'Travel confirms what I've always known: that people are essentially good, and if you travel with that feeling, you'll get back what you give out.'

Who impressed you most on your travels?

'People like the truck driver in Colombia who took me and my crashed Triumph nine hours out of his way, then set off to drive home through the night, or Oscar, a van driver who we met on the outskirts of Medellin (Colombia). He took us to a cash machine, led us all the way through the city and recommended somewhere to stay for the night.'

Where to next?

'Outer Mongolia in a Citroen 2CV as part of the Mongol Rally, and back from Siberia on a Ural, a Russian copy of a 1930s BMW motorbike. And possibly around the world in a light aircraft with Steve Derwin, who was left in a wheelchair by a bike accident and is now the UK's only qualified disabled gliding instructor.

IN SEARCH OF FIDEL CASTRO AND CUBA

Christopher P Baker

Author, lecturer, photographer and tour guide, Christopher P Baker has ventured a long way from the gentle hills and dales of Yorkshire in England where he was born. His love of travel has a long history and, ultimately, took him to the warm and tropical climate of Cuba where he spends much of his time, as well as to the West Coast of America where he now lives. When I first contacted Christopher he had just returned from leading the first-ever group of US motorcyclists around Cuba and was due to return to Havana the following day to lead yet another all-Cuba, 14-day motorcycle tour.

Christopher always had a deep love of geography and, after acquiring a BA degree in the subject from the University of London, he went on to obtain Master's Degrees in Latin American Studies and Education. During this time as a student he travelled widely, including on two research trips to the Sahara. He spent time hitch-hiking around North America, too, and, while there he wrote his first travel stories about Latin America for a local newspaper in England. The trip married his love of writing with travel. But, little did he know where this would take him.

He settled in California, gained a scholarship in journalism to U.C. Berkeley, and in 1982 after a brief period working in the adventure travel industry (during which he led trips as far afield as New Zealand) he launched his travel journalism career. Back in the 1980s, Christopher also briefly operated deluxe tours of Great Britain, specialising in gardens and stately homes, as well as serious shopping tours of Hong Kong and Korea. Then, in 1993, Christopher visited Havana as a participant on a boat excursion from Jamaica. It was this trip that ignited his long and lasting love affair with Cuba.

He loves Cuba for its 'eccentricity, eroticism and enigma'. He never wants to sleep for fear of missing a vital experience. He also loves it for its 'socialism and sensuality, secret police and sexy showgirls'. It's almost surreal. And then there are the Cuban people, gracious, genteel, and generous to a fault. Cuba's socialist experiment has been unique in the western hemisphere. Wed that to a legacy as a virtual US colony, the wealthiest such tropical isle in the world, and an era when it served as a Soviet bulwark in the Cold War. These, and Fidel Castro's pathological genius and a five-decade long legacy of antagonism between two nations separated by a mere 90 miles of ocean water. 'How could I NOT be smitten?' Having fallen for Cuba, it seemed a natural progression to write about it.

He was contracted to author the *Cuba Handbook* (now *Moon Handbooks Cuba*), shipped a motorcycle to the island, and penned his first travelogue: *Mi Moto Fidel: Motorcycling through Castro's Cuba*. Not only did his book go on to win critical acclaim and two national book awards, it was published by the National Geographic Society – the beginning of Christopher's long association with the prestigious organization. He has since escorted tours of Cuba on behalf of National Geographic Expeditions, Moto Discovery Motorcycle Tours, and Santa Fe Photographic Workshops.

Christopher currently specializes in Central America and the Caribbean and is highly respected around the world for his vast knowledge of Cuba, Costa Rica, and Colombia. To date, Christopher's feature articles and photographs have been published in more than 200 publications worldwide, as far-ranging as National Geographic and Newsweek. His more than 20 books in print include guidebooks for Frommer's, Lonely Planet, and National Geographic, and include several titles on California, including his latest book *Back Roads California: 24 Scenic Drives*, in the Eyewitness Travel series. An accomplished public speaker, he has addressed the National Press Club, World Affairs Council, and National Geographic Live, has appeared on dozens of radio and TV shows, In 2005, he was awarded Travel Writer of the Year by the Caribbean Tourism Organisation; in 2008 he was named Lowell Thomas Award 'Travel Journalist of the Year'—the Pulitzer Prize of travel journalism. He is a member of the Society of American Travel Writers (SATW) and the American Society of Journalists & Authors.

THE INTERVIEW

What are your early travel memories?

'Perhaps my earliest memory is a family vacation that I took when I was about seven years old. We spent two weeks in Torquay – a southern England resort. It rained virtually the entire time. Plus, I had mumps. I also recall with great fondness the family vacations in my grandfather's Bedford 'dormobile' [campervan]. Although lacking much formal education, my dour, salt-of-the-earth working-class grandfather was seminal in inspiring in me a keen early desire to travel. He and my grandmother set out every year in their dormobile for forays through Europe, and upon their return they gave slide shows that held me spellbound. I'm going back almost 50 years.'

I ask if his own travel experiences make him feel nostalgic or does he have a more clinical approach to travel?

He tells me he has so many trips he wants to do, but also longs to get hold of a time machine to re-experience all the trips he has done previously.

'I feel nostalgic for many trips, such as my first ever trip outside England as a participant in a university research expedition to Morocco. What an eye-opener to live among Berbers and nomads. I've spent time sleeping on beaches in the Greek Islands, six months hitchhiking around the USA, journeying to the Marquesas Islands by copra freighter, exploring India on sleeper trains... and, of course, my motorcycle journey through Cuba.'

Christopher has written several travel guidebooks. I ask him how much work was involved in writing them and how he dealt with the responsibility of getting the facts right and up to date.

'I take great pride in producing the absolute best guidebooks in the market. I'm dedicated and passionate rather than a dilettante. That means giving the time required to do an outstanding job. I literally go the extra mile for my Moon guidebook research. I'll often drive miles down a lonesome rainforest track to spend a few minutes at a remote lodge or attraction rather than rely on second-hand sources. Seeing is believing.'

It must be quite time-consuming producing a guidebook. How long, for instance, do you have to spend in each place as part of your research?

'Actually, I have more than 20 guidebooks in print, although a few no longer carry my name. Again, guidebooks vary greatly, from small pocket guides that may not require personal visits, to comprehensive guidebooks. I spent at least five months in Cuba to research the first edition, which took two years to complete; on average, I spent two to three months in Cuba and Costa Rica for each subsequent edition. But you also have to factor in the mammoth amount of work that goes into organizing and writing the books.'

In 2003, he attended the first US Cuba Travel Summit, in Cancun, Mexico. At the end of the summit, the *Cuban Ministry of Tourism* flew a small group, including Christopher into Cuba, where he met Fidel Castro. I ask him to recall the event.

'From Cancun, about 40 attendees of the conference were flown into Cuba for the day. No announcement was made that we were going to meet Fidel, but I read between the lines of the written itinerary, which had allotted two hours to visit the convention palace. By then I'd made dozens of visits to Cuba and had been close to Fidel on several occasions at official functions. I knew certain of the routines, such as the "confiscation" of all bags for a behind-closed-doors inspection. When that happened as we pulled up to the convention hall, I knew what it meant, so I rushed ahead to ensure a front seat. Sure enough, I got to briefly talk with Fidel when he appeared minutes later and went person to person down the front row. What was most fascinating was gaining a close-up insight into what I've called Fidel's pathological genius, his astounding grasp of statistics, his fanatical determination never to be wrong. And even more fanatical determination never to apologize. All these played out when he had to correct himself while quoting a statistic on education and asked the Minister of Tourism (with whom we'd spent the morning touring Havana and who was seated next to Fidel at the meeting) to double-check the figures with a calculator. When the calculator showed that Fidel's was wrong, he was furious. We witnessed a bizarre 20-minute long charade of Machiavellian proportion until Fidel was "proved to have been correct".'

Chris tells me there was a photo taken of him with Fidel Castro but he hasn't been able to get hold of it. Although it must be difficult for him, I ask what place had the most profound effect on his life. Could it be Cuba?

'It is most certainly Cuba. I've spent so much more time there (about three years in total, adding up the months) than anywhere else, and it's played such a big part in shaping my subsequent professional life and direction. I've also become more closely attached to the Cuban people than any other culture on earth. Genteel, gracious, gifted and giving sums them up.'

The subject of Christopher's literary travelog *Mi Moto Fidel: Motorcycling through Castro's Cuba* was a dream journey come true for him. What made him choose a motorbike as opposed to walking or some other means of transport?'

'When I was asked to write a guidebook to Cuba, I instantly knew that I also wanted to write a literary travelogue of my impressions at the end of what would amount to three years of visits. Two such travelogues had recently been published and, in each, the authors had travelled by car. I wanted something sexier; something more adventurous. I wanted my time in Cuba to be an adventure, and I implicitly knew that motorcycling would bring that dream to life.'

We speak about his most positive travel experience. He tells me it was, without a doubt, the time where he took to the open road and spent three months riding 7,000 miles (11,265 km) through Cuba in 1996. He recalled how he felt saying, 'It was magnificent. I was on a natural high most of the time.'

He met a lot of ordinary Cubans on his journey and I asked him how they coped with material scarcity.

'The Communist system has destroyed an entire economy. While raising several million people up out of poverty and accomplishing a phenomenal amount of good in education, health, and social development, it has also systematically wiped out an entire middle and upper class (and the economic resources that fuel economic growth) and dragged most of them down into a life of paucity. The US embargo hasn't helped.

Theft and graft in the workplace is one way. People get by through the "black market" the under-the-table deal. Parts are manufactured or cannibalized out of anything that can be recycled.'

That sounds quite hopeless, is there anything positive to come out of the effects of communism?

'Cubans display an ingenuity that will amaze you. But for the most part they're also non-materialistic, although that is now changing. Being in Cuba for some time makes you appreciate the positive qualities of a non-materialistic society. Currently, under Raúl Castro, things are easing up considerably. I'm very hopeful that the Cubans will resolve their own problems... if the USA will get out of their way.'

Of all the places in the world, what drew him to Cuba?

'Well, firstly there was my youthful flirtation with socialism, and my idolization of Che Guevara during my university years (1973–78), when I was a political activist and very involved in Latin American leftist causes. But, when I finally visited in 1993, I discovered that I crossed a threshold to a realm of eccentricity, eroticism and enigma. It's also an intensely sensual isle. The combination of mystery and allure proved irresistible.'

Do you think Barack Obama's presidency has changed American relations with Cuba for the better?

'I think a lot of people are disappointed. The aspirations they had for President Obama to initiate a new direction for relations hasn't happened. But we need to recall that he is hampered by a virulently and powerful anti-Castroite Republican lobby, intent on not permitting any new openings with Cuba. The law in the US also restricts the ability of the president to initiate change; much of that prerogative, such as lifting the US embargo, now resides with Congress. But strides have been made. President Obama has lifted the unjust restrictions on Cuban-Americans, who are now free to visit their family in Cuba as often and whenever they wish. And the new people-to-people educational exchange provision announced in 2011 opens the door for every US citizen to exercise, at least in part, their constitutional right to unrestricted travel as part of the licensed group program.'

US tourism to Cuba is likely to increase, do you worry that Cuba may become Americanized and lose its individuality?

'That won't happen any time soon. On the one hand, several studies suggest that as many as one million US visitors will go to Cuba in the first 12 months after travel restrictions are lifted, constituting a 50 per cent increase in tourism to Cuba. The numbers are said to be likely to increase by one million each subsequent year until five million Americans will be visiting annually. That will have a profound impact. But where are they going to stay? Cuban hotels are already full. The rental fleet is already maxed out – rented to Cuba's three million tourists, including 400,000 Cuban-Americans who visit each year so the Cuban government will find a way to regulate the flow. Not least, it understands that the recent people-to-people provision is couched in the US administration is a way of spreading democracy on the island. So that must give them concern. I expect we'll see a gradual increase.

Yes, there will inevitably be changes. But the greater impact will be when real reform of the economic system takes place within Cuba, when Cubans have the financial means to improve their lives materially. Under Raúl that is finally beginning to happen, assisted by President Obama having lifted restrictions on the amount of money that can be sent to family on the island by Cuban-Americans. Until that time, you're going to see the ox-carts and old cars still trundling down the streets. Plus, one of the positive impacts of the Revolution has been the impressive degree to which even youth are proud of their Cubanness, their Cubanismo. I must say the old cars add a touch of charm to the place; it would be a pity if they were to go.'

Who are the people in Cuba that inspire you?
'It's the ordinary people who inspire me; people who demonstrate amazing generosity in the face of adversity. Friends who, when invited and asked how they want to spent their Saturday nights, reply they want to go visit their ailing aunties.'

I ask what he thinks the wider world could learn from Cuba?
He tells me in no uncertain terms, 'The world could learn the art of simplicity; the fleeting unimportance of materialism. The Cubans know what the true meaning of community is. Added to that, the perspective that adequate health care and education is an individual right to be cherished. I admire the Revolution for all these exemplars to the world.'

So where does the man who travels for work go to unwind?
'That depends. For total relaxation I like to get to sea. I love cruising and nothing is as relaxing to me as lazing on deck. If I'm travelling with a lover, I'd opt for a romantic resort. And I've recently rediscovered my passion for motorcycling.'

Christopher says that, with all his travelling, it can be hard to find the time to read. However, when time allows, he likes a good travel book. He tells me, 'I've always admired Paul Theroux for his perspicacity in penetrating national cultures and I still fondly connect to the old school of English travel writers, such as Eric Newby and Colin Thubron.'

The time has never been better to travel to Cuba and I felt I should take full advantage of his expertise on the country of Cuba. I ask that if one were to travel to Cuba for three weeks, what itinerary would he recommend?

'In three weeks you can cover much of the island. You would want at least three days in Havana, focusing on Habana Vieja (Old Havana). There is so much to see here in this city built around the port of Havana at Havana Bay. The narrow old streets offer some of the most unusual old colonial-style architecture with approximately 3,000 buildings all steeped in history. It's no secret that the city is very easy to walk around and is compact. There's an open-top bus tour option as an alternative for a generic overview of the city.'

He goes on to recommend two days in Valle de Viñales, with its dramatic scenery and tobacco farms. Valle de Viñales was founded by the Spanish in the early 1500s. Built in baroque and neoclassic style, it used to be a stopping point for the Spanish galleons crossing with their goods between the New World and Old World. It is surrounded by beautiful sheer-faced mountains known as Mogotes, enhanced by the vernacular architecture of its farms and sleepy colonial villages. Traditional methods of farming are still used here since modern mechanical methods produce an inferior tobacco. It has a rich heritage in music and crafts. The most unusual thing about it is that it has a number of very large caves, evidently lived in before the Spanish colonized the area but also used by Che Guevara for military purposes during the Cuban Missile Crisis of 1962. Despite its rich history, it also has the dark history of slavery. Viñales Valley was used for military operations during the War of Independence and the Cuban Revolution.

Follow Valle de Viñales with three days in the old colonial city of Trinidad, says Christopher. It's a 'pickled in aspic' colonial city and UNESCO World Heritage Site dating back to and, seemingly, still operating as it did in 1514. For beach time, he recommends you allow two days on the Cayos de Villa Clara. This area has been declared a biosphere reserve and has miles of stunning beaches with turquoise waters and coral reef. Cayos de Villa Clara is in the heart of northern Cuba and is perfectly integrated into the lush flora and fauna of Cayo Santa María.

Next, Christopher advocates taking a full week in Oriente (the eastern provinces), a rugged place surrounded by the Sierra Maestra Mountains and the place where Fidel Castro grew up and the Revolution was born. Oriente is equally important historically for it was here, too, that the wars for Cuban independence were launched. Christopher also suggests taking in Santiago de Cuba with its rich musical culture. Santiago de Cuba has a distinct Caribbean feel and atmosphere, which is reflected in its unique culture and architecture. He reckons you would need two days there in Cuba's second largest city. If you still have the energy, for another two days he suggests visiting Baracoa, an unspoilt, isolated colonial village (dating from 1511) surrounded by thickly forested mountains and secluded beaches. The town is lined with brightly coloured buildings lining cobbled streets. Cocoa trees are plentiful and Baracoa sells specialty chocolates, including cucuruchó – a coconut, honey, and chocolate dessert encased in palm bark.

Christopher's itinerary takes in two days hiking in the Sierra Maestra, an area that formed Fidel Castro's centre of operations during the war to topple brutal dictator Fulgencio Batista—a hike to La Comandancia de La Plata (Fidel's former headquarters) is de rigueur for the hale and hearty. This wild place, setting for Cuba's highest mountains, is a haven for wildlife peculiar to Cuba, especially colourful exotic birds. Finally, he recommends a few days around Holguin. Christopher Columbus landed here in 1492 and referred to it as the most beautiful land that human eyes have ever seen.

I asked Christopher if he had any holiday plans for the future and was surprised to hear that motorbikes weren't on the agenda. He told me he has the strong desire to cruise around the Greek Islands on a yacht and then 'do the grand tour of Europe in a nice sports car.'

What valuable lessons in life have you learned about travel?

'As Westerners, we take too much for granted, perhaps because of our comfort. We have as much to learn from people in other cultures and countries as we have to give. Plan ahead but go with the flow and don't sweat the small stuff.'

SUMMER IN DUBLIN AND ROUTE 66 ON A HARLEY

Ken Doyle

On approaching the driveway to Ken Doyle's large Victorian home, a sign reads: 'Anything other than Harleys will be crushed.' Ken, together with his bandmates Liam Reilly and John O'Brien, has had major success with rock group Bagatelle, sharing the stage with many international artists through the years. They have had two number one hit singles, 'Summer in Dublin' and 'Second Violin', the former of which has been covered to date by 85 artists worldwide, The band has had a positive influence on the music industry in Ireland, with Bono praising them for the impact they had on U2 in the early days of their career. They also won an Irish World Award for their contribution to Irish music worldwide. Their Bagatelle Gold album, a collection of their special hits, won platinum discs from Polydor Records. The year 2013 marks their 35th anniversary as a band.

Ken's love of bikes and music goes hand in hand. Not only has touring with Bagatelle taken him all across Ireland, Europe, the US, United Arab Emirates, Malaysia, Hong Kong and China, the huge success he has achieved has also afforded him the opportunity (financially) to realise his motorbiking dreams. Travelling, he says, can also inspire the creative process of songwriting. At the time of writing this, Ken gave me a preview of a song he had written with Bagatelle after completing Route 66 – a dream bike journey that took him to Illinois, Missouri, Oklahoma, Kansas, Texas, New Mexico, Arizona, and California. Called Mister Harley and Mister Davidson, it goes like this:

Live to ride, ride to live, it's my way of life it seems,
Let these silver wings release you to the highway of your dreams

Ken is a happy-go-lucky guy who, when not on tour, loves to be at home tinkering with odds and ends that he can use to customise his bikes. He can often be seen walking along the beach or cliffs, dogs in tow. Then of course, there is always the chance you'll catch him whizzing around town on one of his many Harleys.

THE INTERVIEW

The thought terrified me but, after much coaxing, Ken took me for a ride on his Harley Davidson. I figured that if he was competent enough to complete 4,000 miles (6,400 km) of Route 66, a short ride wouldn't kill me. Evangelical about the heavenly Harley bike world, he used all his powers of persuasion.

'You'll be fine, trust me,' he tells me. My mind flitted, thinking of the journey and the cliff roads we would navigate. How on earth would I endure this if I couldn't bear to go faster than 15 miles per hour?

There was a holiday vibe to the day and, later as we chatted, Ken's early memories flowed.

'I remember going down to our relations in a Standard Ten car. It was green, like the British racing colour. My father used to borrow it from a neighbour called Mr Devitt. It was so exciting in the eyes of a child. Later, when I worked on the railway, I had a privilege ticket that allowed me to travel on boats and trains to England. I remember going all the way to London. You could pay an extra pound and get a place to sleep on the boat.'

It seemed natural to chat about his life as a musician and how that has manifested itself into a lifetime of travel. Where has he been?

'England, Holland, Germany, Channel Islands, Dubai, Hong Kong, Malaysia, Macaw. On the American side there was, New York, Philadephia, Conneticut, Rhode Island, Boston, Cape Cod, Detroit, Chicago.'

Hold on Ken, I say, where did you get time to live?

He continues, 'Portland Maine, Portland Oregan, Seattle, Atlanta, Washington DC, Florida, Los Angeles, San Fransisco, Arizona.'

At this point I say there must be only one place left for Ken to visit. It must be Mars I suggest.

We both laugh and he says, 'Wouldn't I love to?'

What's your favourite destination?

'I liked Florida. I was there at the right time of the year, in October, when it was more like a beautiful summer, instead of being there in July and August when you would just melt.'

I ask about the various musicians he met while travelling.

'Without a doubt the abiding memory for me was Bob Marley, when we played in Dalymount Park, Dublin, on the same bill. To be in the presence of the one and only Bob Marley – incredible. His music has stood the test of time. It sounds every bit as fresh now as it did 30 years ago. We've played with lots of band, artists such as David Gates from Bread, Bono and U2, Van Morrison, The Pogues, Rory Gallagher, Thin Lizzy and Phil Lynott. It's been an incredible pleasure to share the stage with them and have the craic behind the scenes. At this stage of my life, I love getting to my destination. Beam me up Scottie.' He laughs.

Route 66 is known as the Will Rogers Highway and colloquially known as the Main Street of America or the Mother Road. It consists of 2,448 miles (3, 900 km) visiting the US states of Illinois, Missouri, Kansas, Oklahoma, Texas, New Mexico, Arizona, Nevada and California. We speak about his desire to journey on Route 66.

'When I was a younger, I had this fantasy that I wanted to ride down Route 66 on a Harley Davidson. I think it was a combination of *Easy Rider* and there was another television programme called *Then Came Bronson*. It was about a guy who used to ride around the States on a motorbike and he'd sort out everybody's problems and ride off into the sunset. I just had this fantastic notion that, someday, I would love to do it. Yet time goes on and you have your family and stuff like that.

I happened to be on my old Harley Sportster and this man came up to me and said, 'I never knew you liked bikes.' I told him about my collection of old Harley Davidson bikes and he told me he had a friend organising Route 66 looking for guys to ride a Harley Davidson. I told him, 'It doesn't matter what it involves, just count me in.'

We talk about his preparation for the journey.

'Well, we were trained by the police and a combination of riding instructors and people tuned in to their bikes. Ken was to spend hours of training for his own safety and others. We rode through cones and they gave me a few tips that have definitely contributed to saving my life many times. I have also passed on some of the tips to a few of my fellow riders.'

The terrain was going to be extremely rough and dusty in places. Ken had heard about its diversity and he knew he would be traversing a route that was commissioned in 1926, which was a collection of many bits and pieces of existing roads all pieced together to form what is known as Route 66. This would mean varying conditions and stretches of road and he would contend with extreme heat. At times it was unbearable in the hot sun. Some of the riding would be long and monotonous, other parts more interesting. He knew he was about to cross eight states and three time zones. Route 66 starts in Chicago and one of the first most notable things to be seen is Navy Pier, which is a 1 km long on the Chicago shoreline of Lake Michigan.

'That was incredible. The sheer length and vastness of it was stunning. Zipping along on the bike made it more special. I loved going through Missouri and seeing the enormous iconic image of the St Louis Gateway Arch. I've heard it's one of the tallest monuments in the US. There were panoramic views stretching for miles –up to 30 miles (48 km) on a clear day. In Kansas there were quirky places to stop such as old gas stations turned into shops with memorabilia, selling all sorts including antiques, Route 66 souvenirs and crafts made by the locals.

A high point of the trip was getting to Texas where we reached the mid-point sign known as Mid-point Café Adrian. The mid-point café is at the exact geo-mathematical centre of Route 66 and is 1139 miles (1833 km) from the starting point in Chicago to the finish in Los Angeles. It was a cause for celebration to have come so far and the café is well worth a visit.

We took Route 66 from Joliet, Illinois to Arizona, and while we were there headed to the South Rim of the Grand Canyon, which was spectacular. It has to be seen to be believed. The vastness and the colour of the rock made it look mysterious and beautiful. It seemed to go on forever. There were vast areas of pink rock at every angle and that coupled with the deep blue sky and sunshine made it unique. I took plenty of photos and a video; it never ceases to amaze me. It was the most incredible sight passing the Petrified Forest National Park Arizona known as the

Painted Desert. It really looks as if it has been painted with the different colours in the rocks. I had to stop for a photo. The amazing thing is, it's all natural, and apparently the colours in the rock are from iron and manganese. In the sun the rock looks orange and red.

Travelling Route 66 from Kingman to Oatman, Arizona will take you through a very interesting and historic section of the highway. We ended up at the famous corner in Winslow Arizona, which inspired the well-known Eagles song *Take it Easy*, a few of us hung out for a photo there.'

The most outstanding part about the journey for Ken was the sheer sense of freedom on the open road and being carefree with no pressures of work schedules. 'It was like another world; to be able to get out there, hear the roar of the engine, feel the breeze and get the sense of freedom of space as well as plenty of aromas as you pass the different areas. After the hot sun it was like a little piece of heaven.'

There must have been some funny incidents?

'One very funny thing happened when we ran into some road works and everyone had to take evasive action. Two of the guys went down a slip road but we stayed on the highway. We pulled in at the next slip road, hoping that the rest would find us. It just didn't happen. I decided to go back up on the bridge in the hope of finding the others and, hopefully, flag them down. There I was sitting on the bridge, drinking coffee out of a stainless steel canister and, the next thing, I saw the state trooper car coming towards me. The guy got out with the palms of his hands out. I thought he was going to push me.'

Ken laughs. 'He looked at my flask and I said to him, "It's only coffee," and he said, "What's happening here, man?" I told him I was with a party of bikers and explained we had lost some of them. I could see him looking at my strange attire – my shorts, tunic and big boots – as if to say "This guy is a nut". I could see he was going to make a lunge for me to drag me off the bridge. I pointed down to the other bikers. He said, "Here's the deal man. I've just had ten calls to tell me there was a jumper on the bridge."

"I'm not a jumper," I explained. Eventually he accepted this and we ended up swapping badges. We swapped Irish police badges for Oklahoma police badges and he gave me a teddy bear with an Oklahoma police badge and I still have it.'

I ask Ken how people behaved towards him in general.

'The people were hugely supportive. Police and ordinary bikers would join in and ride with us. Police would just stop and swap their badges for Irish ones. I still have some amazing badges, including little sheriff badges from different departments.'

Which country was the most friendly to visit?

'Hong Kong, they were lovely people – very friendly. I also find the Arabic countries very hospitable. If Arabic people take to you, they will invite you into their homes and feed you. They would also take out their phones to show you pictures of their family. Maybe that's where hospitality came from? It's a very ancient culture. We probably stole it from them,' laughs Ken.

I ask him about food and travel.

'I love to experiment, but not eat the weird stuff such as eyes and brains. My favourite food is always spicy. It can be from any corner of the world. It makes western cooking seem quite bland.'

I raise the issue of Ken's strange habits when travelling and ask about the time he was stopped at Miami airport because of some strange implements in his case. He brings a protector for his banana to stop it getting bruised. He puts baked beans into the kettle to heat them and has a toaster which ejects a little too high, and once popped its contents out of the window of a hotel. Ken tells me, 'Well, just so that people don't think I'm completely mad; I'm only 99 per cent mad. With the hours I work, I can never get a proper meal when I want it, or if I am served a meal late at night, the quality is usually poor. About 25 years ago, I decided that I was going to bring my own kitchen on the road. I got this big old black case, a bit like a briefcase but deeper. It was for tools and I loaded it up with a toaster and a cappuccino machine which, if I leave the lid off, doubles as a kettle.' Ken exploded with laughter again. 'That's not all that was in it. I'd have ciabatta bread, good quality cheeses, red onions and garlic. There would also be fruit and such like. I took it all around the world and I've made breakfast in various locations, even hotel lobbies, to the amusement of some people in reception. They would say, "Oh my, he's really crazy," or some would say, "You can't do that around here". I remember making breakfast on the front porch of some hotel. It was like something out of *The Waltons*. Someone even filmed me while I made the cappuccino. When 9/11 happened, we were in the United States. You can imagine the security panic back then at the airport when we had to take our shoes off. All our cases were taken over three different security checks. We were flying from Miami to New York and back to Ireland. This big black guy with a burgundy jacket, white shirt and black trousers held up my case and said, "Who owns this?"

I said, "Eh, I do".

So the man said, "Come over here, man".

I went over and he scratched his head, looking puzzled.

"What is all this, man?" he said.

Well, it's my kitchen, I said.

The security man turns to his colleagues and says, "Man, this guy has just brung his kitchen".

I asked him, "Is that so unusual?"

He scratched his head again and said, "It's the first time for me, man".

In the kitchen was a small flask with the remains of a bottle of red wine and the security man said, "Drink it".

"But it's nine o'clock in the morning", I said. But he insisted that I drink it.

In the second vessel I had soya milk and he opened it, asking, "What's this?"

When I told him he said, "Drink it".

In the next vessel I had cider vinegar. The same thing happened. I had to drink some. He went through everything in the case, even the coffee. That kitchen has surfaced in every part of the world.'

Do you think that travel is easier now?

'Travel is much more difficult now. I've never seen anything like the security. If you are in a warm country or airport and if the air conditioning isn't working, or if there are too many people, it really is stifling hanging around in queues. When 9/11 happened, it changed travel and the world forever. Before that, I remember I flew from Gatwick to JFK Airport, New York, on an out-of-date passport. I got into the country and the guy at passport control said, "Do you know your passport is out of date by three months?"

I said, "No".

He said, "Do you mean to tell me that the British let you through with an out-of-date passport?"

I said, "They must have done. I'm here."

He said, "This is very serious. Sit down here."

The guy with the silver badge on his lapel then got the guy with the golden badge on his lapel. He appeared very surprised that I got into the United States with the out-of-date passport. Next thing the man in the Armani suit arrived from upstairs and he looked at his watch and said, "Hey it isn't that much out of date, only three months". Then he said, "OK, we'll get you in. We just have to run it through because you could be the mad bomber for all we know."

Luckily, I went through. I couldn't see that happening now. That's how different travel is. I love travelling. There are so many places I want to see. I loved Michael Palin's programmes; I thought *Around The World In 80 Days* and the return journey he did 20 years later were brilliant. I loved Jonathan Dimbleby's *Russia* programme. I like the documentary the guys did on the motorbike called, *Long Way Round*. I like Charley Boorman; as I recall, he took part in a motorcycle adventure from London to New York via Europe and Asia with Ewan McGregor in 2004. The series was shown around the world and the DVD and book became bestsellers. The trials and tribulations the guys went through were tough going. Route 66 was a major endurance test.'

What would your ultimate journey be?

'I'd like to ride a motorbike all over the world. I don't know about some of the roads in Africa. They might be a bit dusty. That wouldn't be any fun, but sticking to the main highways and waking up goodness knows where, I might like something like that. I'd like to explore Africa. I've never been and all that stuff you see about Africa on TV might not give an accurate picture. I've been to India and it's very different, so Africa might also be.'

Were there any scary moments?

'On Route 66 we were heading to Amarillo, Texas. We had to drink so much water. The heat was intolerable and I had an empty bottle that was flopping around with the wind. I thought it might fly off and hit someone so I took the bottle, crushed it and then threw it down low into the central reservation. The wind caught the bottle, whipped it up in the air and it hit a guy on a motorbike behind me right between the eyes. Fortunately, he had his visor down. It smacked him at about 80 miles (129 km) per hour. He was the biggest, meanest, and toughest of our whole team. By trying to avoid a problem, I created one. I thought he might hit me when we pulled in. He went bananas and said to me, "Just stay behind me from now on and keep out of my way". I replied that I'd transfer to another team and then he came over and we shook hands. We've become very good friends since.

Word spread like wild fire among the riders. I was the last one out the next morning and they all waited around to see what the reaction would be. Shane, the guy I hit, came up to me and said, "I wonder what's going to hit us today".'

Ken is in hysterics again but just about manages to compose himself as I ask him my next question.

What is the most valuable lesson travel has taught you?

'Generally speaking people are good wherever you are. To me, it's the minority that screw it up for the majority. When you do charity runs you realise there's a lot more good people in the world, thankfully. Poverty makes people do a lot of dreadful things, but it's also a unifying factor. In some poverty-stricken countries, people give you what little they have for no reason other than hospitality.'

FROM LAW TO LYRICS

Kieran Goss

'A journey of a thousand miles begins with a single step' – *Confucius*

Kieran Goss was born in 1962. He hails from a large family of eight brothers and seven sisters – that wasn't unusual in Ireland in those days and coming from a large family with diverse musical tastes meant that he heard all sorts of music from an early age, from Johnny Cash to Willy Nelson. He got his first guitar when he was nine and taught himself how to play. Later he studied law, supporting himself financially by playing gigs and managing to land support slots with Elvis Costello, Christy Moore and Joe Jackson along the way. Qualifying as a solicitor in the mid-1980s, a career in law ensued, albeit a short one since his love of travel and adventure took him away from the security of a steady job. He moved to France and then Germany, returning home in 1989 to record his first album 'Brand New Star'.

Kieran has come through some tough times in the past few years with the loss of both his mother and sister-in-law to cancer. His wife Annie, is a graphic artist and a fine vocalist who often accompanies him on stage. She also developed an illness and fortunately has made a full recovery. Kieran has turned these tough experiences into inspirational songs, the culmination of which led to his latest album "I'll Be Seeing You". The love of travel is never far away and he spends quite a lot of time in Nashville, where he has written songs and performed with country singer

Don Williams. He has his own record label, Cog Communications, markets his own material, and manages his own gigs and tour schedule.

Kieran had an amazing ability to reach out to his audience and connect with them in a very unique way. Indeed, much has been made of Goss's masterful stage-craft and Rodney Crowell, Grammy-award-winning American musician, summed him up when he said: 'I've seen him win the hearts of everyone in the room, not just with his great songs and instinctive musicality, but with his warmth and humour. It's the performance of an artist at the top of his game, delivered with intelligence and integrity.'

THE INTERVIEW

It's a crisp, bright and sunny morning and I am sitting in a quiet alcove of a plush Dublin hotel waiting to interview Kieran Goss. His new CD is playing in the reception area. He arrived right on time peeping around the alcove with a cheeky grin set off by dimples.

'How are you doing?' He greeted me in his soft Northern accent. We seemed to be a curious spectacle for a woman sitting within earshot who most likely recognised Kieran. My hand-held microphone was also attracting quite a bit of attention. Nonetheless we continued talking and he was more than happy to tell me about his most treasured travel memories.

'I suppose there's a lot of different ones. Travel is a kind of relative term. You talk about family holidays. I remember as a child, because we were a big family, my father bought a house that was on the coast, only five or six miles away from where we actually lived. In order to make us think we were going further than we really were, he drove the long way around the mountains. We thought we were on the other side of the world. To be in a town was an amazing thing and during the holiday we would get pocket money; living in the country we had no use for it – what were we going to buy?' Kieran laughs and continues, 'unless we were going to buy a cow or something. We used to run up to a little shop in Warren Point to spend it. I remember the secret code for finding our way home again. We remembered the things in the windows of houses. As we passed we might notice an HP sauce bottle in the window of a house. Another landmark was a Bed and Breakfast at the top of the street where my father had bought the house and that was our code. God forbid anybody should ever move the HP bottle or put in a ketchup one instead.

My very early memories are of being by the sea. Ever since then I've had a mad love of the sea. I now live in the west of Ireland, but when I was a teenager we'd go to places like Westport, Galway and Sligo. I remember thinking then, "I'm going to live there". I went off to live in France and Germany and places like that, but I knew I'd always come home. In my mind the west of Ireland was where I had some kind of calling to and it's where I met my wife Annie. She felt the same. Now we've been living here for ten years and love it, so that early travel exposure made more of an impression than you might think. I loved it as a child, you know, I'd spend a day just sitting on the beach throwing stones [at the water] and nearly everywhere I've gone since then has been by the sea. I'm a coastal type of person.'

Did you travel mainly to escape the Troubles in Northern Ireland?

'In general, I don't think so. I think the opposite is true. A lot of people who live in Northern Ireland loved it, even during the Troubles. Home is home, you know As a student I'd gone off and busked with a friend of mine, Frosty. We were both studying law in Belfast and if you managed to pass the exams you could get away and travel. I loved the idea of experiencing new things.'

I ask Kieran about the countries he travelled in during his studies.

'We started off in France. We'd both studied French at school, so we just literally got a ticket to Cherbourg and made our way all around. We wandered into Switzerland and went to Germany. Germany is somewhere that I've gone back to a lot since then. We were young and were able to stay in hostels. Sometimes we didn't even bother; we slept in parks you know, if the weather was nice. In my first year at university, I went off to the States. I just worked on building sites. I loved that, there was a romantic notion to it. You know, I literally got on a Greyhound bus and went to Cleveland for no other reason than, "let's go to Cleveland". I got the travel bug very early on. I was lucky and could travel. It was harder for the generation before. There were fewer opportunities. My father really started travelling after he made money in his 50s. He's in his late 80s now and this year has been on three or four holidays, you know he's been to Hawaii, the south of Spain, Iceland; he's been all over the place. Travel can give you a lack of fear. Even if you don't like a place, you know it takes away one's fear of travel. Travel opens the world.'

What do you find inspiring about travel? Is it the landscape or the people?

'Not so much the landscape or places, but the people I meet. An important place for me was Saint Armel, near the southern coast of Brittany. I went there at a stage in my life when I needed to clear my head. When I was at school there was a guy from France who really inspired me. He was a really cool guy, into music. He opened us up to French as a language and not just something you learn at school. He agreed that if I taught him the guitar, he would teach me French. He also taught me to bake. I have this great vocabulary on baking in French.

I worked as a solicitor for a year and a half and I realised I was a bit too young to be doing it. Not law, but too young to be so entrenched in the lifestyle, to put on a suit and represent people. I loved the prestige and position that being a solicitor in a small town can give you. It wasn't me but only a part of me, so that got me thinking about and actually travelling to France where I did a bread round. Off I went in my little Renault, which was literally two cars welded together. It was fantastic. I got to experience how other people live. I saw what a little village in France was like at six o'clock on a wet Monday as opposed to the middle of July and I made great lifelong friends. More than anything, it gave me breathing space.'

Having spent so much time in France, he must have a good grasp of French culture and I wonder what it is about this country that he finds so endearing. Kieran is in no doubt that he loves France and more importantly loves all the people he met there. He feels that, like all cultures, it works on a few levels; on one level he says his life there was simpler with more focus on good food and wine, but he also found the country to be quite bureaucratic at times.

Can he recall any funny incidents while on his travels?

'Well yes, I'd given up law and was busking in Germany. I was like a nomad, you know, a man of the world and I'd fallen for this beautiful blonde German woman,' he recalls, laughing heartily. 'Anyway, I'm busking on the street corner and a crowd gather and I could see this well-dressed man who threw in a lot of money, so when I had done my set and the crowd dispersed, he wandered up to me and says, "I'm Lord Justice O'Donnell. The last time I saw you, you were presenting a case in court in Belfast." It taught me that nothing in life is black and white. For me travel has made me understand the value of kindness. Everything is measured in profit and loss these days and measured in who you are and what you can do for me. For me, the things that stand out are the little acts of kindness along the way, like a man in Switzerland who gave us a lift on a rainy night and who phoned his wife to ask if it would be okay to bring home these two people. She said "no", so he pulled into a motel and paid for a room for us with his credit card and then gave us money. To him we were two young guys on a motorway in Switzerland. On the other hand, I saw well-dressed guys trying to grab money out of my guitar box, a bit like the story of the Glen Hansard movie and I learnt to watch them. In certain towns in Germany it was a wee bit rougher, but the value of kindness is stronger and that is something that is very hard to measure. It very often goes unseen but it makes all the difference in anyone's day, no matter who you are.'

Having looked at Kieran's tour schedule I notice that many are scheduled in Germany and Switzerland. I wondered what it was that kept him returning again and again. Kieran knows exactly what it is, as he reminisced about the time he lived in Cologne for a year in his 20s. He tells me he always makes a point of touring Germany and Switzerland every year. He has a good grasp of the German language, which is useful, but ultimately he has a strong desire to see the country and to play in those small towns, villages and out-of-the-way places, which are more intimate.

His travelling has extended to the USA, including Nashville, Tennessee, which has long been associated with the recording industry. He was so taken with Nashville he tells me, that he has a house there and is planning an extended stay in the near future. But he's very quick to point out that it's not home.

He must have other parts of the USA that impress him. What is it that keeps taking him back there again and again?
Kieran has no hesitation in saying that he really loves Nashville, primarily because he has made some great friends there. The USA is such a large country and each place and town is so different. He recalls how he loved New York for the sheer buzz of the city and the feeling that anything was possible, but equally he loved Livingston, Montana, which is an hour's drive from Yellowstone Park, a place of spectacular natural beauty. The town is so unspoilt that it would be easy to imagine it in earlier era.

If he were to take one more journey where would he go?
'That's a difficult one, because I've learned different things in all the places I've been and it's very hard to filter out the hard times. As much as I've spoken fondly about France, there were days when I'd think, "Is this travel? Is this it? It's all to and fro". It's hard to pick one place. I'd like to go back to all of them for a day or two, even that building site in America. I'd go back and spend some time with that lovely family in Brittany again. I'd love to go back and have the freedom of my busking days in Cologne, Germany. You know, I wandered off your question Mary, but you can learn a lot in different places. The reality is you can't get the plusses without the minuses. A lot of artists are down about the economic climate. Buying

a CD isn't a priority for many people, but here's what I know: I've played on tour and travelled the world and am still enjoying it. The tide goes in and the tide goes out, and what defines you is how you cope with that tide. I think, "do the best you can" and the experience of travel keeps you to that.'

I get the very strong impression that travel is very important to Kieran. He confirms this telling me that travel is an education and broadens the mind and even more importantly, often gives perspective to problems. He speaks of the love that he and Annie have for their home in Sligo, but he says there are times when they need to be in Amsterdam or Berlin or New York. When you travel as much as Kieran it must be really tough to pick out any one journey. Kieran thoroughly agrees. He realizes how fortunate he is to do what he loves, especially incorporating making music into travel. He emphasises real travel – not tourism. He philosophises that he may never have got to Stewart Island, New Zealand, or Shetland Island were it not for his music and travel combination. One thing he was really certain about was that all journeys are amazing if you open up to the possibilities of new adventure. Bad days are part of the experience.

SINGING AROUND THE WORLD FROM BELFAST TO BROADWAY

Brian Kennedy

He shared an apartment block with Monica Lewinsky in New York while singing eight shows a week for nine months on Broadway at the Gershwin Theatre. Brian Kennedy was born in 1966, one of six children – five boys and a girl. His brother Bap is a respected musician in the UK so there is obvious musical talent within the Kennedy family. Brian left home and wound up in London at the age of 18 where he busked in underground stations, played in piano bars and even lived rough in squats until landing on his feet. It seems that it was only a matter of time before he would be 'discovered'.

In 2002 Brian's literary ambitions were realised when he contributed two short stories to the collection *Breaking the Skin*. The editor, knowing nothing of his already burgeoning musical career, chose the stories he submitted on merit. Today, Brian is known as a critically acclaimed singer songwriter, guitarist and interpreter of song. He is also a published author with two novels of fiction under his belt and a third one in the pipeline. He has hosted television and radio shows.

The legendary Van Morrison recognised Brian's singing talent and invited him to join his blues and soul revue where they duetted on stages around the world for six years. Brian's easily recognizable tones can be heard on the now classic, 'live' album, 'A Night In San Francisco' and then the subsequent studio albums, 'Days Like This', 'The Healing Game' and 'Back on Top'. On one of these tours with Van Morrison, Brian met and performed with Joni Mitchell, one of the artists he credits with being instrumental in shaping the way he approached his unusual guitar style and the way he writes songs. It was also not unusual to share the stage with legendary performers Ray Charles and Bob Dylan.

Brian's solo career has been a rollercoaster of creative twists and turns, highs and lows. To date he has released eleven solo albums and also guest starred on numerous other artists albums. But as Brian says, playing live gigs is closest to his heart. In 2006 life took another unexpected course and he was approached to represent Ireland in the Eurovision Song Contest in Athens, Greece, where he performed his own composition *Every Song is a Cry for Love*. Brian appeared briefly in a film with a cameo role as a nightclub singer in *This is the Sea* starring Gabriel Byrne and Richard Harris.

Music and travel are bound closely together for Brian. He tours extensively, taking his lyrics and melodies to the growing number of fans across the globe. Brian was rapturously received at The Basement in Sydney, a prestigious music venue and with a captivated audience and positive media reviews, his reputation as a top class performer was sealed. Travel has taken him on tour with The Corrs, flying to New York, Dubai, and Australia to name a few. He also makes time to fit in charity benefit concerts for organizations such as Disability Action and Contact Youth, the latter of which he is a patron. He was awarded a Lifetime Achievement Meteor Award in Dublin in 2010. He was a coach on the first series of *The Voice of Ireland*, a global franchised singing contest.

For Brian life is very unpredictable, but it seems he prefers it like that. For him there are always new songs to be written. Currently living in Dublin, he was able to indulge his passion for renovating an Edwardian townhouse that he calls home. For now, like his song says, he is the wandering kind.

THE INTERVIEW

I first met Brian Kennedy at my local East Coast radio station; his dulcet tones ringing out through the station speakers where he was singing live on air. Hitting all the notes with ease and with total clarity in his voice I could swear it was pre-recorded. When the radio interview finished, the man whose voice has been described as that of an angel, came in for a chat. He was casually dressed and greeted me with a warm smile and a firm handshake. A Celtic icon and yet he struck me as

Above: Jonathan Dimbleby in Dagestan.

Above: Rosie Swayle Pope pulling Icebird.

Above: Zoë Sallis filming *The Bible* in 1960.

Left: Simon Majumdar in the San Blas Islands.

Above: Simon Reeve in India while filming his *Tropic of Cancer* BBC series.

Above: Carol Drinkwater stands inside the trunk of a 5,000-year-old olive tree in Bethlehem.

Above: Marianne Du Toit in El Salvador.

Above: Tracy Piggott in Kenya.

Above: Nigel Meakin on location.

Above: Geoff Hill and Colin O'Carroll on the Great Ocean Road, Australia.

Above: Christopher P Baker

Above: Ken Doyle in Hackberry, Arizona.

Above: A promotional photograph taken for *Out of My Head... The Best of Kieran Goss.*

Above: Brian Kennedy at the Brandenburg Gate.

Above: Conor Woodman stood, appropriately, in a market.

Above: John Mole.

Above: Gary Finnegan with security guards at the Graduate University of the Chinese Academy of the Sciences, Beijing.

Above: Paul Kilduff with Michael O'Leary, CEO of Ryanair.

Above: Patrick Smith with the *Spirit of Moncton*.

Above: Paul Wilson and a wayward donkey.

Above: Fran Sandham reaching the Indian Ocean near Zanzibar.

Above: Dervla Murphy at home in Lismore, Ireland.

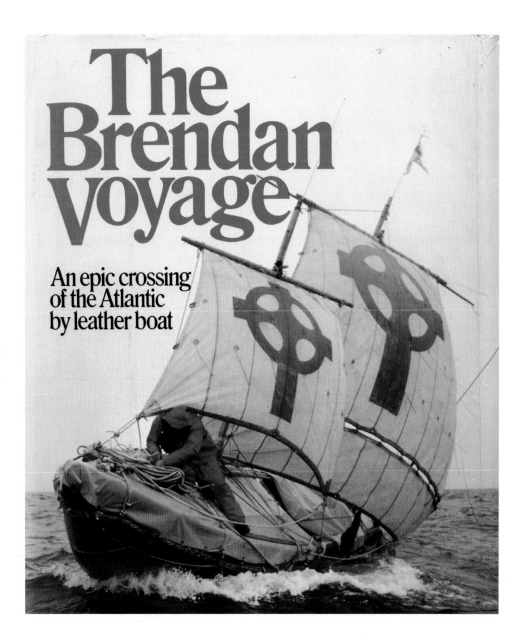

The cover of Tim Severin's book *The Brendan Voyage*.

Above: The cover of Tim Severin's book *The Brendan Voyage*.

Above: Stephen Clarke outside The Abbey Bookshop in Paris.

Above: Ardal O'Hanlon on the right, playing cards, in Rome, Italy.

Above: John Simpson filming in Libya.

the boy next door, approachable and friendly.

Brian was asked to sing at footballer George Best's funeral. What was that like?

'I remember getting there very early in the morning because security was so tight. It's hard to do the atmosphere justice because it was such a bittersweet experience. On one hand, I felt so honoured to be part of the soundtrack of the celebration of the life of one of the greatest footballers to have ever lived, and on the other hand, it was such a sad loss to the disease that is alcoholism. We were all very nervous because the service was being broadcast around the world and we wanted to do him proud. I remember singing the chorus of "You Raise Me Up" just as his coffin was lifted onto the shoulders of the pallbearers and I nearly lost my breath because it was as if the moment had been choreographed to coincide exactly with the lyric but, of course, it was pure magical coincidence. It remains one of the proudest moments of my life. To think that as a little boy on the Falls Road I would grow up to stand in that parliament building that shaped our city and my voice would circle that room as the body of the legend that is George Best would make his final journey out of this world...' Shortly after, the live recording of *You Raise Me Up* was released to raise money for the George Best charity, helping people with alcohol addiction.

When Brian and I made contact I was curious to know how a guy who started off in the back streets of war-torn Belfast wound up on Broadway. I asked Brian how travel started for him.

'It was a school trip in an overheated bus. I was a terrible traveller in those early days and would always get sick. For a few years in a row we went to Butlins holiday camp and it felt like it took nearly all day to get there. The delays were unbelievable. I dreaded that journey.'

Having grown up where bombing was a normal part of everyday life, did this give Brian the desire to travel as a means of escape, or would you have travelled anyway?

'Yes, our childhood mantra was "don't leave your area" because it was just so unsafe and although I was initially suspicious of travelling, I soon got the wanderlust that is still with me today. I was curious and nosey about the rest of the world especially after watching a David Attenborough programme about some kind of forest in the Congo.'

I ask if there's a particular journey he can recall and what made it memorable?

'There have been many, but the one that comes to mind is when I went to the Gambia in West Africa one Christmas and that was just such a culture shock. You think you know poverty until you visit that part of the world and yet I met some of the kindest, most generous, people ever. What a beautiful country and gorgeous people they are. Every child had a smile for us and they wanted to share with us what little they had.'

Brian recalls a time a few years ago where he sang on a cruise ship, which made a stop along the coast of Morocco. 'It was horrific and heart-breaking to see so many kids with missing limbs begging in the streets. Some had their legs bound by their parents so that they could beg.'

He's had so many positive travel experiences too and thinks that New York is hard to beat.

'I love the mix of cultures [in New York] and the year I spent on Broadway meant I got to know it very well, in a very privileged way.'

He loves it so much, he tells me, that if he had one more journey to make he reckons it would, 'probably be to New York because I have so many good memories and there are always new ones to be made. I'd go and see as much theatre as I could. Then take a horse-drawn carriage around Central Park before heading out for an incredible dinner somewhere. Not forgetting a martini at the Four Seasons. Otherwise I'd choose Melbourne or Sydney.'

Brian moved to the USA to perform with Riverdance on Broadway and also sang in Carnegie Hall. He tells me, 'it was a dream come true to find myself living on the Island of Manhattan because it felt as if the streets were drenched in rich musical history. A young Joni Mitchell played in coffee shops and Bob Dylan changed the shape of folk music back in the late '60s. The Clancy Brothers could be heard wherever I went and I really got a sense of the continuing love affair the Irish have with America. I was lucky to meet Kevin Killen who had worked with U2 and he produced my album, "Get On With Your Short Life", which is very much my New York album. I couldn't wait to take the train to Broadway and clock in at the theatre. It was surreal to be singing there and I loved every second of it.'

Songs were written and tailored for his voice by Grammy-award-winning composer Bill Whelan and performing live for former president Bill Clinton was just part of what he did. At one fundraiser they ended up duetting Carrickfergus to an astonished crowd.

A large part of his life is and has been music. Do the places he travels to inspire him to write music and influence his melodies and lyrics in any way?

'Definitely, I wrote a song called *The Ballad of Killaloe* about a time spent in the hills of Tipperary. *Christopher Street* and *New York* were penned while living in the west village of Manhattan.'

I remember seeing footage of Brian walking the Glens of Antrim with his guitar and him singing an Irish ballad called *The Green Glens Of Antrim* as part of a BBC television series, called *On Song*, featuring a duet with Sinead O'Connor and Moya Brennan, among others. This series examined the origins of the great ballads and their history. It was set in the most exquisite places with breathtaking scenery and sunsets. In one episode Brian sings *Peggy Gordon* with the legendary Lulu.

Of all the places Brian filmed, which was his favourite?

'It is a hard question to answer because it really brings home to me just how beautiful our own country is. I loved Cobh in County Cork because of the history, but Galway has always been a favourite too because I have made many friends there over the last few decades and I jump at the chance to visit when I can.' All of these places featured on the BBC series.

So how does Brian prefer to travel, is it planes, trains or automobiles?

'I probably prefer planes because I love the idea of flying and of course, it's the fastest way to travel the greatest distance. Never mind what Phileas Fogg.' He particularly likes the airline which asks, 'Would you like an upgrade?'

Another memorable experience Brian recounts was when he was sent to the Blasket Islands to report on the status of sea eagles, whichfeatured in a series on RTÉ television. The birds were facing extinction and a few were spotted on the island. Eagles, however, turned out to be the last thing on Brian's mind having had to battle constant seasickness on the choppy seas. He remembers how inclement it was.

'When we reached the Blasket Islands we weren't allowed to land because the seals were pupping and we were caught in the strong currents throwing the boat in every direction. A few of us were sick over the side of the boat. Seasickness is horrible, though, and I was never so relieved once we were on solid ground again.'

He also recalls being given the opportunity to make a documentary called *Wild*

Trials for RTÉ Television about white-tailed sea eagles, found in Norway.

'My challenge was to try and get the best picture I could on my camera so as part of my training I was treated to a hot air balloon ride to experience what it might be like to have an eagle's view of the earth. Going up was easy, but landing was another story and we careered sideways before coming to a halt upside down in a field; it was exciting and terrifying at the same time.

I eventually ended up on the freezing fjords of Norway and on the second day I got a beautiful picture of an adult sea eagle catching bait. Mission accomplished.'

So what was the highlight of the trip?

'Seeing the sea eagle in its natural habitat from our little aluminium boat in the middle of the sub-zero temperature fjords. We were surrounded by little islands thick with forest and lucky to be accompanied by an eagle expert who had the most amazing knack of knowing where all the nests were and when to throw the bait.'

What is it that makes you want to keep travelling?

'I enjoy the freedom of it. It's such a privilege to fly somewhere to sing for a crowd of people. It takes around 24 hours of various flights and cars to get to New Zealand and just when I'm at the end of a momentous journey I'm actually just beginning a new one. It's not lost on the audience either, what an effort it takes for an artist like me to undertake such a journey that far afield. I love the idea that I'm on the other side of the planet immersed in a completely different culture yet there's common ground, too, when it comes to music. It either moves you or it doesn't.'

What lesson in life have you learnt from your travels?

'Get on with your short life.' He advises, 'don't wait. Book that ticket now and always have a secret supply of antibiotics because long-distance travelling can be exhausting and there's always someone on the flight with a cold.'

What country do you like to tour?

'Australia, because the audiences are true music fans whatever their taste and I love winning new fans over. Each time I return there is a growing sense of appreciation and loyalty and more and more people attend the shows. In this day and age it's very much a "word of mouth" thing. People will spread the word when there is a good concert coming up and Australians are not shy to give a new artist a chance. I've been lucky to play the continent far and wide and it's easy to underestimate just how many miles you need to travel. Each place has its own charm. There's something about Sydney that is just so welcoming. It must be said it's a very cool place to be a gay man. I love that there's so much acceptance there and I think the rest of the world could learn a lot. Melbourne is also a favourite mainly due to the people I met there. I think the people make the place. It's all about the company.'

HE'D BUY AND SELL YOU FOR TRAVEL

Conor Woodman

Author and television presenter Conor Woodman took a gamble when he gave up his job in corporate finance to travel the world. After completing his studies in economics, he worked in London for nine years as a market analyst for a credit broker. While still working in the financial sector, he had a yearning to try some television work. He was disheartened at the ruthlessness in the financial industry and was caught up in a job he wanted to leave. During this time of turmoil he was given the opportunity to do some work for television.

One of his assignments was working on a travel documentary with a friend in Nepal. Conor was intrigued by how the people were trading there. 'It was like going back to ancient times. They carried their goods on the backs of animals just like the ancient traders who used yaks as transport for their goods and sold anything from spices to carpets and furs. These were traded between the Nepalese and Tibetan border.'

He felt it would be fascinating to make a television programme about economics mixing the old ideas of trading with the new. Only this time he wanted to have a go at trading himself. He made the decision that he would sell his flat and trade with some of the proceeds to see if he could make a profit. He pitched his idea to a production company with the hope that it would one day be a television series with a book to accompany it. They accepted his idea. Now all he had to was to quit his job in corporate finance, sell his flat and go. He decided there and then that television and travel was for him and now he was ready to devote all of his time to that.

Conor was on a mission. He wanted a travel adventure with a difference. His mission was to see how people operated in ancient market places, and compare it to the tough and harsh world of corporate finance. His plan was to travel to off-the-beaten-track locations and trade goods face to face with the market traders. In doing so, he was aware that he may be exposed to life-threatening dangers, hardship and embarrassment, but also to excitement, experimentation, adventure and new cultures.

His chosen route took in Sudan, Zambia, Botswana, South Africa, India, Kyrgyzstan and western China. From Shanghai he travelled by train to Hong Kong, Taiwan, Japan, Mexico and Brazil. His travel experiences were translated into the television series, *Around the World in Eighty Trades*, which was followed by a book.

Following on from this success a new series, *Unfair Trade* (long listed for the 2012 Orwell Prize) was commissioned, which was to take Conor all over the world. His focus was to determine if it was possible for businesses to be ethical and profitable. For the series he spent time on lobster boats in Nicaragua; and in the Congo saw sweatshops that supply the Western world.

Another television series, *Scam City*, followed, in which Conor visited ten popular holiday destinations to uncover the sinister side of tourism. Deliberately seeking out scammers, his mission was to find out who these people are as well as how they operate. Using hidden cameras, he exposed those trying to rip off tourists in Rome, Prague, Rio de Janeiro, New Delhi, Barcelona and Las Vegas. He encountered unscrupulous taxi drivers, pick pocket scams, prostitution and different criminal underworlds. He discovered corrupt doctors treating sick tourists, fraudulent rug makers in Marrakesh who dye rugs to make them look antique, a process that makes them seemingly more lucrative. He uncovered the gangs that operate all over the Metro in Paris at night, and in Rome he found corrupt and untrained tour operators controlled by the mafia. Counterfeit currencies in that city were passed to unsuspecting victims by taxi drivers. In Bangkok, he encountered the tuk-tuk gem scammers who divert tourists away from their desination to very expensive jewellery shops. And in Istanbul, he uncovered the fake friend scam whereby drinkers with astronomical bills will befriend someone in a bar, only to adandon them, and their bill, a while later.

According to Conor, it is possible for travellers to avoid falling prey to tourist crime, so long as they bring their common sense with them. 'You need to look after yourself and your stuff with the same vigilance as you do at home.'

THE INTERVIEW

Conor Woodman's book, *Around the World in Eighty Trades* caught my attention some months before I made contact with him. This was no ordinary man. Here was an adventurer and risk taker. I was looking forward to meeting him. I found Conor to be easy going and gentle, not the over-confident city slicker I thought he might be. I ask him about his early memories of travel.

'My first overseas trip, I suppose, was when my family moved from the west of Ireland to the UK when I was seven years old, but my first real holiday was the following year when we went to Sidari in northern Corfu. Back in 1982, it was a little Greek village with a tiny beach with a choice of two tavernas. I remember it was the first time I'd ever been in warm sea. I couldn't believe it, it was a far cry from the freezing Atlantic where I learnt to swim.'

Where did his interest in travel to Asia come from?

'I was studying economics and my Master's degree thesis was on the South-East Asian currency crisis of 2007, but I had no idea what that region was like until I'd finished writing and went there. While there I went to a small bucket shop to book a flight out of Malaysia to Indonesia. The guy who owned the shop started talking about why things had got so bad in the region while he printed the tickets. The conversation was really interesting, so much so, that he invited me back to his house to meet his family and they asked me to stay for dinner.'

What gave you the inspiration to want to trade?

'I was making a documentary in Nepal for National Geographic in my spare time. I was still employed in corporate finance but looking for a way out and, while I was waiting for the cameraman to get some more shots of a monastery on the Tibetan border, I noticed some traders taking meats and furs over the border loaded up on yaks. I felt I should make a documentary about what they do, but do the trading myself. When I thought about it some more, I started to think about whether I could apply myself to make a profit in the same way. From there a small idea just snowballed and the whole challenge "went global".'

Wasn't it drastic, selling your flat and leaving the country in order to trade?

'The idea to sell my flat came from a couple of places. First, I wanted to have enough money to play with so that anyone reading about the story could picture themselves in the same situation. I decided to raise £25k sterling. I'd made a bit more than that on my flat during a very buoyant period in the property market and it was enough to risk. Actually, at the time I didn't regard it as a risk because I was pretty confident that I could make money on the journey. The second factor was that the property market was beginning to look like it was faltering – and it was. It was a good time to sell up.'

Selling a flat adds up to a lot of preparation and organisation for a trip. What other preparations did you need to make?

'Because the whole thing was being filmed, the route had to be nailed down. Global events did force a few changes. For example, I'd planned to go through Kenya and Tibet but civil unrest in both countries meant that I had to change my plans. What wasn't set was what I was going to trade. It was really important to me that I was free to explore opportunities along the way and so I had to convince the production company that nothing was to be set up by them – not easy in telly land. I managed it though and, so, what you read or see is what happened. I had no idea before I left that I would trade chilli sauce, (which he called hot as hell sauce), or jade, for example. Other than that, I just packed a passport, a toothbrush, and a film crew – and set off with a one-way ticket to Khartoum, Sudan.'

Conor chose Sudan as the starting part of the journey because like all the countries he chose, he wanted to visit newly industrialised countries where he might find the best opportunities for business. He was looking for places where there was some disposable income, which ruled out the poorest of the countries, but he also wanted to avoid the more sophisticated economies. Added to this Sudan has a thriving camel trade. He aimed for Khartoum, the capital, and then planned to move to the market place in El Obeid.

It must have been very complicated obtaining visas?

'Visas were difficult because there were so many countries involved. I had to get a second passport so that I could be using one while the other one was off at some far flung embassy being stamped with visas for the next leg of the trip. This is standard practice for journalists.'

I'm not for one minute suggesting that Conor looks shifty or shady in any way, but I ask if people were suspicious of him. I mean, he arrives as a stranger in a community, with no fixed abode, and the intension to trade in all sorts. He doesn't have time to become a part of the community. What sort of challenges did you have?

'The first challenge in every situation was to convince people that I was for real. I was always the new boy trying to sell something or buy something in an environment where everyone else knew each other and had done for ages. Then I had to convince them that the camera played no part in it. Suspicion has become something I am used to living with. Once I had got over that they were still suspicious because I was trying to make money out of them.'

One of the most unpleasant incidents happened while Conor was in Egypt. He was with a small production team and needed to hire a Land Rover. They were hoping to go to Dongola in Sudan. It seemed like they had negotiated one at a good price of $100. It was to come with a driver included in the price. Unfortunately neither the Land Rover nor the driver showed up. Naturally they wanted their money back but the car rental man was reluctant. Things turned nasty when the salesman's friend called to say that he was going to report them. There was the real threat of arrest. He told them that he had reported them to the authorities as spies.

'That was the only really nasty bit of the trip. There were three of us travelling with a Sudanese translator and driver. When the accusation was revealed to us we laughed it off until our Sudanese colleagues explained that we would all be arrested first and questions asked later. While we would get help from our embassies, the other two would have been in a really bad situation so we took the decision to leave. We all left for Egypt the next day.'

That must have been very scary. What would the punishment have been if he had been convicted? Don't they still carry the death penalty? And being inside a Sudanese prison would be no picnic either.

'I dread to think. You don't mess around in war-torn countries.'

Were there any language problems?

'With language barriers, I just hired a translator. The hardest thing was often the authorities.'

Which was the most outstanding and interesting place and why?

'I still have dreams about the jade mines of Xinjiang, China. I'm not sure how much longer they'll be there because the jade is running out – it has a very Wild West feel to it with guys scrabbling around in makeshift open mines dug into the dusty old river bed looking for a rock that will make them rich overnight. I doubt I'll ever see something like that again.'

Can you recall your most positive travel experience?

'The whole 80 trades experience was very positive. I found that people from so many different cultures were happy not just to do deals to make money, but to engage and share experiences as well. I've always said that having something to trade was the first reason that anyone ever bothered to travel down the road to the next village. And because of that trip, we found out a little bit more about what happened in the next village. Trade was the reason the world opened up for people back in Marco Polo's day and it's still true today.'

Has working on your book *Unfair Trade* influenced the way you live and the purchases you make?

'Very much so. I buy all my coffee (and I drink a lot) from Ethical Addictions. They source all their coffee direct from the farmer so they pay way more than any Fairtrade-certified coffee on the market. I always try to buy goods that give the greatest benefit to producers and that means I almost never buy Fairtrade certified goods.'

If you could return to the life of trading on a more permanent basis would you do so?

He laughs saying, 'No definitely not. It was a personal challenge for me to see if I could do it. Now that I've proved to myself it can be done, well that's enough. It was an incredibly difficult way to make money and I think I'll stick to writing and television. In Mexico, I hatched a plan to get some surfboards endorsed. I'd bought them in China and they were new to the market so I needed someone who knew what they were talking about to say they were alright. I found a surf champion called Angel Salinas and asked him if he'd try them out. He and I went out together on the Mexican Pipeline – the biggest shore break in Mexico – to test out the boards. Angel managed to surf a couple of 15 foot waves (4.5 m) with utterly amazing courage and skill. He was a genuine hero.'

Conor doesn't appear to be sentimental about home?

'I've travelled a fair bit now. For most of my adult life, I've spent long periods of every year overseas and, although I miss my family and friends, I'm happy to know that I'll see them when I get back.'

What valuable lesson did you learn from travelling?

'I have learned that making a living is about more than just making money, it's about living.'

I ask how he managed to discipline himself to write about his travel experiences.

'I didn't really have time to. I returned from my trip in September and, because my publisher needed the book finished in time to have it on the shelves to coincide with the accompanying television series, I had to get my head down and get on with it. I rented a cottage in the middle of nowhere for six weeks and lost myself in reliving the past five months.'

What advice would you give to someone planning a trip like his?

'Firstly, don't be mad. Second, if you're still determined to do it then I'd say be realistic about your goals. Leave enough time to do the trip justice. Each thing you buy needs to be researched properly if you're going to make money and that may take longer than a day or two. Other than that, enjoy it and don't start with more money than you can afford to lose.'

It wasn't all plain sailing either. He says, 'Most of the food in Sudan was poor. It was mostly gristle and stale bread. There was one point when I stopped at a truck stop in the desert and had a stew from a big pot. Let's just say I was glad it was too dark to see exactly what it was I was putting in my mouth.

Local food is always best. Of the local food I'd say the winners were in Japan eating sushi at the Tsukiji fish market or in Brazil at the churrascaria.'

How has Conor changed after his travel experiences?

'I'm fundamentally the same person but I do take an enormous sense of satisfaction from having completed the travel. It was such a big project and I invested so much in it – almost three years from having the idea to seeing it in print and on the screen.'

Working on *Scam City* must have given him an insight into the characters to be wary of when abroad. It doesn't appear to have made him suspicious of people or changed his perspective on travel, but he says he is certainly more careful and cautious. Every city, both at home and away, has its fair share of hoodlums. They are part of the experience of travelling and often poor people who've made bad choices in their lives. Conor affirms he isn't excusing what they do; only saying we need to be aware of their existence.

Could he contemplate going back to an office job?

He tells me that the office is not on the agenda, but books and television are.

PLAYING RUSSIAN ROULETTE WITH SPUDS

John Mole

I was hooked by the title of the book, *I Was A Potato Oligarch* and became fascinated by the idea of an English man going to Russia with the aspiration of becoming an oligarch. I was intrigued. What was he up to?

It was only one of the inspired but calamitous ventures that John embarked on after his 40th birthday present to himself – quitting international banking for a more precarious but interesting career as a writer. His first comic novel had been published and he went on to publish three more.

Meanwhile he was interested to find out what effect the management techniques he had learned and practised as a manager had on the people managed. He took various temping jobs as a clerk, typist and messenger and discovered that they had no impact. He wrote about it in *Brits at Work: Inside Job on Management*.

His other book *Mind Your Manners* is based on John's business experience in Europe, the Middle East and Africa. It is about the different behaviours and expectations people have about work and working together. It's helpful to know what they are if you are in a multi-national organisation or project team. The book became a bestseller and has been published in Japanese and Latvian.

Research for his books required extensive travel and took him around Europe, the USA, the Middle East and Africa.

John Mole has an abiding love of Greece. There, he converted a stone ruin into a family home on the island of Evia back in the '70s. It proved to be an ideal setting to experience life in rural Greece at a time when old Greece was moving into the 'new Europe'. His story of the trials and tribulations of building relationships and transforming his house is told in *It's All Greek To Me*.

As for Russia, John was curious about the New Russian revolution after the collapse of the Soviet Union. Starting a business was a good way to find out what was happening. With technical advice from a South London fast-food restaurant, he set up a joint venture with the Russian union of private farms and co-operatives in Moscow to create a potato take-away, only to stumble across the Russian Mafia, who wanted a piece of the action. Before leaving on a plane in a hurry John discovered a lot of what was going on under the (potato) skin of the New Russia.

John is still writing and in between likes to play his miniature bouzouki. He still loves to travel, especially around the Middle East and the Mediterranean.

THE INTERVIEW

John has visited so many interesting places so I ask him to describe some of his treasured memories.

'In 1951 when I was six years old, my father went on a business trip to the USA. He flew there and sailed back on the Queen Mary. My mother, little sister and I went to meet him and we came back by train. I had never been on a train before. The memory of that train compartment filled with American toys, which my father brought back is still, to this day, vivid in my mind.'

Curious to know what took him from South London to Greece I ask him how his interest in Greece started.

Since early childhood I've had a love of Greek stories, where that interest came from, I have no idea. I still get a thrill from standing in places that have been part of my mental landscape for more than 50 years. This year I went to Pergamon, Sardis and Troy and although there's not much to see there, these places continue to live in the imagination, and provide me with a feeling of "coming home" when I visit.'

'I was transferred by the American bank I worked for to Athens to open a Middle East Representative Office – the conventional location, Beirut, was at war. We had three children at that time and our fourth was born in Athens.'

What was living in Athens like?

'In those days, before the Euro, rampant commercialism, pollution, traffic and over-building, it was very pleasant and easy. Now, less so.'

How different was it from life in the UK? Was it difficult to adapt to the culture? If so what aspect?

'Life in Greece was so different from Britain. Foreigners and children are welcome. Families and family values are predominant, also good humour, cheerfulness, optimism, obsession with food and talking about food, sociability and lack of snobbery. It was a most engaging and refreshing place to be.

We lived there for five years until 1980 and since then have gone back every year to our house on Evia. I have a US Green Card so over the years we have spent a lot of time in the United States too, but home is London.

It was so easy to adapt to the culture; so easy to flee from Thatcher's Britain; so easy to throw off English snobbery and stand-offishness and food and weather and introversion and xenophobia and... you name it. Athens was a small town in a big city. The rest was a rural society with rural values. The islands had a distinct character. Televison had not yet destroyed communities and community life. It wasn't Arcadia by any means – poverty, emigration, corruption, and also right and left-wing political fissures were woven into society.'

Are things any better? How has it changed in these latter years?

'It's hardly changed at all. Greeks have stumbled from one political and economic catastrophe to another since their independence. Their ideals and aspirations have often outstripped an ability to realise them. They are the instigators of many of their own problems and blame foreigners for them, sometimes with justification. The basic Greek social unit is the extended family and the network of mutual obligations and loyalties that bind it together. The net stretches very far. The dark side of this is the mistrust, the desire to outdo and do down other families. It makes the kind of civic society we have in Northern Europe very hard to replicate. For example, the idea that an elected representative should defend the interests of their entire constituency and not just of those who voted for them is alien in Greek politics.'

John has practised and written about cross-cultural management. I ask him what advice he has for doing business in Greece.

'Find a Greek partner you trust and who will do it all for you.'

It appears that travel has brought John a wealth greater than money can buy. I remind John about his original dream of owning a little white-washed house with a blue door and blue shutters on an unspoiled island in a picturesque village near a beach with a taverna around the corner. I ask him to describe the reality.

'Dream on; a tumbledown stone house with a wonky floor and mice.'

I ask him to recall some of the most memorable characters he has encountered.

'The Mogho Naba, King of the Mossi tribe, sitting under a baobab tree outside his palace in Ouagadougou, surrounded by courtiers and a woman killing chickens. Since childhood he was fed millet beer and he was the fattest man I ever met. He filled his outdoor throne, a two-seater G-plan sofa. We discussed his investments; he was intelligent and charming too.

I also remember a driver I had for a week in Sanaa. He learned his few words of English in the British hospital in Aden when it was still a colony. He'd greet you by snapping to attention, saluting and booming in home counties English, "Good morning Sir. Have your bowels moved?" He was an expert at catching snakes and summoning the Haji eagle.

Then there was Pat O'Connor of the British army catering corps. He saw plenty of action in the Korean War. Forward troops did not have ration packs but were supplied from the corps kitchens. Pat's job was to guard deliveries of Irish stew and spotted dick from Chinese ambush. Their motto was "the stew must get through". Now he's a sprightly octogenarian and full of stories.

Another who made an impression was Elpida, the wise woman of our Greek village who cured my back with a raw egg, herbs and incantations. I also remember Mother Shyama (Guru Shyamadevi), a lovely lady who founded the Radha Krishna Temple in Balham. She radiated goodness and welcome and is credited with the gift of bi-location having simultaneously attended weddings in Leicester and South London.'

His life has taken him on many journeys. We focus on the most memorable.

'The most eye-opening was the train journey from Abidjan in Cote d'Ivoire to Ouagadougou, capital of what was still then Upper Volta and is now Burkina Faso, then to Niamey and northern Niger by bus and taxi. It was fascinating to see the transition from tropical forest through Savannah to the Sahara and how people adapt to their environment. The country I find the most expensive and the best value for money for a curious tourist is Japan. Everything is different or odd or baffling.'

Why did you choose to go to Russia for business?
'My so-called business was a way of getting deeper into what was happening in Russia at the time, other than by journalism or tourism. Russia is a fascinating country. It was a fascinating time. There was a revolution going on and I wanted to get stuck in; be part of it.'

Apparently John hadn't seen much of Russia before that except for a ten-day package tour to Moscow and St Petersburg. I understand he used unusual forms of transport. While viewing a farm he was carried pig-gy-back style. Did this take him by surprise or is this the norm in Russia?
'It's definitely not the norm, especially for the western development consultant I was taken to be. The normal transport was Latvian mini-buses.'

What did you think of Russia? What most impressed you about it?
'Where do you start? History, geography, politics, society, culture... full of contrasts and contradictions, run by gangsters and inhabited by generous and cultivated people. The sheer size impressed me, matched by the resilience of a people subject to the most appalling acts of tyranny and war over the past century.'

It intrigued me to know how he managed to enter Russia in a business sense.
'At that time, the end of the Yeltsin era, Westerners were thought to have dollars bursting out of their briefcases. The problem was not getting in but getting out without being fleeced.'

Is it easy to break into Russian life as a foreigner?
'Yes, if you are white and speak Russian and resist getting on a high horse about how things are done. There is a Russian proverb: "don't go into someone else's monastery with your own rule".'

Did you go to Russia with the purpose of writing a book or would you have gone anyway?
'I never do anything with the prior intention of writing a book. I write about it

afterwards if there's a good story but often there isn't or I can't be bothered.'

Was it a good business idea?

'I reckoned the raw material would be easy to come by. Russia was the biggest potato producer in the world. I was told by the man responsible for co-ordinating Soviet production of potatoes that I wouldn't find a single one you could serve up in its jacket. He was right.'

How did the mafia become involved?

'The coup de grace was being summoned to meet the mafia over breakfast at nine o'clock in the morning at a topless restaurant. They wanted ten percent of the takings in return for protection against other mafia or the police, who were just as bad.'

Were you bothered by the corruption?

'It's a blow to my self-esteem that no-one has ever tried to bribe me.'

What do you think about modern Russia?

'It's wonderful for a minority of wealthy middle class people. It's not much different from the old one for many and a lot worse for some. There's as much graft and bribery and official corruption and violence as there ever was. It's now institutionalised, official and centred on the Kremlin and the government. If you do business or go to court or deal with the tax inspector it's who you know and who you can, let's say, influence. Things are less chaotic, more organised. You know where you stand. In the big cities people have jobs and salaries and flats and cars and can lead a more or less normal life. Look at the millions of ordinary Russians who go abroad on holiday. In the old days it was bankers and business people who were most at risk of assassination. Now it's journalists.'

Were the Russians welcoming in general?

'Yes, very much. In general, I found people very hospitable and to have a great sense of humour.'

What was his impression of Moscow?

'It was and still remains a great imperial capital full of people from so many different nations and ethnicities.'

There is an expression "I'm on the pig's back", meaning to be in luck; in a prosperous happy state. It was literally true for Mr Mole who found himself at one point wearing very muddy boots with pigs underfoot. I ask him to recall having literally landed on the pig's back when he went to Russia.

'It was my first official visit to a Russian farm. I was dressed up like a bank manager in a dark suit and tie and shiny shoes. It was an old fashioned farmyard with lots of animals except that it was two feet deep in thick, black mud. The first indignity was being carried across the mud, piggy back by the farmer. Then we were treated to homebrew vodka and raw pickled piglet tails. I sneaked outside to get some fresh air to keep the piglet tails down and there in front of me was a wonderful Russian landscape like something out of *Dr Zhivago*. Struck by the beautiful surroundings, I instinctively walked forwards, across some stepping-stones in the mud. Except I discovered too late they weren't stepping stones. Do you remember the scene when James Bond skipped across the backs of crocodiles? Well crocodiles swim flat and their backs are knobbly but pigs are slimy and buck up and down. It was a wonderful adrenalin rush; pig surfing in a sea of mud, but I'm no better at surfing on a pig than a board. Everyone was very nice. I had a hose down to get the worst mud off and then went inside for a shower and a change of clothes. When I went back into the kitchen dressed like a farm labourer they all clapped. "Oh Ivan, Welcome to Russia."'

What's the most hilarious experience you had while travelling.

'I went into a church in Moscow where a service was going on with a lovely Russian choir. It was packed except for a side chapel. I think this was because the main occupants were two dead old ladies, lying in open coffins. One of them had lots of mourners congregating around her, surrounded by flowers and candles. The other woman had nothing and nobody. I felt sorry for her being on her own. So I lit a candle and stuck it on her coffin and stood there for a bit. When I backed off another little old lady grabbed my arm. I got a shock because she looked just like the dead one. "She knew you'd come", she said. She dragged me off to an old man leaning on two sticks. I was scared in case it was my putative father. But she stuck his hand in mine and told me to take him outside to the soup kitchen next door. He was a horrible yellow colour and covered in bright red scabs and had the worst case of the shakes. We shimmied and shook down the aisle and when we got outside he steered us to a whitewashed shack that was a makeshift lavatory. He had a lot of trouble undoing himself and he said "hold it please". Lord, in for a penny... so I took it out for him. Remarkably, and very conveniently, it was the only bit of him that didn't shake. I tried to think beautiful thoughts. I tucked him back in and he looked up at me and said, "I only wanted you to hold my stick, but thanks anyway".

What have you learned from travelling?
'Never leave home without a six-foot piece of string. So many daily uses from a tourniquet to a washing line.'

After his failed attempt in the potato business, he set up a protection and remediation company in partnership with an institute of biochemistry of the Russian Academy of Science. I ask him about it.
'They had bacterial technology for purifying industrial air emissions that was ten years ahead of anything in the West. I set up a British company to market it. Russian bugs help to keep the air of Wolverhampton and Wigan sweet.'

Does this make you an oligarch?
'Every man is an oligarch in his own mind.'

He is environmentally aware and active, setting up, and implementing a project to control the spread of water hyacinth on Lake Victoria, Tanzania, in 1995. The water hyacinth is considered to be one of the most noxious weeds in all of Tanzania. It has become a real problem as it is a threat to the marine life. A regional project was set up in the '90s to try to control it. As well as Tanzania, Kenya and Rwanda were also a part of this project. This project was set up to establish ways to control aquatic weeds in east Africa. The future of more than 30 million people is at stake as their livelihoods depend on Lake Victoria. It also forms a thick carpet-like layer of plant causing difficulties to transportation, as well as hydroelectric power generation.

The weed has blocked fish landing sites on the lake and cuts off the oxygen supply, destroying the aquatic life. A regional training course was set up to educate people on the control of aquatic weeds and national policies were developed. It's an on-going battle but would have been much worse had John Mole and others not got involved to try to eradicate it. John says, 'I had more success with INBIO Ltd, which imports Russian biotechnology for environmental protection and with a project to control the spread of water hyacinth on Tanzania's Lake Victoria. The campaign involves a combination of mechanical, manual and biological control methods and is on-going in the fight to eradicate the weed.

However, after a concerted effort between the three East African countries as well as the international community, the weed, started declining in 1997. By 1999 it almost became extinct so the hope is that they will be able to achieve that again.'

When did he become aware of this as a problem to the environment?
'When sitting on the shore of the lake with fishermen who couldn't launch their boats.'

Did travel inspire him to write his book *Mind Your Manners*, which examines managing business cultures in Europe?
'Not so much travel, as studying and working with foreigners.'

What was your most amazing discovery?
'That other people didn't want to be like me.'

He spent many years in New York. What was that like as an experience?
'I actually spent 15 years working for an American company all over the world, including a few years in Pittsburgh and New York. The striking thing about the USA is that, compared to other countries, it's so homogeneous. You find more variety over a hundred miles of Europe than a thousand miles of the USA.'

John tells me that he still spends a lot of time in London. I ask if there anything he'd miss about London if he stayed in Greece permanently.
'I'd miss the British library. I collect library reader's cards in preparation for my old age – Bodlean, Bibliotheque Nationale, Lenin Library. There's always a warm radiator, something to read and somewhere quiet to doze off.'

Does he ever go on conventional holidays?
'I like reliving youth and anticipating old-age pensioner poverty by trundle casing – the bus-passer's equivalent of backpacking, a step away from shopping-trolleying, then zimmering.

'Travelling on buses and staying in rooms with no bedside light and mosquito splats on the walls also appeals. I love the sound of a trundle case outside my window, so romantic, like a ship's siren.'

Who is the most influential person you've met on your travels?
'I once lectured a room of politicians about entrepreneurship. They included one of the two new deputy mayors of St Petersburg, a certain Vladimir Putin. He's a

little chap so in those days you wouldn't pick him out in a crowded room. Perhaps I gave him an idea or two.'

I ask him to tell me about his latest book.

'A couple of years ago I came across the diary of a young Elizabethan organ builder called Thomas Dallam. In 1599 he took a self-playing organ and automatic clock decorated with moving figures to Constantinople as a present to the Sultan from Queen Elizabeth. It took six months to get there. He encountered brigands, pirates, Moors, Turks, Greeks, pashas, eunuchs, slaves and finally the Great Turk himself. He made the first recorded crossing of mainland Greece and is one of the few men who peeped inside the harem and lived. I loved it and thought he deserved an audience today. So I translated it into modern English. It's called *The Sultan's Organ*. It's a brilliant insight into the Elizabethan world and a wonderful story.'

Any words of wisdom he learned from his travels?

'Avoid airports. My millennial resolution was never to fly over anywhere I hadn't seen on the ground. Six weeks later I was invited to Korea. I took the Trans-Siberian to Beijing and then trains and buses. I've stuck to it ever since. Then when you have to fly it's very satisfying to look at the little map in the back of the seat in front of you and to know what's down there.'

BETTER IN BEIJING

Gary Finnegan

What happens if you send an Irish man to China? What happens if the language is so confusing that you could be saying four different things depending on the tone you use? What happens if you are misunderstood and unwittingly call a person a weird gummy elf? They might spit at you. Oh, but they do that anyway in Beijing. Gary Finnegan had to grapple with the odd and the disgusting in China where he went to live and work for a year. On a diet of choking smog, Chinese phlegm, chicken's feet and caterpillars on a stick, he braved the elements, not to mention hitting the Great Wall of China, and a developed a greater understanding of modern China in the process.

In Beijing, Gary took his life in his hands. Even crossing the road was an ordeal. He treated it as a game, and described it as an art. He advises thinking of crossing the road as a war game, where you assume everyone on a bicycle is out to get you and where your paranoia is your ally. So far so good, he managed to stay alive long enough to taste the Chinese cuisine and to experience a dodgy stomach or two. One such incident he recalls in his book *Beijing for Beginners: An Irishman in the People's Republic*. 'My funny tummy is no laughing matter when the next day we make our way to Zhanshan Temple, a mountainside Buddhist enclave high above Qingdao's coastline. As fascinating as the temple is, my mind is far too busy to achieve nirvana, as I'm totally focused on finding a toilet. I have no interest in desecrating a religious site but if a bathroom doesn't present itself very soon, I'll have to run the risk of angering Buddha and probably the monk.'

In his book Gary recalls how on many occasions he was required to show great bravery, often with hilarious results. He also manages to display his knowledge and insight into Chinese history, culture, corruption and a changing society, as well as detailing the complete culture shock he experienced when he moved there.

THE INTERVIEW

After discovering Gary's book *Beijing for Beginners: An Irishman in the People's Republic*, I was intrigued. I was curious to know where his interest in travel began.

'We drove from Dublin to Kerry for what seemed like an eternity when I was around three years old. Destination: Banna Beach, just outside Tralee in County Kerry. The car journey seemed longer than the holiday but the drive was passed playing "I spy", which must have been maddeningly tedious for my parents. When they tired of that, the rules would be changed so that I would let out a shout when I spotted a red car. If it was happening a bit too frequently, the new rule would be that only green-coloured cars were worth shouting about. It sounds a bit boring now when I think about it but it was outrageously good fun at the time. Things got more interesting once my younger, noisier sister was old enough to chip in.'

Travel took Gary into a teaching job in Beijing where he was worshipped. Did this hero worship make his job easier or was it uncomfortable?
'It was a bit bizarre – and I'm sure I'd be in for a shock if I tried teaching in a school in most other countries. I'd done a crash course in teaching and prepared for classroom management, crowd control, mini-riots, that kind of thing. So when they all sat obediently looking up at me expectantly, it was a much different kind of pressure to what I'd anticipated. It made the job easier but Chinese students had an entirely different concept of what teachers are about. They didn't just expect me to be an expert in English writing; they see teachers as moral guardians, fonts of knowledge on all things from grammar to culture, history and family values. They wanted to know what I thought about having children, sex before marriage, balancing study with social life. There were curious too because most had not had any direct contact with a foreigner before. Overall, I presume hero worship is better than students throwing pencil sharpeners at your head while you're trying to explain phrasal verbs.'

Beijing is one of the most polluted cities in the world, so what made him decide to move to there?

'Ignorance. I hadn't much experience of living in a polluted atmosphere so I didn't appreciate that it could be a daily irritant. I had quit my magazine editing job, found somewhere to live and work in Beijing and mastered chopsticks before I gave serious thought to what life would be like in China. All the research in the world couldn't have prepared me for the reality that waited, particularly because I found myself on the west side of town, which is about an hour away from the east-side expat paradise of the Chaoyang district. That's where all the embassies, bars and restaurants are. The west side is a concrete jungle where foreigners are a rare sight.'

Did you regret making this decision?

'Oh yes. There were definitely days, particularly in the winter, when I wondered whether I'd done the wrong thing. It's a horrible feeling and I usually had to bury it unless I was in a position to leave. I went to Australia for a few weeks during the break for Chinese New Year and it killed me to go back to freezing temperatures and dodgy food. I had a one-year contract and, although I could have broken it, I was always likely to see it through unless it became absolutely unbearable. In hindsight, now that I'm in back in Europe, breathing freely and not having to deal with a censored media and all the other downsides, living in China seems like the best thing I've ever done. But I still wouldn't be in a rush to go back.'

Gary mentions in his book that 400,000 people die in China every year. A new report suggests the figure is even higher. One effect of air pollution, is that traffic police die on average at forty-three. As a journalist who has written health articles, did he feel threatened by this?

'What is harder to ignore is the black stuff that gathers at the back of one's throat and the inescapable taste of exhaust fumes you get when you step outdoors in Chinese cities, but I was careful not to seek employment as a traffic cop. Working as a health journalist is a great way to become a hypochondriac. I'm worried about diabetes, cancer, my triglycerides, my pelvic floor muscles. I wrote a piece about hypochondria once – it's rampant; I've probably got it. In truth, most of those statistics just wash over me.'

'Girlfriend' featured quite a lot in his book also. Was she instrumental in helping him stick out tough times?

'I would have found it very difficult to be alone on the far side of western Beijing. It's quite an isolating place because the Chinese are friendly and welcoming but can be hard to crack – they don't let you into their inner circle too easily. Plus, there's the language barrier and other cultural differences so we probably kept one another sane. I should add that Liz – or "girlfriend", as she is referred to in *Beijing for Beginners* – wasn't overly keen on being named in the book, hence the decision to give her a moniker. This suited me fine as I was able to steal all her jokes and observations and claim them as my own.'

What was the hardest part of Chinese culture to adapt to?

'The language is something I just never got close to mastering. I had three teachers and can still only order dinner, a couple of pints and get a taxi home. Obviously I had wanted to discuss the role of Confucianism in modern China or the paradox of operating a market economy in a nominally communist state – but I was mostly happy if waiters understood it when I asked for 'no MSG (monosodium glutamate) in the Kung Po chicken please.'

What part of the Chinese culture could you never adapt to?

'As tricky as learning to speak and understand Chinese was, writing characters is a whole other ball game. It's nothing like our alphabet, of course, and requires a whole new way of thinking. I don't want to say I could never learn to write Chinese but it would be a major project. The other thing that was slow to grow on me was the food. That was quite a surprise, but the food in Beijing is a lot different to what we in the West often associate with Chinese food. Even those long-term expats who loved Beijing food are usually glad to grab something more familiar from time to time. Naturally, Chinese people feel the same way about potatoes and baked beans. The other thing that irked me was the often hilarious media propaganda and censorship of the Internet.'

Did anything upset you about China?

'The poverty. Before and since my visit I've seen so many news reports about China's economy showing its brightly lit mega-cities. Beneath the neon glow is a very poor – and very large – population. Beijing and Shanghai can look swish but it is run on the backs of literally millions of migrant workers who live below the poverty line. Some Chinese people are getting richer and buying up big-brand cars and handbags but most are still extremely poor. It gets worse when you leave the big cities. On top of that, students who work every waking hour to get ahead are in an almost impossible struggle against 100 other hardworking students for every job vacancy that comes up. The government is genuinely trying to improve living standards for everyone but, for most people, a decade of double-digit economic growth has had no real meaning.'

What really impressed you about China? Is there anything we in Europe could learn from the Chinese people?

'At the risk of generalising about 1.3 billion people, the Chinese have a strong sense of self-sacrifice when there's a higher goal to strive for. That can either be the grand project of building a great nation or of giving your offspring the chance of a better life. They are not as self-centred or cynical as we are. Although, the flipside is that there's a general lack of scepticism and questioning of authority.'

Did moving to Beijing give you a deeper insight into China?

'Yes I'm still glad to have some concept of what China is like, especially because it looks as though its global importance will continue to grow. I would probably have done more homework on which areas of the city were best to live in, but otherwise I now feel like I had a narrower concept of the world before going to Beijing. Such a huge chunk of the population lives in Asia and I have a better appreciation of that now.'

Did you visit any other parts of China? If so, what did you think of them?

'I went to Shanghai for a few days – it's a glitzier version of Beijing and has some great old colonial buildings. But I have greater affection for the capital, probably because it was home for a while. We took a trip to Hainan, a resort island in the South China Sea, and stayed in a relatively fancy hotel. But Hainan is a weird place and it's easy to feel uncomfortable. There are rows of shiny new hotels along the coast with people living in shacks and run-down old blocks of flats just across the street. It's a slightly exaggerated version of what we found in other cities we went to like Qingdao, Penglai, Yantai, Weihai, and Xidan: a construction boom has seen hundreds of modern buildings spring up in the past ten years but most people still live in dilapidated communist-era blocks. It's like they built nothing for 60 years and are now in a mad rush to make up for lost time. The result is a yawning gap between the better-off and the less fortunate.'

Are the Chinese generally as happy as they look on the surface?

'Despite often living in harsh conditions, there is a justifiable sense of optimism in China – things are getting better. I taught postgraduate students, aged between 22 and 30, who lived in cramped six-man dorms with no shower and no cooking facilities, but they never complained.

They felt fortunate to be getting an education, and confident that they would eventually reap the rewards of Chinese progress. They may wind up disappointed but, for now, everyone is looking forward. Whatever we may think of China's government, it must be comforting for people to believe in their leaders.'

Were there any funny or bizarre incidents?

'There were many bizarre moments. One of my favourites was the night a local restaurant owner joined us for dinner and ordered the chef to entertain us while he bullied us into eating roast caterpillars, chicken neck and fried cow tendon. The chef stood at our table staring intensely at the bowl he was holding in one hand. Then, in an instant, he smashed it using the index finger of his other hand. He proceeded to chop bricks in half with his bare hands and wrap copper wire tightly around his chest before snapping it with a flex of his pecks. It helped take our minds off the food.'

Were there any scary moments while travelling?

'China is one of the safest places to travel, even if it's not used to catering for foreign tourists. I was never particularly worried about being in the city late at night, and it was the same in more remote towns. It can be slightly eerie to see such a heavy police and military presence sometimes, but violent crime against tourists doesn't seem to be a major problem. We came back to Europe via South-East Asia and there are plenty of dodgy places along that route – certain quarters of Bangkok and Ho Chi Minh, for example, have plenty of horror stories to tell.'

Where else have you travelled?

'Vietnam and Thailand were great in different ways. The islands in Thailand are amazing but they're a holiday resort; you couldn't live there. Hanoi was fantastic: a bustling city, beautiful old buildings, and a stunningly sad recent history. As a student, I spent summers working in Chicago and Paris, with the latter being infinitely more appealing. But much to my own surprise, I found Australia to be one of the most attractive places I've seen. It wasn't the land of uncouth yobbos I'd expected. If Melbourne wasn't so far away and full of killer spiders, it'd be ideal.'

Have you revisited Beijing?

'I left Beijing in the summer of 2008 and have yet to return. There's a lot of the world left to see so it might be a while before I make it back but it's definitely something I will do one day. It'll be fascinating to see how much it has changed. Even in the year I spent there the changes were visible and dramatic.'

In your book you mention public spitting and chaotic queuing as some of the things visitors find hard to get used to. Do you think Beijing will always be a land of queue-jumpers and spitters or are the Chinese trying to improve on these for the sake of tourism?

'In preparation of the Olympic Games in 2008, the government dreamt up some typically insane ways of coercing the populace into behaving as tourists expect: they have established a Spiritual Civilization Office, drawn up a Civic Index to measure public etiquette, and launched Voluntary Wait in Line Day. You couldn't make it up. They also trained volunteers to smile manically at foreigners to make them feel welcome. To me, it smacks of effort and is a bit creepy.'

Would you say that living in Beijing was a character-building experience?

'It surely was, but I didn't give it much thought until it was behind me. We developed as individuals and as a couple but perhaps that would have happened elsewhere too. Family and friends seem relieved that we survived the challenges that China threw our way, but it never really felt like a test to us.'

Do you think you'll uproot again to explore another country? If so where?

'We currently live in Belgium, land of chocolate and beer. Things could be worse. I was reminded recently that I said in an interview last year that Cuba's current transition could make for a fascinating book and, although I've been busy in Brussels and always have one eye on a move back to Dublin, Havana is still at the back of my mind. India is also intriguing for its sheer scale and the pace of change but I'm not sure I could live there.'

Have you learnt any valuable lessons in life through travel?

'Going to China teaches you a lot about scale. It's enormous. Getting from one side of Beijing to the other could take hours; and neighbouring cities are sometimes an overnight train ride away. There are cities I'd never heard of which have twice the population of my home country. Travel gives you perspective. You also learn to make do with whatever you are presented with in terms of food and accommodation – you can't afford to be fussy. Travelling certainly helps reset your values. You appreciate a good night's sleep and decent food, and worry less about trivial things. Hopefully I'm less materialistic as a result.'

HIGH FLIER IN THE TRAVEL ZONE

Paul Kilduff

Paul Kilduff's favourite haunt is the check-in queue for Ryanair (a Europe-based low-cost airline that operates 1,500 flights a day). Not because he enjoys it, but because he wants to 'get even'. Stung by a ten-hour delay and an expensive €300 fare to Spain, he seeks 'justice', and he tries to 'get even' by flying to every country in Europe for the same total expenditure suffering every low fares airline indignity possible to man but enjoying it at the same time.

Armed with no more than 10 kg (22 lbs) of carry-on baggage, he endures 6 am departures, boarding scrums, lengthy bus excursions, terminal anxiety and dubious cabin crew service. It's almost an addiction and the only cure is to fly.

In Paul's early days, he had success writing financial thrillers, inspired by his six years of working with international banks in the City of London. From there he graduated to travel writing, specifically tales about low-fare air travel. His first travel book, *Ruinair*, was a number one non-fiction bestseller in Ireland for nine weeks. In his second, *Ruinairski*, Paul discovers the countries of Central and Eastern Europe: he meets the Latvian politician who refers to Ruinair passengers as 'savages'; he searches for a second vowel in Brno; he learns there is more to Gdansk than a shipyard wall; finds beauty in Bratislava; and he endures Romania's native low-fares airline. He is not finished with low-cost airlines by a long shot.

THE INTERVIEW

I was looking forward to meeting the man who caused me to laugh out loud while reading his books. I didn't quite know what to expect. I had this image in my head of a city slicker, somebody very cocksure and assertive. How wrong was I? Paul was casually dressed, sported a neat and tidy haircut and was softly spoken, gentle, chatty and open. I was completely taken aback and relieved.

Paul had taken a huge risk with *Ruinair*; after all it was a controversial book. He's exposes the hidden costs and tells it as it is. Even calling his book *Ruinair* was controversial. He risked legal action from the airline if the book damaged their brand and reputation. The book was checked and cleared by a libel lawyer before publication.

I ask Paul if he has any cherished travel memories.

'I recall my first ever overseas trips when I was probably only about ten or eleven years old. My parents used to take myself and my brother away for two weeks every May – it was cheaper to travel then, before the summer rush. One of the best parts was delivering a note to my school teacher to confirm that I was going to be absent for two weeks, and there was nothing that she could do about it. We always went to Majorca, which in those days, back in the late 1970s, was a very exotic destination. There was some loose arrangement with our school that we would do a few hours of homework each afternoon to keep up our education, but I recall we didn't learn much in those few hours spent sitting by the pool or the beach. We dined sumptuously nightly on omelettes, French fries and fantastic crème caramel or fruit salad deserts. Those two weeks every year were the foundation of my desire to travel in later life.'

What sort of family holidays did you have as a child?

'Apart from the joyful Spanish holidays, we also had to endure, as some sort of familial payback, a week in a mobile home, which was owned by a friend of my parents. It always amazed me how the home was referred to as a mobile home since it was supported on bricks and never went anywhere. We spent the time trying to stay out of each other's way in a very small space. It often rained every day and the rain hammered down on the tin roof making sleep at night time next to impossible. The highlight of each day was a trip to the communal bathhouse for a wash; a building which we somehow referred to as "The Ha-Ha", though I don't know why. The mobile home had gas lights, which were lit by matches. They were always going out and it was my job to relight them as soon as possible, to prevent us all being asphyxiated while having our evening meal. When I became big and old enough, I pointedly refused to take the annual trip. I finally escaped.'

At this point I'm in stitches laughing. There is Paul making me laugh out loud in the cafes again. Had he always wanted to write a travel book or did the low-cost airline drive him to it?

'I don't think I initially wished to write a travel book – in fact my first four financial thrillers, were set in the City of London, but they also featured scenes in the world's financial capitals such as New York, Hong Kong, Singapore, Tokyo and Frankfurt. At the time, my editor said that my books had a strong sense of place, so maybe she knew – before I did – that I would later write a travel book.'

Paul has travelled quite a lot. I ask if he has a favourite place.

'I liked Ljubljana, the capital of Slovenia, possibly because the city has no Ruinair flights so there are less tourists and certainly no stag or hen parties. The city might be (another) new Prague – it's full of history, markets, castles and medieval squares, plus rivers and canals with boat trips, and there are lots of cheap open-air bars, cafes and restaurants – just avoid the fillet of foal on the menus.'

Where would you least like to return to?

'That would be Brno, the second largest city in the Czech Republic and badly in need of a second vowel. Ruinair fly there via London Stansted; but don't do it. Despite being a large city of 300,000 people, there really is nothing to see or do there. When I returned, I wrote a letter of complaint to Ruinair Customer Service who replied to me advising that Brno is more exciting than some parts of Dublin. They also kindly enclosed a two-page printout from the Yahoo travel website about Brno.'

I'm thinking that he could have gone to the Cabbage Market, opposite the Capuchin Monastery and stocked up on edibles. Apparently the square in Brno has hosted the best fruit and vegetables market dating back to the 1300s. Then again, with only a 10 kg (22 lbs) luggage allowance I imagine his suitcase was probably already filled to the brim.

What about your most frustrating travel experience?

He doesn't hesitate and says, 'Without doubt having being abandoned in Malaga airport for ten hours waiting for a €300 flight home on an alleged Irish low-fares airline. It was a frustrating, but not entirely fruitless, experience. While spending the time reading every English language newspaper I could get my hands on, plus the text on my boarding card, I plotted revenge using my modest literary talent. First, I wrote a fuming letter to the airline's customer services department, only to receive a useless cut and paste reply. But the idea was planted and I decided to see 15 European countries for the same price as my total holiday fare, thus extracting a modicum of retribution.' So it was to be €20 ($26) return fare for each excluding taxes, fees and charges.

I ask Paul about his most positive travel experiences.

'The ability to work and travel at the same, by living the life of a travel writer, is a great positive experience. Some people think that being a travel writer is not work at all, but it is, and it requires a lot of research, planning, writing and hanging about in airports and railway stations. Not all destinations are as grand as Venice, Barcelona or Berlin. And after all that travelling and writing, I'm convinced that I need a holiday.'

I ask about the most inspirational person he has met while on his travels, or the person he couldn't forget in a hurry. Paul's answer comes quickly.

'I was fortunate enough to see, rather than meet, Ruinair's Chief Executive Michael O'Leary once on a flight to Stansted. I was impressed that he queued up like the rest of us at check-in (before they charged us for the privilege) and that he helped board the flight. I avoided him since I was writing a book about his airline, which was not all positive, and I didn't wish to be banned from the flight. You have to admire Mick saying: "You can look at us as a small Irish company stuffing it to British Airways and Lufthansa and Air France. This is not work for me. This is sheer fun at this stage."'

With all the travel Paul does, I ask him what's his favourite way to travel.

'I have to admit, despite having flown all over Europe, the aircraft is still my favourite way to travel. I was fortunate to have a job some years ago that allowed me to travel all over the world on business and I got used to the highlife in every sense. Once I flew British Airways to Tokyo and was upgraded to First Class where I sat in a cabin and couldn't even see any of the other passengers. I flew First Class once on United to the USA and we were served an eight-course meal that lasted three hours, way too much to endure. I still love flying, but nowadays it's on low-fares airlines. I am like Tony Ryan, founder of Ruinair, who said he was always happiest getting on or off a plane.'

I imagine Paul must read during some of the journeys so I ask him what his favourite travel literature is.

'I read other vaguely humorous travel books to either get inspiration or get a shock as to how good others are at their craft. Bill Bryson remains the master of the genre: *Neither Here Nor There* is the first good travel book I can ever remember reading, way back in the 1990s. It made me want to get out there and see all of Europe up close. *The Art of Travel* by Alain de Botton features unparalled observations by the Swiss professor on why we travel, including his tales of being stuck in a hotel room in Madrid, and even the beauty of signage in Amsterdam's Schiphol Airport. *McCarthy's Bar* by the late Pete McCarthy is about one man's quest to visit all the bars in Ireland with his surname over the door. A simple yet hilarious idea, but especially when executed in Ireland because Ireland revolves around pubs and it is a common name in Ireland. Why didn't I think of it first?

I like *Stamping Grounds* by Charlie Connelly – I too have been to Liechtenstein on my travels and any man who can write an entire book about a country that's as dull and small (population 35,000) has my genuine undying admiration. *Continental Drifter* by Tim Moore is written by one of the best current exponents in the UK of the humorous travelogue – Tim takes an old Rolls Royce across Europe to relive the Grand Tour, but with disastrous results. As John Cleese once said of *Fawlty Towers*: "It's only funny if something goes wrong."'

So, what of Paul's future travel plans?

'I'll visit the countries that are likely to join the EU in the coming years, including Croatia, Moldova, Montenegro, Serbia, Iceland, Ukraine, Albania, Macedonia, and I might go to Morocco too. The only problem is that Ruinair only fly to two of these destinations, so I hope that they'll open some new routes or else I'll have to pay exorbitant air fares.'

What is your ideal holiday?

'It has to be somewhere hot and sunny, with a beach and the sea, somewhere with some history, culture, great food, vino in the evening and cheap.'

What's a not-so-perfect holiday?

'Any charter package that would confine me to two weeks of ordered chaos with a lot of other people whom I don't know well.'

I'm quite sure Paul must have had some funny incidents while travelling, so I ask him to recall one.

'I was served a bowl of soup on Air India, Business Class, while flying from Bombay to New Delhi – not so easy to enjoy during turbulence.'

That leads me on to my next question of any embarrassing incidents?

'Losing my luggage on a Virgin Airlines flight to Tokyo meant I was one very whiffy passenger hanging around a hotel lobby for two days.'

What changes would Paul make to Ruinair if he were to become head of the airline?

'If I led Ruinair, I'd teach the staff how to smile. It costs nothing so it shouldn't be a problem. Every other low-cost airline, from easyJet to Air Berlin to Germanwings, can do it already. The solution lies in the staff recruitment process.'

Any tips for surviving the lower-cost airlines?

'You have to play by their rules all the time. You must accept that you cannot change your flight or get a refund. You must check-in online if they charge you to check-in at the airport. You must be at the airport in very good time because they don't wait for passengers. Only bring one small piece of carry-on baggage, and always travel light. Bring or buy your own food and drink. Try to board first and grab one of the larger emergency exit row seats if it's a long flight. And research in advance how to travel from your destination airport.'

What luxury item would you not be without when travelling?

'As a writer, I always carry a pen and paper. No heavy laptop for me – I don't even own one. I scribble manically and then decipher it at home. I also remember to take the aerial and earphones for my mobile phone so I can listen to a local radio station when I'm stuck in airports.'

Has life changed since you became a full-time writer?

'It hasn't really changed at all. I just took a few years away from a banking career to write and travel and it was a very good time. People think writers are all multi-millionaires but that's not the case. I do have 1,400 fans on Facebook which is 1,400 more than I had before I became a writer.'

In the light of all the destinations to which you have travelled, what would be your favoured travel itinerary?

Paul tells me he would consider Venice worth a visit saying it always has the wow factor on arrival, but of course, you would fly to Treviso, if you fly with a low-cost airline, 'so expect a long bus trip'. He also thinks that Berlin 'is the most happening capital city in Europe with oodles of history, mostly involving the tragic events of various world and cold wars'. In his opinion an 'all-in-one' summer trip to Nice, Monaco, Antibes and Cannes is always a winner using the excellent TGV train connections.

Where have you travelled to in the past year and what place impressed you the most?

'I took a trip to the Middle East for the first time and was very impressed. Everyone should visit at least once and air fares to the Gulf are lower than ever. I'd recommend a dual city break. Fly Emirates to Dubai and stay near the new air-conditioned metro train system so that you can see the entire city cheaply and in comfort, from the old Dubai Creek and markets and river, down to the glitzy shopping malls and beaches and marinas. With 40°C (100°F) plus heat in summer; it's best to visit in another season. Then, take a frequent public bus from Dubai for 90 minutes down the desert coastal highway to Abu Dhabi and explore its unique history and character. And on the last night stay on Yas Island, which is reputed to be one of the most exotic in Abu Dhabi.' Many go there for golfing pursuits and the Ferrari World theme park, which Paul reckons would be well worth a visit before flying home from the nearby Abu Dhabi airport on Etihad.

It must take a lot of courage walking onto the low-cost airline after writing the books he has written about them. I wonder if he gets recognised by the crew. Paul tells me that sometimes those nice 'Ruinair' cabin crew ladies and gents do recognise him on flights yet they still allow him to board and fly. 'Unfortunately,' he laughs.

I ask him if he has plans to write any more books. He mentions that he was approached by a serving 'Ruinair' cabin crew member to jointly write a book about life on the inside 'warts and all'. He's not sure if the book will progress but if it does, he plans to name it Armed & Cross-checked. The crew member expressed her concern that she might get fired from her job if the book was published. He grins and says, 'I told her that could be a mixed blessing.'

What lessons in life has travel taught this frequent 'Ruinair' flier?

'Travel has taught me that there is so much more to the world than the place where you grow up. It's true that travel broadens the mind; it gives you more ideas and conversation topics, it builds inner confidence and can often make you appreciate what you have. But ultimately I believe that home is where you belong most.'

PLANE CONFIDENCE

Patrick Smith

The events of 9/11 changed the face of air travel, and the downturn in the airline industry that were the result of the atrocities led to Patrick Smith losing his job as an airline pilot. Redundancy made him re-evaluate his life and he turned to writing in the hope of making a new living. Using his great knowledge of aviation, in November 2001, Patrick sold his first article to Salon.com, a travel column website.

The timing was perfect: many people had fears about flying at a time when terrorism was a significant threat. Patrick provided the healing balm that would remove the anxiety about travel for ordinary people. He continued to share his expertise with Salon.com for ten years. He wrote his first book in 2004 called *Ask The Pilot*. The book tackled passengers' silent fears – those moments when you might hear strange noises and the alarm bells start ringing in your head, or maybe the engines go quiet, or your flight experiences terrible turbulence; he answers all the questions you may have about flying.

He went one step further in releasing his latest book, *Cockpit Confidential*, which was published in April 2013. This book is full of original and new material, offering a reassuring voice to the nervous passenger, and an insight for anyone interested in finding out more in the aviation world. He is currently a pilot and host of Askthepilot.com.

THE INTERVIEW

Patrick doesn't think that air travel is glamorous by any stretch, but he reckons it can still be dramatic.

'You can step onto a plane in New York City, and 16 hours later step off in Singapore or Bangkok, halfway around the world. That's pretty incredible when you think about it.'

It really is. A lot of the time we take it for granted. It's mind blowing how aviation has developed in such a short time span. Take yourself back to around 1900, when flight was created. Then to the time of Orville and Wilbur Wright who mastered lift, propulsion and in-flight control. On the 25 July 1909, Frenchman Blériot set off across the English Channel without any navigational instruments, making his way from Calais to Dover in just over 36 minutes and gaining worldwide notoriety in the process. Years later Captain John Alcock and Lieutenant Arthur Whitten Browne took off from Newfoundland on 14 June 1919 and landed a day later in western Ireland. Charles Lindbergh made the first solo flight, non-stop from New York to Paris in 1927, a remarkable 16 hours and 27 minutes across the Atlantic.

The Boeing 707 entered commercial service in 1958 and the Pan Am airline flew from New York to Paris in 8 hours and 41 minutes, twice as fast as the propeller plane. It had four engines and travelled at a speed of 575 mph (925 km ph) In November 1962 France and Great Britain signed the Anglo-French Supersonic Aircraft Agreement to construct Concorde. It could travel at 1,490 mph (2,397 km ph) and at an altitude of 60,000 feet (15 miles) The contemporary Airbus A380 is the largest airline ever built, almost as long as a football pitch and accommodates 840 passengers.

I chat to Patrick about his earlier memories of travel.

'I can vividly recall my first-ever airplane ride. It was 1974 and I was eight years old. It was on board an American Airlines Boeing 727, flying from Boston to Washington, D.C. We were served sandwiches and a cheesecake dessert, I remember. By today's standards – for a 90-minute flight, in economy class – that meal is almost unfathomable. The flight made the trip so memorable. Granted, an eight-year-old kid is by nature more excited by flying than some jaded million-miler, but to this day I remain captivated by the idea of getting on a plane, and I would never have traipsed to 70 plus countries if I hadn't fallen in love with aviation first. I see the airplane as more than just a convenient means to an end and I wish more people did as well. It's so easy to take flying for granted, but how can a traveller not appreciate the fact that countries and cultures, separated by once insurmountable distances, are now so accessible – and it's these beautiful machines that make it happen.'

Where did American people holiday in the 1970s?

'We went to Florida, the Caribbean and California – the standard American holiday circuits. It wasn't until high school that I felt the desire to travel abroad. Though actually, my first international holiday was in 1982, when my mum took me to Israel. I remember much about that vacation, including many thrilling details (to me) about the El-Al jet that took us there.'

I study the picture Patrick has given me of him as a boy getting on that plane; it captures a moment of sheer nostalgia. I wonder if that early travel instilled a desire in Patrick to take up flying.

'My infatuation with planes led to another with the world's airlines, which in turn led to a fascination with the places they flew to. For example, I would eventually visit India. Why? Because I grew up with a thing for curry and an obsession for ancient Sanskrit? No – because I grew up with an obsession for Boeing's iconic wide-body jetliner, the 747. In my mind, the 747 became an Air-India 747; Air India became a line on a route map between New York and Delhi; Delhi became India; India became a place I wanted to visit. So I did.'

What is your favourite country?

'I have to say Botswana, because more than anywhere else it exceeded my expectation. I wanted to experience remote, primordial wilderness – the kind of idealized African safari a person might dream about but presumes no longer exists, except it does exist, in Botswana.'

What was the most peculiar airport?

'I worked a flight into Brussels. A passenger left some valuable items in one of the overhead bins. One of the flight attendants suggested to the station manager that a public address announcement be made down at baggage claim to help the person retrieve his belongings. "We can't do that", she was told. "This is a silent airport." A silent airport? Brussels doesn't allow public address announcements of any kind, except during emergencies. I have to admit, walking through the arrivals hall; it was hard not to savour a cathedral-like peacefulness. This, in stark contrast to the sonic bombardment experienced at airports in the United States. If you've read any of my articles, you'll be familiar with my disdain for the noise levels inside US terminals, where a hurricane of public address announcements and the chatter of gate-side TV combine to push already frazzled nerves over the edge. Over in Brussels, I thought the refusal to make a single announcement, in the interest of helping a passenger recover important belongings, was extreme. Here at home, the problem is the sheer number and uselessness of announcements. It's not uncommon to hear three or more announcements blaring simultaneously from different speakers.'

What's your favorite city in the world?
'I'm not a city person, though Istanbul is my favorite and whenever I'm asked by a potentially adventurous American as to where he/she ought to visit, beyond the usual confines of Europe or the Caribbean, my answer is always Turkey.'

I ask him to tell me about other memorable journeys.
'In 1998, when I worked for DHL, I flew a charter from Gothenburg, Sweden, to a place called Sondrestrom, in Greenland, just above the Arctic Circle. The first time I spent about three hours there. It was May and the weather was mild. This time, as we flew over the island, I pulled up the current weather for Sondrestrom. It was 35 degrees below zero.'

Is there a place you wouldn't wish to return to?
'Travellers hate saying negative things about a country, but I'll tell you this: the people in Bulgaria were rude and extremely unhelpful. I've also been very disappointed by the amount of pollution and litter encountered in some countries. El Salvador, Morocco, Romania and Senegal are some of the filthiest places I've ever seen. I understand that poverty and pollution often go hand-in-hand, but conditions in many places seem so needlessly awful – the result of nothing more than abject irresponsibility.'

I recall Jonathan Dimblelby, a journalist from the BBC, telling me about his fear of flying. There must be a lot of people in this position and it must be extremely tough if flying is part of your job. Is there anything Patrick could say to allay such fears?
'Everybody, be it a first-timer or a seasoned veteran, is on some level afraid to fly, and contemplates his or her mortality when stepping onto a plane. That's our nature, and nothing to be ashamed of. Flying is not natural for humans, and while it

doesn't quite violate the laws of physics, it does seem to violate any and all common sense. Soaring through the air at hundreds of miles per hour, high above the ground, in machines weighing hundreds of thousands of pounds, is something many people cannot understand.

On the other hand, technology has made it work to an almost flawless degree. We so often hear that flying is meant to be one of the safest modes of transport and I guess, considering how many airplanes take-off daily, there could be some truth in it. The number of serious annual accidents can be counted on one hand. I realize that not everybody's anxieties can be addressed rationally, and for many people this is a psychological issue that cannot be solved with statistics or a pilot's fancy explanations, but those numbers are astonishing and should offer some comfort.'

I'm curious to know why Patrick generally chooses a window seat. I have often wondered if there is a safer position to sit in the event of an accident, also I had heard that the wing seat was the best if going through turbulence. Is that the reason for his choice?
'No there's something comforting about sitting at the window – a desire for orientation. Which way am I going? Has the sun risen or set yet? For us lovers of air travel, of course, it's more than that. To this day, the window is always my preference. Even on the longest and most crowded flight after a trip to Istanbul, I remember the view of the ship-clogged Bosporus from 10,000 feet as vividly as standing before the Blue Mosque or the Hagia Sofia.

To me, the greatest thing ever to be seen from the window of a plane, whether as pilot or passenger, is the skyline of Manhattan seen from the vantage of flying low along the Hudson River – that "quartz porcupine" as writer Kurt Vonnegut termed it. You can still catch some great panoramas, weather and flight patterns depending, flying out of Newark, New Jersey or LaGuardia, New York.'

What does a pilot on the move eat?
'Well unlike so many people these days, I'm not a foodie. Street food serves me just fine – a kebab or falafel sandwich from a corner vendor. One of the most memorable meals I've ever had was a bowl of noodles from a sidewalk cart in Cairo.'

What would you not be without on your travels?
'It has to be a good guidebook (usually it's Lonely Planet), a wind-up alarm clock, a notebook and pen, and some Cipro tablets in case that occasional stomach bug

gets severe.'

Despite Patrick having been to many countries, he still wants to explore Bolivia, Ethiopia, Madagascar, Kyrgyzstan and Iran. He spent two days in Ireland on a work stayover. He ended up at Shannon Airport.

'I was surprised and quite amused by how green the landscape was. In America, we associate Ireland with the colour green, and I always assumed this was just a silly cliché but man, it was green.'

I ask Patrick what he has learned from travel.

'Not to leave this on a negative or depressing note, but here goes: If I have grown more cynical in recent years, it is travel, I think, that has pushed me in this direction.

Exploring other parts of the world is beneficial in all the ways it is typically given credit for, and I remain appalled by the average American's geographical know-nothingness and disinterest in visiting foreign countries.

Travelling can also burn you out; suck away your faith in humanity. You will see, right there in front of you, how the world is falling to pieces; the planet has been ravaged, life is cheap, and there is little that you, as the western observer, with or without your good conscience, are going to do about it. There are those who say the world is slowly righting itself. We are, the thinking goes, on the cusp of some great, inexorable push toward social and ecological justice. We are moving this way because, with our backs against a wall of human-engineered oblivion, we have to. Well, based on what I've seen, I'm not sure I agree with that.

On a positive note, many places are just knock-your-socks off cool: Kaieteur Falls, the Suleymaniye Mosque, and the Okavango Delta... where can I begin? The flight to Kaieteur Falls, in the remote highland jungle of central Guyana, was one of the most breath-taking flights I've ever taken. I have been to the rapidly disappearing rainforests of Borneo, Ecuador, and Brazil, among other places, but I've never seen wilderness of this expanse untouched. Kaieteur Falls stands 741 feet (225 m) high from rim to riverbed – the height of a 70-story skyscraper. Incredible.'

I ask Patrick about the most inspirational person he met while on his travels or the person he couldn't forget in a hurry?

'It has to be the guy in Ghana who gave us directions late one night, when we were hopelessly lost at the Kumasi bus station – then refused to accept a tip.'

THE SILK ROAD

Paul Wilson

Paul Wilson's 'big story' happened when he and another English guy were set up and arrested within a few hours of arriving in Chile in 1994, aged 21. A few hours later he found himself in The Castle – notorious as Pinochet's main prison. Paul tells me they were never specifically told which prison they had been taken to but could only guess that it was the city's largest: San Miguel prison (this district of Santiago has a castle on its crest/coat of arms, hence the nickname). He found himself with the friend of a friend, whom he had only met that night. They spent the night in captivity, but eventually were released. It was quite a big story in South America for a few months and they kept bumping into people who had heard about them as they travelled through Chile, Peru and Bolivia. 'It's a great story but lots of twists and turns in the telling drag it out so it usually takes a couple of hours to tell.'

Paul first came to my attention when mentioned as a friend in Conor Woodman's book, *Around the World in Eighty Trades*. In the past, Conor had taken advice from Paul when travelling and found him to be a great support. Paul's travel guidebook, *The Silk Road*, fell into my hands at my local library. I was intrigued. Just what was this Silk Road?

I had always thought of it as a dusty, arid and endlessly long path, linking the Mediterranean with the Orient. I had heard it was a major trading route for hundreds of years. Trading took part en route, before the journey was over. The Silk

Road became Paul's passion and he has travelled the route five times, cycling it once in 2008. People are being enticed back on to it including Persians, Greeks, Mongols and Romans. If you want to travel the Silk Road, this guide is about as good as you can get. It covers the network of ancient trading routes, extending from Turkey and the Middle East, across central Asia to China. The fourth edition of his book, *The Silk Road* is on its way.

Paul tells me he fell into travel writing by accident having met Bryn Thomas, founder of *Trailblazer* magazine. He is now an editor for *Trailblazer's Great Himalaya Trail Guide*. When not travel writing, he teaches English to foreign students. Paul has lived and taught in San Francisco, Santiago (Chile), The Dominican Republic, as well as Sydney, where he has been for the last ten years.

THE INTERVIEW

How did travel start for you?

'I was brought up in a non-car family. My earliest travel memories centre on public transport, particularly trains. I'm sure this is why I still choose trains over flying and buses whenever possible and I continue to enjoy train journeys. I think it's no coincidence that all my travel writing has been about land-based journeys. Most family holidays were spent in Scotland, particularly the Inner and Outer Hebrides, and we spent the summer in the UK. Probably the highlight was an epic train, boat and bus journey (two children aged eight and eleven) from the northwest of England, up through Scotland, out to Lewis and Harris, and then island hopping down to the isle of Barra, the Wilson family's favourite island. We returned there as a family to see in the millennium on top of Heavel, the small mountain that dominates the island.

I also fell out of my third-storey window aged two, which I always cite as my introduction to unusual journeys.'

Why did you move to Australia?

'Funnily enough, I'd never been to Australia before I moved to that country and I think that was part of the attraction. Previously, I have jumped on a plane and gone to live and work in Chile, the US (San Francisco) and The Dominican Republic, without ever having visited them before. I hope to live in a new country again at some stage but probably one I have been to before (in Europe). I love Australia for the outdoor lifestyle. I cycle everywhere and, although the UK is not as bad as it's often made out to be weather-wise, in Oz it's very easy and relatively cheap to spend a lot of time out of doors, be it at the beach, walking in mountains or just having a good old Aussie barbie.'

What do you miss about home?

'Newspapers. I have to read *The Guardian* every day and then *The Week* over the weekend. I always missed the news on previous pre-Internet stints working and living abroad and, without the Internet, I'm not sure I'd have been able to stay out here for so long. Everything else I was worried about, in terms of culture, has been fine. There is not quite the selection I enjoyed during my ten years in London but, these days, culture like everything else is going global, and I see as much drama, comedy, opera and live music here as I did back home.'

He has travelled the Silk Road from eastern Asia through to south-eastern Europe. Any favourite parts?

'Choosing favourites on the Silk Road is almost impossible. The mountains of northern Pakistan took my breath away and continue to do so. Istanbul is the best city on the planet for me. It has everything: history, culture, dramatic beauty, parties and friends. It is impossible not to climb up onto the Great Wall of China for the first time and not pinch yourself to check that you are really there.'

Having travelled the Silk Road five times, has the experience been different each time?

'I am very lucky with the Silk Road. There are so many routes and sub-routes; it's very easy to choose a new one each time I go. Often, the new route can take in a brand new country (I retraced the Caucasus route for the first time last year) and it always includes a fresh city or region. I am also trying to give myself new challenges each time I do it, to make sure it never goes stale. For example, I cycled the route last year, previously I hot-air ballooned a stretch for the first time. In the future I want to climb one of the big peaks en route and do an archaeological dig on one of the many sites. Also, having revisited this route many times over a ten year period, I am starting to gain a depth of understanding that allows me to see how much the route has changed and is changing: in places like China, this can mean it's like visiting a country fresh for the first time.'

There must have been a lot of preparation for the trips?

'Preparation is quite straightforward these days. I know someone in most of the countries now so, in many ways, I just let them know I'm coming and get on a plane. Transport and accommodation isn't a real problem as I am never in a rush and still there aren't too many tourists. The biggest headaches are the visas, which can be very frustrating, but I have learned to live with that. I never take any particular medical precautions as it's not really necessary and I don't have special travel insurance because, if something goes wrong, it is likely to be really bad and none but the most expensive policies would cover me anyway. Also, I quite like the idea of being self-sufficient so I prefer to rely on myself, and try to turn any setbacks into positives.'

What are the dangers of this route?

'The route is dangerous and you can't pretend it isn't but, like most things, when you are there it never feels too bad. We had to evacuate out of Georgia during the cycle ride because Russia invaded. The Uighurs of Xinjiang started rioting a few days after I left the province this year. Tajikistan, Afghanistan, northern Pakistan and Iraq are all "off-limits" to some degree. I've never been shot at, though, or anything like that.'

What are the safest areas on the Silk Road?

'Turkey (apart from the Kurdish separatists), Uzbekistan (apart from the Islamic Caliphate separatists) and China (apart from the Uighur separatists) Seriously, there have been problems of tourists being targeted by groups in Turkey and Pakistan, but usually they are welcomed everywhere they go.'

What was the most exhilarating and exciting part of this trip?

'Definitely crossing the border from Kyrgyzstan to China on my first trip back in 2001. We had been kicked out of Syria and had to skip round to Turkmenistan. China was the last border crossing so we knew that once we were in and had reached Kashgar, we were going to make it and complete our target of making it to Beijing.'

What kind of transport did you use?

'All sorts, from hot-air balloons, to donkeys and bikes. But buses and trains get you almost everywhere you need to go.'

How long did it take to cover the route?

'You need at least three months to get across Asia (one month Middle East, one month Central Asia, and one month China) but you would need to go at a fair pace to do this and would need an incident-free journey or you'd be slowed down. Four months is best and six months ideal.'

Did you take a survival course?

'No survival courses – just Scouts (my mum is a Brown Owl). My dad used to take me with him walking the length and breadth of Scotland, sleeping in bothies as we went, so I've never been worried about being able to survive in the wild.'

What sort of weather did you encounter?

'The Silk Road is unusual in that it follows a straightish line of latitude, so the weather is pretty even along the way. In winter many borders are blocked by snow as they are high up in mountain chains but, as most travellers go in summer, it's the heat of the various deserts that gets to you. High 40°C (104°F) is the norm and it hits 50°C (122°F) in places such as Turfan in north-west China.'

What sort of difficulties did you have grappling with borders and visas?

'Borders and visas are a nightmare. As you are likely to be away for more than three months, you will have to apply for some visas while you are on the road. This can take up to two to three weeks in places and some, like Iran, are notoriously fickle, meaning they cannot make a decision or abide by it and some embassies, like those for Iran, are notorious for delaying or rejecting visa applications for no apparent reason.

Turkmenistan is second to North Korea in terms of visa difficulties. Often borders don't allow public transport to cross, so you often have to get as close as you can, then hitch, walk or take a taxi across to the next town.'

During the times he hitchhiked, you must have met a few characters along the way?

'Hitching as we know it isn't actually an option. Plenty of people will stop and pick you up, but they will expect you to pay for the petrol to cover your bit of the journey. Almost everywhere, however, you won't have to wait long and they are fascinated to find out why you are there and want to know what you are doing. Sometimes they can be too friendly and you will spend hours chatting and drinking tea, desperate to get on with the journey.'

How did people react to you on the route?

'Everybody is so happy that you have come to their country, it's incredible. Except for the Chinese who, on the whole, were very unfriendly and unhelpful on my first trips but, post Beijing 2008, seem to have had an about-turn and latterly were far, far more welcoming. Most countries are Islamic so part of their religion is that they must always welcome strangers into their lives/homes/societies.'

Is it safe for women to travel alone on the Silk Road or would it be risky?
'I wouldn't recommend women travel alone, at least not the whole way. Most women are travelling in groups or with friends/boyfriends. Even single women usually wear a "wedding ring" and pretend they are married to avoid hassles. Women I have met there have said it is a hard part of the world to travel in.'

Is the wildlife dangerous?
'Dangerous wildlife isn't a problem. In fact, you are pleased to see any, as many are endangered. If you are lucky enough you might see a snow leopard, but these are not known to attack humans.'

You must be brave to travel on a route such as this?
'A bit of Dutch courage always helps and, apart from Iran and Pakistan, your hosts will be keen to toast your arrival long into the night.'

How about communication, was it difficult?
'I speak French (badly), which is useful in Syria and Iran, and Spanish (very badly), but this is not of any real use. I have a smattering of all the languages I need, but mostly I rely on sign language and meeting locals who want to help. This is not a big problem as you can always find someone who speaks English (most under-30s you are likely to meet, plus anyone involved in tourism, understand some English in all Silk Road countries).'

Where was the friendliest place?
'Turkey. Iran and Pakistan are equally as friendly at a one-on-one local level, but can be unfriendly at government/police level.'

Has travel increased your faith in human nature?
'Travel has completely reaffirmed my faith in human nature, although I had a camera stolen once on a train in Italy. I can't think of any other bad experience, except The Castle in Chile. I place myself at the mercy of the local populations and I have never been let down. I have some real friends out there who look out/after me for no other reason except that they want to. Whenever possible I try to return

the favour when anyone visits me.'

Why were you kicked out of Syria?

'For trying to be too clever. As we were retracing Marco Polo's journey, we wanted to start in Jerusalem and then work our way through Jordan and Syria to Turkey and Iran. The only problem is that Syria and Iran, as part of their refusal to acknowledge Israel's existence, won't allow anyone who has previously been to Israel to enter their territory.

We managed to persuade the border guards at the Israel/Jordan border not to stamp our passports but, when we arrived at the Jordan/Syria border, we hit trouble. We had valid visas for Syria. We were allowed through the first border check but the second one stopped us and asked us how we arrived in Jordan. We said we had flown into Amman but, as there were no Amman airport stamps in our passports, they didn't believe us. They couldn't prove we had come via Israel (there were no Israeli stamps in our passport) but we couldn't prove we hadn't (there was no Jordanian stamps either). Needless to say they won and we were refused entry, which meant an expensive cab ride back to Jordan.'

Was there anywhere you felt awkward and wanted to leave in a hurry?

'On my first trip, a guy on a bus in Iran offered to find a hotel room for me in the next town as it was out of season and many places were shut. The only place he could find was quite expensive so he offered to share the room with me and halve the cost. He ended up sleeping on the floor insisting I took the bed. The next day he offered to change his travel plans and accompany me for a few more days, after which he wanted me to stay with him and his wife in Tehran. I panicked as it was my first time in Iran (although I had travelled alone many times before) and I didn't realise how hospitable the people were. I presumed there must have been a catch and clumsily made my escape but, looking back now, I know it was yet another great person just going out of their way to try to help.'

I couldn't wait to hear the funny incidents.

'The funniest part was right at the beginning of our first trip in 2001 (with my best mate, Rick). My sister's husband is Israeli so we were staying with his grandparents in Tel Aviv on the way to Jerusalem. They didn't speak a word of English and we had never met but it had been arranged that we would take a taxi from the airport to their apartment and go on from there. All they knew was that two young men were coming to stay before embarking on a four-month epic journey.

They knew we would be writing a guidebook and so, no doubt, have lots of equipment. Sabena Airlines managed to lose all our luggage (and never find it) so, after waiting fruitlessly for various searches and checks to be made, we arrived at the apartment 6 hours late and with just our passports and hand luggage.

Moses and Estha were really worried and had been calling their grandson in England. They couldn't understand why we were so late and had no bags (I think they thought we had been robbed) and, as no one spoke each other's language, we couldn't explain. By this stage Rick and I had seen the funny side (lots of "travelling light" jokes), which only confused them more. In the end we had to bring in some English-speaking neighbours and make several phone calls to English speakers, but still they thought we were crazy.'

Can you recall any embarrassing moments?

'The worst moment was in a university type of hostel in Bishkek, Kyrgyzstan. During the night, I had managed to roll out of bed and I woke up stark naked on the floor. For some reason the door to the room had also swung wide open. Realising that various students were walking past all the time and could see straight in, I asked Rick what had happened. He just laughed. I said "At least I was lying face down."

"Not for the previous five hours you weren't", came the swift reply.'

What other trips have you embarked on?

'My other big trips were Western Europe and Morocco in 1990, Canada coast to coast in '91, Eastern Europe Inter-railing in '93, Chile/Bolivia/Peru (teaching and travelling) in '94, USA West Coast in '96 (started real writing on this trip) and Southern Africa in '98.'

How did you meet Conor Woodman of the Channel Four series *80 Trades*?

'I met Conor by chance. He was researching a book, which became a TV series, then changed into a slightly different TV series and ended up being a book again. He had read my stuff and asked me to look over his ideas and make any suggestions. We had never met but it sounded interesting and I have a policy of always accepting any invitation to get involved in a project as you never know what might come of it. We hit it off straightaway and, although various others pulled out over the course of the project's various transitions, we saw it through. Today, we continue to enjoy bouncing ideas off each other even though we never see anything like as much of each other as we would wish.'

What travel literature do you like to read?

'I read lots of travel/history books, primarily connected to The Silk Road but not always. I studied Ancient and Modern History at Oxford so still enjoy going back to primary sources (Marco Polo's *The Tales*, Arrian's *The Campaigns of Alexander*). I think Peter Hopkirk's assortment of books on and around *The Great Game* are fantastic.'

Which travel author do you most admire?

'My favourite travel writer is Eric Newby – genius, yet doesn't take himself too seriously. Favourite authors are Waugh, Greene, Wodehouse and Maugham – so probably no real surprise.'

Did you bump into any interesting people along the way?

'The most fascinating guy was Japanese; we met cycling. He had cycled around the world. Then, on returning to Japan, he decided he hadn't seen enough and went around again. In fact, when we met him he was seriously considering doing a third lap. The best advice on the writing side was from an old friend, William Harvey. He warned me there was no money in writing and even less in travel writing, "So don't give up your day job". Obviously, I didn't quite follow his advice to the letter but it really put things in perspective. I have vowed never to chase a book deal or a magazine front cover and, instead, take what is offered and enjoy it as much as I can. This has meant I have spent some years writing full-time, others teaching and following other pursuits, and for me that has worked well. The day I stop enjoying it, I'll hang up my pen – if not my travelling boots.'

What kind of food was available on the journey?

'Food goes from the sublime to the monotonous to the ridiculous on the Silk Road but the key factor is probably the concept of vegetarianism being anathema to almost everyone you meet. Fortunately, I enjoy kebabs, as they are a staple in most of the countries. Also, I am lucky enough to have inherited a cast-iron stomach.'

What travel plans do you have for the future?

'I'll keep travelling both on the Silk Road and off, bringing out a new book on the Silk Road every two to-three years, and whatever else I can in between. My big travel dream is to follow the Pan-American Highway from Alaska to Tierra del Fuego (joining up several routes I have done previously) in one trip, by a combination of bike, motorbike and public transport.'

I can't finish without asking Paul a question about The Castle. Was it as bad as it sounds?

'Yes, I suppose it was. As one of our fellow prisoners told us while we were being taken from the central police station: "Where you've been is heaven. Now you go to hell." It really was the classic South American jail you'd expect from a movie: dusty courtyards, perimeter walls with watchtowers and gun positions, sentries with German shepherd dogs. As two six-foot (1.8 m) gringos with blonde hair, it was always going to be a problem and, in the end, we had it all: strip search, chain gangs, intimidation from guards, razor blade threats from fellow inmates. Fortunately, every time it looked like getting really bad, something or someone intervened and we emerged just about unscathed.'

Would you ever go back?

'To Chile? Yes, for sure, great country. To The Castle? Let's just say, I don't think I'll ever be able to watch *Midnight Express* again.'

Does travel provide a positive learning experience?

'I have learnt patience. At home I hate any sort of inefficiency, for example, waiting in queues, but while travelling everything always takes longer and I have learnt to roll with it. Also, I've learnt that no setback is too bad and you can always bounce back.'

A STROLL THROUGH AFRICA, IT'S ONLY 3,000 MILES

Fran Sandham

Imagine the drudgery and dullness of Fran Sandham's existence; the daily commute to the bookshop in London's West End where he worked for a measly wage, then going home to a tiny flat with a two-bar electric fire. It was hardly an awe-inspiring lifestyle. The only reward was the opportunity to read some of the epic journeys made by Victorian explorers such as Dr David Livingstone, Sir Henry Morton Stanley and Ewart Grogan. These adventurers really influenced and inspired him.

Yet reading about them could neither satisfy his hunger, nor substitute for his own experience. Surely there had to be a better life than this? A life with more freedom, excitement and adventure and the possibility to escape routine; to live a little. This sums up the way Fran felt before he decided to embark on a solo 3,000 mile (5,000 km) walk across Africa. The plan he hatched was about to change his life forever.

Fran had experienced backpacking, but nothing on the scale of this trip. His life took on a new purpose and in order to save up he started to economise. He spent months researching, preparing and planning as best he could for this epic journey.

Yet no amount of reading maps or books could have prepared him for the year-long adventure that lay ahead. Fran's walk was to take him far from the tourist trail. He picked what many people might consider a difficult, even dangerous, route, starting at Namibia's Skeleton Coast, and finishing at the Indian Ocean near Zanzibar.

The Skeleton Coast is known to be one of the most unfriendly places on earth. It is littered with skeletal remains and shipwrecks, casualties of heavy fog or worse; but that didn't put him off.

Fran's attempts to train first a donkey and then a mule to help carry his belongings were in vain, so he carried a rucksack the size of Kilimanjaro. At one point it weighed 100 pounds (40 kg). That's no mean feat in a hot desert where the midday temperatures can reach more than 40°C (104°F). He soon learnt to travel light but, still, he suffered all manner of foot trouble on a daily basis. In fact, his foot blisters were so large, they looked like clusters of grapes.

Blisters weren't the only nuisance. As his journey progressed, Fran was tormented by every kind of fly, insect and small flying creature imaginable. Not only did large greedy ants like the taste of his tent, many insects also liked the taste of Fran. He also endured a succession of bad haircuts en route, courtesy of local village barbers unused to dealing with straight European hair. To shave, he used a cup of rationed drinking water. And washing was a pure luxury that only happened once in a while, given the constant threat of a diminished and polluted water supply.

His funds, or lack of them, also presented Fran with a daily challenge, even though it was a conscious decision not to have too much materially for his journey. He was determined to support himself on a meagre budget without sponsorship or any financial safety nets. Doing things this way meant not having to justify everything he did: if he failed he'd have nobody to answer to but himself. The trip was entirely his own.

Fran's book *Traversa: A Solo Walk Across Africa* is an engaging account of his remarkable journey. Despite the hardships and discomforts endured by Fran as he trudged and slept rough through the seemingly never-ending wilderness, he gained much from his trip. The things he had been craving all along: freedom, adventure, excitement, diversity and challenges, to escape the daily grind were now within his reach. Things weren't easy, but the sense of adventure was enough to keep him motivated. Now all he had to do was to leave the book shop and set off.

Following his epic African journey he worked as an editor at Rough Guides.

THE INTERVIEW

Hatching a plan can sometimes be almost as exciting as the journey itself. I ask Fran if he found the research before the trip as exciting as the journey, or was it the actual journey that excited him the most.

'The actual journey – reading from a book doesn't really compare. Although, in some ways the research itself brings you closer to the explorers than you can get by merely visiting the places they went, usually because these places have changed beyond recognition. It's not so easy today, for example, to imagine how Dr David Livingstone felt when he first arrived at Victoria Falls in the 1850s when today every Tom, Dick and Harry can go white-water rafting, microlighting over the falls or bungee jumping off the bridge.'

I can imagine embarking on a journey like this must have stirred a reaction in friends and family. Did you receive positive feedback or did they try to discourage you?

'Most people weren't too keen and tried to talk me out of it. One or two suggested it wasn't worth going because I would inevitably have to come back home afterwards only to pick up where I left off. But it seems daft not to do something simply because it won't last forever.'

On his journey Fran was tormented by flies and gained a morbid curiosity about them: Did they live in nests? Where did they go at night? Do they go hungry and starve? At one point in his book he planned to research the answers. Did he manage to get around to this?

'Researching flies afterwards? Certainly not, I'd spent long enough in their company already.'

What differences did you find between African people and Londoners generally?

'You can't generalize about Africans as a whole, it's such a big continent with so many races and people of different ethnic backgrounds living side by side (same with London, for that matter), though at the most simplistic level I found that a lot of Africans tend to smile rather more than Londoners do, especially during a recession. I like London and I like Londoners, although I'd struggle to believe that most Londoners are as generous and welcoming toward strangers as a great many rural Africans can be.'

Did you encounter any strange customs?

'Strange is comparative, of course – some of the things acceptable to us these days would seriously offend some Africans in certain places, like scantily clad women on a beach. In Zambia, for example, I rather liked the old tradition you still find among elderly people of clapping by way of greeting or to express approval of a passing stranger – at first I thought they were just enjoying the show as I staggered past with a huge heavy rucksack and trekking poles.'

Do you feel that Africans are happier than the British, in spite of economic difficulties?

'Again, you can't really generalise, and I guess happiness is dependent on so many variables at different levels happening simultaneously. But in some ways, yes, you realise that material possessions and comparative wealth can bring as many problems and stresses as they solve – the less you have, the less you have to lose, so at one level there's less to worry about – even if you're worried sick about where the next meal is coming from. In the West, we don't worry so much when we're all in the same boat together, when we're all equal. But we get stressed out and jealous and unhappy when others around us have noticeably more material benefits than we do. We feel hard done by for no good reason. I was very short of money in Africa, but obviously not in local terms – the whole experience was a constant reminder that a poor man in England and a poor man in Africa are not the same thing.'

I know that Fran has a passion for the old Victorian travel explorers. But which contemporary travel writer or explorer does he admire most?

'Ranulph Fiennes for the way he refuses to let advancing years stop him from doing what he sets his mind to do, even though it would be easier for younger guys. I like the way Bruce Parry obviously gets on well with the people in the places he visits – it does help.'

Fran was unlucky enough to contract malaria. Does it have any effect on you today or do the symptoms reappear?

'My bout of malaria, frankly, was on the wimpy side compared to what a lot of people go through. I haven't had too many problems since. Throughout the journey, catching malaria was one of the few things that I thought would stop me in my tracks, but the timing couldn't have been better – I caught it on the East coast, the day after I finished the walk.'

Fran survived on a very bland diet of maize porridge, biscuits, stale buns and green bananas, washed down with 'Shake Shake' beer. This beer had the consistency of a thin gruel made from sorghum, one of the most easily harvested cereal crops in the world. How did you adapt to British food after such a bland diet in Africa?

'When in Rome, do as the Romans do (or however the saying goes)... Pie and chips can be pretty bland too, or trying to decide what kind of sandwich to buy each day.'

At a few places in rural Africa the women and children were so startled by the appearance of a solitary white man walking past their village with a huge rucksack and trekking poles that they ran off. Was this amusing or unnerving?

'It only happened occasionally and, generally, it was amusing, except on the rare occasions approaching a village in twilight or in pitch blackness, when all sorts of misunderstandings could occur. It's obviously more dangerous than in broad daylight, so I tried to avoid doing this whenever possible, though sometimes I had no choice when I couldn't find a suitable spot to pitch my tent for the night.'

It must have been difficult for Fran when he returned to London. Imagine the freedom of walking every day with no schedule and roaming the world at your own pace and then arriving back to the craziness and bustle of London city life. Was it difficult to adapt to life in Britain after experiencing a great sense of freedom in Africa?

'Yes, it was very much a case of returning to the daily grind. I couldn't wait to get travelling again as soon as possible but, as I'd expected all along, I returned to England flat broke and had to spend a while saving up again to do so.'

Could you ever go back to that London bookshop, to the nine-to-five routine?

'Well, I did just that – several times, in fact, over the following few years – but I wouldn't do so again, given the choice. Each successive time was harder than the last – getting back to England after travelling, skint and with nowhere to live, and then doing the same thing all over again. Rather like repeatedly taking two steps forward then the same two steps back – some lateral shuffle seemed called for.'

What was the most embarrassing incident on your travels?

'It had to be trying to sort out a pack animal to carry my gear; first a disobedient donkey and then a psychotic mule. It was a disaster – in two and a half months with the donkey and mule we covered less than one mile of the journey across Africa, literally. A third of the money I spent on the whole journey went on this fiasco, although on the Namibian coast the donkey did become something of a local celebrity.' Tsondab, the donkey in question, took him on a merry ride to nowhere. Fran had to give him away to a farm.

What kind of travel literature impresses you most?

'I tend to read expedition writing from the time of the great explorers more than modern travel writing, though I admire authors such as Colin Thubron and William Dalrymple for their skill.'

What projects are you working on now?

'I'm working on three different books simultaneously, which is definitely not the best way to get things done.'

Have you travelled since going to Africa?

'Yes, I've been to more countries since the Africa walk than I had before it. I've spent a lot of time in Asia, and did some travelling in Columbia and Ecuador. This year I've been doing some writing and photography in Northern India and Cambodia. Sometimes I give lectures on cruise ships.'

If you were to return to Africa, what part would you go to and why?

'Sometimes I've been tempted to retrace the journey across Africa, although with a few more comforts. Somehow I suspect it wouldn't be the same as that first time crossing Africa on foot; it wouldn't be as adventurous and I wouldn't feel so alive. So, there's a good chance I'd go to some completely different part of Africa, possibly Zululand.'

For someone planning a trip to Africa, what advice would you give them in terms of the precautions they should take?

'Malaria is one of the biggest problems. Some people seem to think it's a comparatively minor disease and easily curable these days, but it's still a killer. Just look at the statistics that show how many Africans die of it each year, a high proportion of them children. Despite the side-effects of malaria tablets, I'd say take them religiously and do everything within reason to avoid mosquito bites (easier said than done).

There are problems with theft in some parts of Africa, of course, but no worse than in a great many other countries around the world and, in most places, if you behave sensibly regarding valuables and possessions, you should have no more problems than anywhere else.'

How would I go about planning a similar journey in another part of the world?

'Make something your own; do it your own way. Following in someone else's footsteps is fine, but it doesn't bring the sense of freedom of determining your own journey. And providing it doesn't hurt or exploit anyone along the way (unlike some of the great journeys in history), then that's a positive thing. Despite the discomforts and hardships and setbacks and all the rest, it's a rare privilege to be able to go where you choose to go, in your own time.'

Did the trip across Africa change your life or your perspective on life?

'It certainly provided a change of direction in many ways (literally and figuratively), and has led to some interesting opportunities – for example, a lot of public speaking engagements, radio interviews, and of course, various writing opportunities that wouldn't have arisen otherwise. Regarding my perspective on life, I felt more self-reliant after the walk, perhaps inevitably, although at the same time I became, to some extent, more restless and impatient than I was before, and felt more compelled than ever to get on with things rather than sitting around waiting for them to happen. None of us is getting any younger, after all.'

Is there anything you would avoid next time?

'Yes, donkeys and mules, unless you're writing a book.'

Fran persevered and wrote down all aspects of his journey, but it took many years to get his book published; a struggle that demanded perseverance and bloody mindedness. As for going back to Africa, at the time of writing, Fran sent me an email to say he was heading back there – but this time he was definitely not walking.

A TIMELESS TRAVELLER

Dervla Murphy

Here is a woman who has visited the remotest parts of the earth, and found isolated places of stillness and solitude. I imagine Dervla Murphy belonging to another era; a time when life moved at a much slower pace before the invasion of technology prior to Victorian times. Dervla was brought up in a quiet rural village in simple times and she yearns to live this way. There is little place in her world for motor cars, computers and other technological distractions. If she has to use them she will, but with limitations. She has to have a website as it is expected by her publisher for sales and promotion of her books but any technological gadgets are kept to a minimum. She likes to write in the old-fashioned way using notebook and pen. As for cell/mobile phones, she detests them and will only use them if necessary. The thought or being accessible all the time fills her with distaste. Yet she can see that being bombarded with technology is inescapable; these intrusions infiltrate our lives at alarming speed.

Dervla reckons there may be more wisdom in getting back to nature, using the old ways. Now with mass tourism, it is increasingly challenging to find cut-off places that offer solitude. This is something Dervla feels very strongly about and she says she feels sad when she thinks how her grandchildren may miss out on the travel experiences she has had. In this fast and busy world, it's difficult to hear the sound of silence. She speaks about how exploration began with little reliance on technology, where people used their senses and intuition to guide them, bringing them closer to nature for example. Before the compass and sextant for ocean navigation, people relied on their observations using their senses and logical mind to problem solve. She appreciates that early explorers didn't go off on a whim and did have to plan for their journey but a lot of that planning incorporated using their senses to guide them. Dervla would rather be close to the natural elements rather than to rely on 'gadgets' as she calls them and would much rather have a bike than a motor car which she isn't too keen on. Walking, going by donkey, or slow train are modes of transport that give her pleasure and for which she has a preference. These methods of travel have formed the basis of her journey.

Born in Waterford, Ireland in 1931, and an only child, Dervla's childhood was consumed with caring for her mother who suffered from painful and debilitating rheumatoid arthritis and, when she was 14 years old, she left school to nurse her full time. When Dervla reached her thirties her mother died. It was only then that she was free to travel. This new-found freedom had a profound effect on her life and may have been a motivating factor to explore and embrace freedom while she had it.

She describes how she felt after her mother died and her responsibility for caring for her.was lifted. It was a huge relief that her mother was out of pain. Dervla woke up the next morning realising, 'I was responsible for no one but myself – that I was free to do what I liked, when I liked, as I liked'. She describes how she felt as currents of appreciation that ran through her body like mild electric shocks. She had been planning a journey in her own head and dreamt of going to India. Now it was going to happen.

Known for her journeys on bicycle and foot, Dervla has explored the remotest parts of all the continents, visiting India, Persia, Pakistan, Afghanistan, and travelling through Ethiopia on a mule. On many different and contrasting journeys she crossed places as diverse as Nepal, Kenya, Zimbabwe and more than 6,000 miles (9,656km) through Limpopo, South Africa.

The path of travel has been rough at times. She was pursued by a pack of wolves in the former Yugoslavia, which she had to shoot in a life or death situation; and was robbed in Siberia, but thankfully the urge to travel was always stronger than the fear caused by these unpleasant incidents. Another time while alone in the middle of the Zimbabwean bush, several miles from the nearest doctor she suffered a severe malaria attack. She has been struck down with food poisoning and on another occasion suffered an attack of amoebic dysentery in Pakistan. It's all a part of the journey and she doesn't regard herself as brave or courageous in the least.

No ordinary octogenarian, she drinks beer in preference to tea and is passionate about issues concerning world progress; issues such as, why people are living in misery while the fat cats in governments and certain organisations get fatter, in particular she has little time for bodies such as the World Bank, and condemns the greed and the corruption that goes on in the food industry. She despises the use of chemicals in modern farming. She frequently condemns the environmental devastation caused in the name of progress. At the time I visited her she was on the lookout for an organic weed killer for her large outside space at her home and was going to leave the growth until she could find something suitable and safe. She pulled up any weeds she could by hand.

Although not affiliated with any political group she has much to say from what she has discovered through her travels, about poverty and injustice and has a keen interest in reading about various countries' regimes. Dervla Murphy could fairly be described as an activist and will highlight the issues that she considers important.

Through her travels she has encountered many issues that affect the wider world and she speaks of these in her many books. She is especially angry about the greed of people in the western world while people on the other side of the world are starving or exploited in industries that mass-produce goods for the western world. Another issue she feels strongly about is waste and the modern mindset to throw everything away in order to buy a new and better model, be it a car, phone or clothes. She reckons we could learn a lot from the Cuban society. Having spent time there she can see that Cubans manage without many of the material possessions that enslave the west. Yet she acknowledges that Cuba wastes a lot of its fertile land and has far too many imports. She's also impressed by the way Cuba manages any weather alerts by evacuating its people in time for the hurricane season.

She hates capitalism and says 'Prosperity squeezes people's traditional way of doing things, forces places to "westernise" and can ruin a country! She is not afraid to speak out and doesn't care if people are critical of her raising these issues in her books. She won't be silent.

One of Dervla's greatest motivation for travel, after her desire for freedom, is to get a strong sense of the place. She tells me that what she looks for is the "feel of the place". She gets this sense from being alone in the wilderness; close to the landscape and even more importantly meeting the people who live there. She has enjoyed the hospitality and goodness of the people in so many countries and that is another motivating factor; that she can enter their world wherever they are and get a better understanding of what's going on out there. Being on the bike or on a donkey is more environmentally friendly and gives her the opportunity to see more while travelling at a slower pace; closer to the ground and opportunity.

She recently visited Cuba with her daughter and three grandchildren and this journey is documented in her book *The Island That Dared*. More recently she went to Palestine to research a book.

THE INTERVIEW

Looking fresh faced in pale blue, Dervla appeared robust and strong for a woman of her years. She had a pleasant countenance and warm manner. For lunch Dervla served up a hearty and thick lentil soup made with courgettes, tomatoes and onions. To go with it was Dervla's homemade brown bread and a large block of cheddar, butter and a relish. She had also filled two pint glasses to the brim with Bavarian beer. Her homemade pudding was rich shortbread pastry with apple, raisins and cinnamon, which she served with a jug of homemade custard.

'So, you enjoy cooking?' I asked.

'No, I hate it,' she said laughing. Not bothering to cook when on her own, she has only one meal a day – breakfast – for which she eats organic muesli, kippers, natural Greek-style yogurt and cheese. She doesn't eat vegetables and although she had prepared a dish using courgettes, tomatoes and onion, that was purely for my benefit. She may tolerate vegetables in a soup but she won't cook them for her dinner. She doesn't eat chocolate either. Bavarian beer is her beverage during the day.

'That's where I get my sugar from,' she says, laughing again.

Horrified by the way the food industry is poisoning our food, she tells me that beef is meant to be grey in colour but that some supermarkets inject it to make it red. She detests margarine, using butter in preference. She prefers spelt flour to white flour because most flour nowadays is treated with bleaching agents and riddled with flour improvers. She can't buy it by the sack load anymore and says it's too expensive in the supermarkets. When travelling, she eats whatever is on offer as it isn't possible to stick to a regime. She took me to the study where she writes. Her love of literature was evident with wall to wall books, many on travel.

I asked her about her writing technique.

'The first draft is done by hand and then it's typed on an ordinary typewriter,' she says.

Her laptop remains out of sight and it's only used to correspond with her friends in far-away countries. She writes until bedtime, which is around 9 pm (she rises at 5 am.

The house struck me as a writer's haven, full of character with its wooden beamed ceilings. Her entire house feels relaxed and lived in; a lovely natural environment. To get to the bathroom you need to go outdoors and across the charming courtyard. In fact, visiting each room involves going outside, which gives the house a less claustrophobic feel.

Dervla is very unassuming and modest. She gets on with things, dealing with challenges as they materialise. From previous contact, I knew she'd had a hip operation and I asked her how she was.

In typical Derlva fashion, displaying her sense of courage and strength, she laughs, 'Oh I'd forgotten all about that.'

I ask where travel began for her.
Her first journey outside Europe was the *Full Tilt* trip in 1963, at 31 years, 'I'd been making short trips on the continent on my bicycle, for maybe five or six weeks at a time. It was then that I left Europe.'

For the *Full Tilt* journey, she travelled overland on a bicycle, which was an intense and challenging journey. She had to contend with some very severe weather extremes from heavy snow to scorching heat. While travelling through Persia, Afghanistan, across the Himalayan Mountains and on to Pakistan and India, she documented her journey in a dairy, which formed the basis of her book. This book has been in print ever since.

She got to the heart of the countries, meeting the people, experiencing the culture and the warmth and hospitality but also suffering the dangers of an attack during which she needed to defend herself. She came up against many obstacles, including hunger, heat exhaustion and personal injury. With her long travel history she has been fortunate to experience many countries before modern disasters, including war and famine, affected them and to witness the Afghanistan before the troubles there.

Have you always been fascinated with travel?
'Yes always, since before I can remember,' she says laughing.

Did receiving an atlas and bicycle at ten years old stir up the desire to travel?
'Definitely, it was the beginning of the planned cycle to India. When I looked at the

atlas, I realised there was only this little strip of water between Europe and Asia, so there was no reason that I couldn't cycle to India. And off I went,' she says with the heartiest of laughs.

Were the '60s an unusual and difficult time for women to travel alone?
'No, it wasn't difficult in those days. Was it that unusual? Actually I don't think so. I suppose in a way, it was unusual for men to travel on their own, but not particularly women.'

Is travel more complicated now?
'Obviously there are more military complications. You couldn't cycle now from Istanbul to Delhi and expect to arrive alive. In a sense it's easier. People just hop on and off airplanes and get cheap flights all over the world.'

Interrupted by growling coming from under the table, two of Dervla's dogs appeared to be having a dispute. There was yet another interval of laughter. I joked that the dogs may be angry about mass tourism too. She hates the idea of all these package holidays and these weekend breaks and all the unnecessary air travel. Mass tourism is making it increasingly difficult to find a quiet place to escape to, In fact, many tourism companies specialise in making the out-of-the-way places accessible for large numbers.

Dervla has one daughter, Rachael, with the late Terence de Vere White, the literary editor of the *Irish Times*. She chose not to marry. After devoting her full attention to Rachael in her early years Dervla was ready to travel again. It was then she decided to travel to India with her daughter who was only five years old.

Did you plan to travel with your daughter?
'Yes, but not until she was five because I thought she needed the stability and to be in one place, although we did travel a little. We travelled on the continent before we went to India, you know, little journeys to the Julian Alps in Slovenia to get her used to the idea of camping.'

Dervla was criticised for travelling with a child so young but she hates the way society instils fear into their children by not allowing them independence. She wonders how they will cope as adults if not given that sense of freedom early on.

Did travelling with a child help break down the barriers between yourself and the communities you visited?
'Yes, I could say that applied everywhere. When Rachael was 18 years old we went

trekking with a pack horse. We were then, as far as the locals were concerned, two adults and that didn't work out so well because two adults, I think, are perceived as able to give each other support, so I'd say there definitely was a disadvantage.'

Do you reminisce about the journeys you took together?

'Yes, sometimes, but not often. Once I've finished a book, I don't think about it anymore. It's gone. I'm like a bad mother. I just have them and then they're gone.' She explodes with laughter. 'I'm too busy thinking about the next one,' she says, laughing again.

'A child's presence emphasises your trust in the community's goodwill. And because children pay little attention to racial or cultural differences, junior companions rapidly demolish barriers of shyness or apprehension often raised when foreigners unexpectedly approach a remote village.'

Can Rachael recall the journeys she took at five years old?

'No, I thought that was very interesting actually, when you think of the development of a child's memory. We were in Coorg, south India when she was five and exactly a year later she had her sixth birthday in Baltistan [north Pakistan]. She was able to write a little diary. She remembers virtually nothing of the Coorg journey and remembers many details of the Baltistan journey.' While away, Rachael wrote some diaries, documenting the journeys.

Does Rachael still have these diaries?

'No I have them. Rachael would tell me what she wanted to write. She wrote beautifully, but I would have to provide most of the spellings, except for the simplest of words.' I wondered if these diaries might be published one day. I suggest there may be another book in that. Dervla laughs at the idea.

Has life changed for the better in general worldwide compared to when you travelled more than four decades ago?

'I think things are much worse than they were 40 and 50 years ago, in the sense of more hunger and destitution. The gap between rich and poor is much wider. When you see how some of the rich live in the world and you know the sort of houses and the rents they pay in certain areas and the fact they are driving around in their big four-wheel vehicles.... I mean it's pretty awful to see an old woman struggle going up a hill with a load of firewood or vegetables on her back in India, and one of these vehicles won't stop to pick her up. There's something very wrong.

I'm just using that as a tiny example.'

Does it ease your frustrations to speak out about these issues especially poverty and perceived inhumanity?

'Oh yes, she laughs. Have a good old rant.'

Through the course of her travels she has seen so much hardship and especially noticed the hopeless political and economic conditions. It frustrated her to see little being done to solve these problems. She has a big issue with the greed that she sees and watching the effects it has on ordinary people upsets her. She wants fairness and justice for all. She believes that much of the problem is with corrupt governments. She believes prosperity doesn't usually make people any happier.

Is it good to study the politics of a country before you go or is it better to discover it as you go along?

'For me, a lot depends on language. For instance, before I travelled to Cameroon or Madagascar in 1989, most of the relevant political sort of writings would be in French, which I couldn't read fluently enough to really make sense of, but I think, yes, if possible it's better to read up on it before you go and also learn about the current social problems so that you understand what you are seeing and why it is, and how it is.'

Do you think that people in the world have the same common thread, with the same sorts of needs and aspirations?

'Yes, as far as the ordinary people are concerned.'

Is it possible to pick out the most outstanding place you have ever visited?

'Oh I don't think I can. There are too many.'

Dervla has a great love for Afghanistan. I ask if this is this one of her favourites?

'Yes, I have a great affection for it. When I hear people talking on the radio or writing in the newspapers, you know, about the poverty especially, and naming Afghanistan as one of the poorest countries in the world, that's complete bullshit because when I was there it wasn't a poor country. That's why I got such a shock when I cycled across the Khyber Pass and down into Pakistan and India, I mean that was real poverty. Afghanistan was a prosperous country in its own terms.

Obviously, not having any of the mod-cons of contemporary society, but people were well fed and clothed, with sound houses, healthy crops, no opium growing; no such thing as a poppy back then and they were making a living exporting fresh and dried fruits to Iran, Pakistan and India. It was a thriving trade. The distorted picture that is being put out about Afghanistan makes me angry.'

What do you think of the changes in Afghanistan?

'Well, clearly the economy is totally wrecked and everybody is dependent on growing opium. With all the corruption, that brings a completely different country.'

She recalls that when she visited Afghanistan back in the '60s it was a primitive country, not poor but very beautiful and peaceful and the hospitality was something she has never forgotten. She says it really saddens her to see what has happened to the country. She recalls religion in Afghanistan was more positive. Her earlier experience of Muslim countries, in Afghanistan and Pakistan were so relaxed without the fundamentalism, which has sprung up of late.

'No I'm afraid countries don't recover from that.' She feels that so much has happened to ruin the country with all the wars and repression that she has no urge to re-visit.

What would you be doing if you weren't a writer?

'No idea. I can't imagine anything else. We were what you might describe as a bookish family. My mother would have read hugely.'

Did you tell your mother about your ambitions?

'Yes. When I was 16 she said to me, 'Well why don't you get on your bike and cycle around the continent'. I don't know too many Irish mothers that would tell their daughters to take off and cycle around the continent.'

I joke with her saying: 'Well my mum told me to get on my bike a few times.' We both laugh.

What advice would you give somebody planning to take a journey?

'Take the absolute minimum of luggage; I think the advice would be not to take any of the things like laptops and mobile phones. Leave all that behind and be dependent on where you are, not always linked to home, you know, really get out there on your own. What I've noticed increasingly in the last ten years is that more and more young travellers are actually going to the nearest internet café and communicating with friends and family and not really able to detach themselves, you know, be on their own in a foreign place. To me that's not really travelling it's just half and half stuff.'

Do you prefer solo travelling?
'Yes, I had said I wouldn't travel with anybody except Rachael but of late I have travelled with Rachael and the grandchildren. We went to Cuba together'.

'So a package holiday would be out of the question?' I joke.
Yet again laughter fills the room.

How do you discipline yourself to write about your experiences?
'That's just my way of life. I mean it is hard work. I suppose there's a certain amount of self-discipline.'

There is a lot of moaning about the recession. Does this annoy you in view of the fact that you have been to so many countries where the ordinary people have so little?
'Oh, of course and also I think, as the affluent West, we deserve the recession. We've been so stupid buying into the whole consumer culture, which was clearly so false and we're still at it, paying out to keep the banks afloat. Let them sink. Why should the ordinary tax payer rescue the banks for goodness sake?

I think that so much of the consumer society has to be addressed. But then, how do we escape from the advertising industry and the millions that are put in persuading us to consume every hour of the day? People have the television and the radio. We're not being left alone to make our own decisions. People have choices but they are brain washed. I mean they must have what's being advertised.'

If you were to move to another place, where would you go?
'I think maybe Coorg. I don't know. It might have changed so much since we were there. No, I think I'd prefer to stay where I am, thank you.'

Who inspired you while you were on your travels?
'Well, so many ordinary people in different countries whose names I don't even remember now – just because of their own obvious integrity. It's all about oneness with where they are, whether it is Ethiopia, Baltistan or Peru. I don't think there is anybody I should really name, but in every country there were quite a few people.'

What was your most positive experience of travel?

'I think Ethiopia; the trek and the winter in Baltistan; the trek in Peru and down the Andes. Also the inauguration of Nelson Mandela was the most amazing experience.' Her face lit up as she recalled that great day in South Africa. There were more than 10,000 people singing and dancing in the streets that day and it was great to be among them. The atmosphere was electric. There were women and children of all ages and races. Suddenly Pretoria came to life. Dervla recalls the atmosphere and joy everyone felt and it will stay with her always, especially Mandela's moving speech in which he spoke of the human disaster of apartheid and advocated forgiveness saying: "We saw our country tear itself apart in terrible conflict... The time for the healing of the wounds has come... Never, never and never again shall it be that this beautiful land will again experience the oppression of one by another." Nelson Mandela at his inauguration 10 May 1994. Courtesy of The Nelson Mandela Centre of Memory'

I ask about her desire, years ago, to settle in the Hindu Kush. I remind her of the deep peace she felt there. Does Dervla regret not settling there?

'Not really. That was just a whim of the moment.'

Have you ever found that same peace elsewhere?

'Later on, I found the same sort of peace in the highlands of Ethiopia,'

On the spiritual side, Dervla spoke about the complexity of Eastern religions. Does she find it overwhelming that people who have so little will share all they have with you?

'Absolutely There's so much fear and suspicion being worked up into the world. I have found the majority of humans in every country I've travelled through to be good, reliable people and many of them very kind, so I think it's horrible that we have this fear and suspicion and overprotection of children that says you've got to travel in certain protected areas. It's horrible.'

If you could have lived in another era in time, when would you choose?

'I think maybe the 18th century. There wouldn't be any mod cons. I certainly wouldn't want to live in Victorian times but I think women, obviously not the wretched working class, had a fair amount of freedom and could travel on their own. That's what I'd go for.'

Have you read much Victorian travel literature?

'Well yes, I suppose the women explorers came a bit later. Well there was Lady Mary Montagu. She was an 18th-century explorer and Mary Kingsley and Isabella Bird Bishop. They were Victorian and yet they went out and did their own thing and I loved both of their writings, especially Isabella Bird Bishop. I really think she is a kindred spirit.'

How did Isabella travel?

'Mostly riding and on her own. She went to California in the days when it was still wild territory, pretty well everywhere you know, Iran, Afghanistan, Tibet, China. Amazing.'

Are you inspired by any of the modern travel explorers?

'Yes, Frea Stark, Paddy Lefarmer, Colin Thubron and William Dalrymple.'

Does it frustrate you that it's becoming harder to find places of solitude on the earth?

'Yes very frustrating. It also makes me sad when I look at my three grandchildren and I think that they will never be able to experience what I did in Baltistan, Ethiopia, or in the Andes. All these places have now been invaded by motoring roads and what they bring with them.'

HISTORY IN THE MAKING

Tim Severin

im Severin's background is unusual. Born in India, he is the son of a tea planter and for him, the seeds of travel were sewn long ago. While at college, he
made his first big expedition by motorcycle along a route taken by Marco
Polo (1254–1324), a Venetian explorer who travelled through central Asia and
China, covering 7,500 miles (12,000 km). It took more than 20 years for Marco Polo to finish his expedition and he recorded his journey with Italian writer
Rustichello while they were in prison. Marco Polo inspired many adventurers,
including Christopher Columbus, though Tim was one of the first people from the
western world to follow in his footsteps. For Tim that was the start of a lifetime
of adventure and discovery. He is greatly motivated by his curiosity to discover
truths and to experiment and uncover mysteries, which led him on a number of
re-enactments and hypothetical journeys.

Can you imagine sailing in an open boat in the freezing and tempestuous waters of the Atlantic Ocean, with waves thrashing about and having to live in close
confinement with a number of crew, while family at home anxiously await your return? There would be no comfort, shelter or warmth, only the unknown and uncer-
tainty hanging over you, day in and day out. That experience is what Tim Severin
and the crew had to face on The Brendan Voyage: no escape and nowhere to run.

As a small child I remember being fascinated by Tim Severin and his numerous
expeditions. I vividly recall watching the documentary about the building of the

boat, destined for this great voyage. The journey was to take Tim and the small crew of five along the west coast of Ireland, through the Hebridean Islands, north to the Faroes, then to Iceland, Greenland, southwest along the coast to Labrador, ending in Newfoundland. Sailing on a boat called *Brendan* in 1976, he retraced the legendary journey, which may have been made by the monks of St Brendan thirteen centuries earlier. Tim wanted to see if it could have been possible to build a boat of skin in the sixth century and take that perilous route. This was to be a significant journey that may confirm new theories of the discovery of the New World, a long time before those made by Christopher Columbus.

Tim and his craftsman team constructed an exact replica of the boat and attempted to build it in the way contemporary vessels would have been constructed. It was a long open boat with an upward curving in the stern. Forty-nine ox hides were stretched over a wooden frame and stitched together by hand with strong and durable flax thread to form 'a patchwork quilt' that made up the hull.

Tim had a theory that ancient boats used two masts but many old pictures depicted only one. As an experiment to see how many masts were needed to sail a boat he made a mast for *Finbarr*, a small wooden boat known as a currach that he had built, and by his own admission stole the linings of the curtains from his dining room to make a sail. The mast he made failed miserably and he concluded that the old boats must have had more than one mast as he had suspected it was a very significant discovery made just before the Brendan Voyage.

Tim has a penchant for recreating legendary journeys. One of his missions was to identify the 'real' Robinson Crusoe. Starting 400 miles off the Chilean coast he began piecing together the events of the past. As children, many of us would have heard about Robinson Crusoe, hero and sole survivor of a shipwreck, marooned on an island, and having to fend for his own survival. Tim's interest started as a boy, when he was told that there was a real character behind the story, namely a Scotsman, Alexander Selkirk, who was marooned on an island off the Chilean coast. It was widely believed that Selkirk was the inspiration for the character of Robinson Crusoe.

Tim discovered some similarities between Crusoe and Selkirk, though Selkirk had never actually explored the island. Also, he wasn't skilled in survival and self-sufficiency in the way that Crusoe was. A vital clue to the real identify of Robinson Crusoe was also provided by an account written by Henry Pitman, a man who had rebelled against the English crown and for punishment was sent to Barbados as a slave. From there he planned his escape to the Chilean island in a boat. Henry Pitman wrote his account of events thirty years before the author of the Robinson

Crusoe story created the tale. Tim concluded that most of the stories in the Crusoe book were in fact inspired by Pitman.

Tim was to travel in a small 100-year-old sailing boat, retracing Pitman's voyage to the island of Salt Tortuga off the north coast of Venezuela. Armed with Pitman's writings, Tim discovered a number of startling similarities between his journey and those reported in Pitman's own account; far too many to be coincidental. He had found the real Robinson Crusoe.

Tim was to undertake yet another epic journey in the 1980s. He examined the mythological voyage of Jason and the Argonauts and his quest to obtain the Golden Fleece. Legend has it that Jason was sent to get the Golden Fleece by King Pelais, who recognised that Jason was a threat to his throne. In his quest he travelled with 50 heroes called the Argonauts on a ship called the *Argo*.

To build a replica of the Bronze Age galley ship that Jason and the Argonauts would have set sail in, Tim enlisted the help of a Greek shipbuilder. Together they sailed from northern Greece, through the Dardanelles, across the Mamara Sea and through the Straits of a very challenging Bosphorus, eventually ending their journey on the Black Sea, 1,500 miles (2,400 km) away. Their destination was Colchis, now known as Georgia. Tim wanted to prove whether or not such a journey may have been possible in ancient times. He proved beyond a doubt that it was.

In another journey known as The Crusader, Tim and a companion set off on a 2,500 mile (4,000 km) trek on horseback, following in the footsteps of Duke Godfrey de Bouillon, his knights and pilgrims who, 900 years before, travelled to Jerusalem leading the First Crusade. The journey was to take Tim eight months. He was to ride past ruined Crusader settlements and ancient battlefields, over dangerous mountain passes and through many countries and terrain, from Germany, Bulgaria and Yugoslavia to the Anatolian Plains, Lebanon, the occupied territories and Jerusalem. His aim was to bring to life the long march of the knights and pilgrims who walked and rode to Jerusalem as well as to tell the tale.

For the Spice Island Voyage, Tim retraced the steps of Alfred Russell Wallace, a Victorian explorer, on board a traditional Indonesian boat known as a Prahu which was built by Wallace's descendants. In retelling the story of Wallace's life and accomplishments he discovered the endangered species that Wallace had recorded in his expeditions and observed how the environment has evolved and developed in the twentieth century.

His 1989 journey involved another ride on horseback, this time accompanied by nomadic horsemen of Mongolia. Together they searched for the heritage of Genghis Khan, the Mongol emperor (c.1167–1227), who ruled over the largest empire in existence. This journey took Tim from the Gobi Desert to the Altai Mountains, a mountain range in East-Central Asia where Russia, China, Mongolia and Kazakhstan come together. He would replicate journeys that Mongolian couriers made in the Middle Ages from Mongolia to France. Once closed to Westerners, with the collapse of Communism, Mongolia now opened its borders visitors. His brief was to investigate the lifestyle of barbarian Genghis Khan and to see how much of the traditional way of life survived in Mongolia.

The China Voyage saw a crew of seven set sail on an extraordinary expedition to see if the ancient Chinese Mariners could have reached the Americas more than 2,000 years ago. This time his vessel was a giant bamboo raft.

Tim Severin is the winner of numerous global awards, including The Christopher Prize and The Thomas Cook Travel Book Award. His many expeditions have been released in print as well as in documentaries, screened on BBC, National Geographic and The Discovery Channel. These documentaries have been acclaimed at film festivals, winning prizes for Best Cameraman, Best Film of the Sea and the Best Adventure Film. *Viking: Odinn's Child*, the historical fiction trilogy, was a bestseller. *Buccaneer* is set in the 17th century and recounts the adventures of pirate Hector Lynch. Other accreditations include the gold medal of the Royal Geographical Society, the Livingstone Medal of the Royal Scottish Geographical Society, and a Doctor of Letters awarded by Trinity College, Dublin and by University College, Cork. Tim Severin is a multi-talented explorer and traveller, author, filmmaker and lecturer.

THE INTERVIEW
I asked Tim what his childhood was like.
He revealed that his younger years weren't typical. 'In my childhood... we were always moving. The company my father worked for as a tea planter would have him move around a lot and I remember that we didn't actually have a home life at all.'

I wondered if having no sense of place in his childhood could have given him the desire to travel. I ask Tim if he has any early travel memories.
'I remember we were going by train from Calcutta for a summer break and my father cut his hand on a can opener.' He laughs when he recalls the holiday mishap.

What inspired you to do The Brendan Voyage?
'I'd studied history and exploration at college and I was familiar with the St.

Brendan voyage story, treated largely as a myth and legend. When I was at university I had done a few projects tracing the route of Marco Polo. I was travelling and at the same time looking at the stories and exploration. By the time I decided to replicate the voyage of St. Brendan, I'd been down the Mississippi River already. Not only that, but I also went in a small boat to look at the conditions there and subsequently wrote five books on the exploration. It seemed right to put that notion to practical experiment.'

I'd been reading that the monks in the 6th century would have looked to providence and the hand of God to look after all their needs. Was this the case with Tim?

'No I'm very cautious, in fact. I like to minimize the risks before I even get involved in a project like The Brendan Voyage. I take a careful look at the risks and then try to minimize them. We tested the boats made out of skin and I believed that they were capable of making the journey; it wasn't a question of just trusting the journey to luck. The tests proved beyond a doubt that it is possible to do such a journey successfully today.'

I reminded Tim of a close call during The Brendan Voyage, which could have been fatal. Visibility was poor and an enormous trawler was heading towards them. It looked as if it would hit them but the wind intervened and carried the vessels away from each other. Did he think that was the end?

'Well collisions in those days were not infrequent, just as they are today. They give you a terrible fright, especially if it's dark. They couldn't see us as we were in a small boat but thankfully it veered out of our way. Firstly, there was the shock of seeing this enormous factory vessel on our path and knowing that if it hit us we wouldn't have survived. A tiny boat would have no hope. Where could we run to? It was less than 100 yards away (90 m) and her bows were sending a massive spray as she slammed down on the waves. If the wind hadn't been in our favour it could have been fatal.

I found out later that radar hadn't picked up *Brendan*'s leather hull and we were completely invisible to other boats and added to the murky conditions, there wasn't a hope if we were to collide. We thought of shining a torch on their mast to attract attention but quickly abandoned that idea as our sail wasn't large enough to act as a light reflector. The vessel's hull passed so close to us that the lights on the portholes covered us but they didn't see us and carried on their path oblivious to the fact that they could have killed five crew members. It was over so quickly and the wind just carried them past. In cases like that you think, "Oh thank heavens".

Did you find it hard to adapt to normal life when you returned from The Brendan Voyage?

'No I had no problem adapting. On any of my expeditions, I always ask the crew to think about what they are going to do after the voyage ends. In my case, I know the moment I hit dry land that I'll be at my desk. I have a job to do, which is writing up the story of the voyage I've just returned from.'

I imagine the writing is an opportunity to re-live the journey all over again?

'Yes, it's like doing the journey twice, but I am using a sense of judgment, as I have to decide what to leave in and what to take out; parts of the journey can be tedious and boring on the ocean, so I need to make it interesting for the reader.'

I speak to Tim about embracing former methods of travel and exploration. Does he believe that modern travel methods are superior or should we revert back to the old ways?

'The modern methods are certainly more comfortable,' he laughs. 'In that sense they are superior. Modern methods of travel are a lot faster. Slowing down generally enhances and gives you more to appreciate.'

In the wandering course of his research, Severin encounters many modern-day Robinson Crusoes, including a small detachment of Colombian soldiers who were posted to defend their country's sovereign claim to a small strip of sand known as the Serrana Bank. This 'low, whale-backed sandbank, barely rising above water level' is named after Pedro Serrano who was shipwrecked there in the sixteenth century, and – so it is told – amazingly managed to survive for seven years, even though the desert island gave no shelter nor had any source of fresh water.

Of the contemporary explorers, is there anybody that you admire?

Tim tells me he admires a Norwegian explorer called Thor Heyerdahl. He also pioneered journeys with replica voyages. 'He had a significant influence on me,' Tim says.

Thor is remembered as the 'Kon-Tiki man'. His journey took him from Peru to Polynesia on a balsawood raft in 1947. The 6,000 mile (9,656 km) expedition proved that ancient cultures possibly sailed and inhabited the South Pacific. He co-ordinated excavations on Easter Island in the 1950s, which set out to prove that inhabitants from South America travelled there. In the '70s he journeyed across the Atlantic in a papyrus craft. The journey concluded that Columbus wasn't the first transatlantic navigator.

Was your family a great support?
'Again, I come back to my own childhood where the child of a tea planter was sent away to school and was hardly conscious of having a family there at all.'

Did you meet any inspirational people during the course of your journeys?
'Each of my journeys is special, whether by land or by sea. I found my crew to be inspirational and I still keep in touch by email with those that live far away. Having email makes it much easier to keep in touch.'

How has travel changed with new technology?
'Someone pointed out recently that The Brendan Voyage I undertook with my team couldn't be done now because we would no longer be out of touch, which I thought was a very interesting observation. Nowadays email has changed things for the better and for worse. The change for the better is obviously to do with safety and if you are somewhere remote and fall ill you can call for help. That's a huge bonus. On the other hand with the type of work I do, where in a sense, you are out of reach, it is rather intrusive. Recently I heard of a crew rowing across the Atlantic and they sent a daily report.' At this point Tim laughs. 'What's the point?'

Will your future be wrapped up in voyages?
'No', he says without hesitation, 'I have reached an age when I don't want to be out in a howling gale and I am well into a second career of writing historic novels.' He is currently busy with The Saxon Trilogy.

Do you think the old way of boat building is a dying art?
He appears positive and says you can still find the craft of boat-building in many countries. Even though the bamboo raft-builders in Vietnam have practically ceased, the skill can always be brought back, he believes.

Which place impressed you the most of all the voyages that you did?
Tim tells me there were far too many places to select just one, though he cited the Banda Islands of Indonesia, which he found to be remote and relatively un-

touched; an extraordinary place with dramatic landscapes and to which he sailed on a prahu, a small sailing boat with a rectangular sail. The Banda Islands, comprising three large islands and seven smaller ones, are well positioned on the rim of Indonesia's Banda Ocean where the waters are deep. The North Banda Basin is 19,000 feet (5,800m) deep, while the South Banda Basin is nearly 18,000 feet (5,394m).

Two of the larger islands, Banda Besar and Naira produce nutmeg and mace, commodities traded by the Dutch, who colonized the islands. One of the islands known as Gunung Api has an active volcano. There is an incredible marine life there ranging from enormous turtles, dolphins, whales and schools of Napoleon Wrasse to exotic fish and coral life. It is a haven for divers.

Having gone to so many places as an explorer, how were you received by the locals and what place was the most hospitable?
'Again just a single example: on the journey by horseback from Belgium to Jerusalem retracing the route of the First Crusade, the hospitality of the devoutly Muslim farmers in the remote villages of the Anatolian plateau was remarkable. In more than two months riding from village to village we never once had to buy ourselves a meal.'

If you could live in another era of history, which would you choose and why?
'I'm happy to be alive now, and to have had the chance to indulge my curiosity about remote places and how they were reached by earlier travellers.'

What have you learned from travelling?
'To stay relaxed about things and not to worry.'

A WALK IN THE MERDE

Stephen Clarke

After studying French and German at Oxford University, Stephen Clarke took jobs in Germany as a washer-upper and a grape picker. He also worked in what he calls 'international diplomacy', teaching French to bored business men. Later he moved to Glasgow to 'put rude words into the French Collins Roberts dictionary'. Then, a life-changing opportunity came his way when he was offered work on a Paris-based English language magazine. This job had attractive working hours, leaving him time and opportunity to do other things. By now he had an interest in writing.

A Year in the Merde is the story of Paul West, an Englishman on a mission to oversee the establishment of a French chain of British tea rooms in Paris. In this fictional work, we encounter a host of French idiosyncrasies and a Brit's observations of life in France. The character and the experiences are loosely based on Stephen's own.

Talk to the Snail, another of Stephen's titles describes French society with his trademark humorous approach. The French, it appears, are compelled to buy his books and there are few aspects of French culture and mannerisms he hasn't covered.

In *Paris*, he takes a close look at the French capital, searching through 1,000 years of history, and at the risk of annoying the French he looks at the love-hate relationship between the British and the French.

THE INTERVIEW

So where did travel start for Stephen?

'I remember riding on the sofa-style front seat of a big, powder-blue Ford Zodiac with no seatbelts, as everyone did at the time, and being allowed to steer the car across a huge beach somewhere in Wales while my dad operated the pedals. I must have been about 21, no, about four or five, rather young to start driving, even in Wales.

My first memory of travel to France was my parents going to Paris for a week-end when I was about ten. They never used to go anywhere alone, and I remember thinking, why Paris? And why are they looking so pleased to be going somewhere without their kids? I didn't understand till much later.'

How did your interest in France come about?

'I must have been eleven. On the first day of secondary school, the head of the scout troop announced that the scouts would be going camping the following sum-mer. I joined up, learned to tie three knots and how to start a fire using only dry wood, matches, firelighters and a flamethrower, then went camping in the Loire Valley. Every morning they used to send us off in groups of three or four with a map and enough money to buy a picnic. We would buy baguettes, Vache Qui Rit cheese triangles and cider, and then get tipsy and lost. I left the scouts straight after the camping holiday, but retained the memories of France as a good place to get tipsy and lost.'

Where did you first encounter the French?

'In a post office in Saumur, during my camping trip. I'd memorised the key phrase "Je voudrais un timbre, s'il vous plait" and went in to buy a stamp for my postcard home, but everyone started jabbering at me, pointing at my money and saying negative-sounding things. Eventually I realized I had an old coin that was out of circulation. I didn't get my stamp, but I learnt an important lesson – if you're going to try and pass off invalid or counterfeit currency, learn the language first.'

Why choose to live in France?

'I was offered a job in France. I'd also applied for one on a Greek island, but it wasn't as good. Otherwise, I could have ended up settling on Lesbos. Not sure how well I would have got on there.'

I ask him how the French react to his books, especially the Parisians.

'Très bien. The Parisians were the first ones to start buying *A Year in the Merde* via my website. I even had one email from a lady saying: "I am French but I have a sense of humour." The French seemed to get the joke straightaway – this was France seen from the inside, by someone who lives there, enjoys it, but sees the funny side of our cultural differences. The French did a Parisian shrug, said, "oui, we are like that," and began reading my books. I still get almost entirely positive reactions, except for *1000 Years of Annoying the French* – that's too painful for them to face up to. And one Frenchman who came up to me at a book fair and said to me, in English, "I know why your book is called *A Year in the Merde*, because it is merde", I couldn't fault his logic. The French are a very rational nation.'

What part of the French culture amuses you most?

'Two things. First the French psyche, their overriding negativity, which is, in fact, a kind of idealism; they so want everything in life to be perfect that they whinge all the time and make life unbearable; and then their view of history, which is astonishingly skewed; Napoleon and de Gaulle both studied military history books that omitted defeats; and if you ask the French about Joan of Arc, the American War of Independence or D-Day, you'll get almost entirely incorrect answers.'

Just to keep a balance, I ask him what part of British culture amuses him the most?

'Stand-up comedians – the strongest part of our culture at the moment – and our general capacity to make a joke of almost anything. Not (as the French do) to show we're cleverer than everyone else, but just for the fun of it. When I worked for a big French company, I used to love cracking jokes in meetings – it threw people completely. Is he being serious? Is he joking? Is he stupid? No, he's English.'

Any more examples?

'If you mean the thing that I find silliest about British culture, it'd have to be our capacity for knowing the exact value of our house all the time. Even friends who have no intention whatsoever of selling tell me, "You know, our house went up in value by 8 per cent last year". We Brits are obsessed with money, I mean with owning the stuff, rather than (like the French) just seeing it as a means of buying the good things in life.'

Of all your discoveries about the French, what was the hardest to come to terms with?

'The way TV journalists treat politicians. Half of the politicos are complete crooks (allegedly), and all of them are only in it for self-promotion, and yet journalists bow and scrape and totally fail to go for the jugular in interviews. On the contrary, TV interviews are more like public blowjobs, "oh thank you so much for coming on to the show, Monsieur le Ministre, now tell us your biased, untruthful version of events, and I promise not to interrupt, contradict or embarrass you in any way, you sexy brute, you". The only journalists who really give politicians a going-over are the ones writing for satirical magazines, and they can be astonishingly vicious, but they don't get enough readers to really influence people's opinions.'

I ask why he thinks that his *Merde* novels are so successful. Does he think it has something to do with the English/French love-hate relationship?

'Well, yes, we Brits do enjoy reading about France, and teasing the French, but it's not just about the British relationship with the French, because my books have been published in German, Czech, Polish, Thai, Chinese, Russian, and more. Everyone seems to be fascinated by the French without really understanding them. They're like exotic animals, a cross between peacocks and walruses – elegant but grumpy. And I try to give an insider's view and talk about real life there, and readers tell me they would love to be able to share the experience (when it's not too infuriating, of course). People also seem to enjoy the fish-out-of-water comedy aspect, the tribulations of being an expat or immigrant. When I go to Eastern Europe, for example, they all say, "we suffer the same things from the Germans". Just to put geopolitics to one side for a moment, though, I don't think my books would work if they didn't have lots of good jokes in them. Without sounding arrogant (or even with sounding arrogant) people tell me that the books are quite simply a good laugh. They're not meant to be serious sociological studies, they're supposed to entertain.'

I'm curious to know if there is any other culture in the world that he would like to examine in the way he does with the French.

'Yes, but I'd only do it if I really understood them. The thing about my books on France is that they're written by a Parisian – moi; I mean not some French ghost-writer. I've worked for French companies. I have been through pretty well everything in life that a French person goes through (except for supporting their football team and liking Johnny Hallyday, of course). I don't think you can write books about a culture from the outside. My book *Paris Revealed* couldn't have been written by anyone who hasn't lived here for a long time. It's written from the point of view of someone who wakes up in bed next to Paris every morning, and, I should add, is still happy to do so. Though I'm hoping to be invited to go and live in the Seychelles for a few years so I can study them.'

Do you have a favourite travel writer?

'Douglas Adams, author of *The Hitchhiker's Guide to the Galaxy*. He's so right about those Betelgeusians. Seriously, though, he really made me want to travel the universe, which is the most important thing about a travel writer. And Gerald Durrell – his *My Family and Other Animals*, about living on Corfu, was the book that made me want to grab a rucksack and leave home in search of adventure.'

Stephen has written so many books on the French. Which is your favourite?

'*What I Did on My Hollidees*. I wrote it when I was six, and did all the illustrations too. It never got published, though, because the dog peed on it. Apart from that, *A Year in the Merde*, because it was the first book of mine that sold, and in a magical way, via word of mouth on the internet, with zero publicity and, this, after it had received a heap of rejection letters and I'd self-published it. It's an amazing thing to happen. It also allowed me to give up the day job and concentrate on what I love doing most – nothing. Oops, I mean, writing. Well, actually, a combination of the two. As it says in the biographic notes in my books, 'Stephen Clarke lives in Paris, where he divides his time between writing and not writing'. I'm not sure exactly what it means, but it's accurate.'

Where do you like to go to unwind from the everyday stresses?

'To my guitar and to my writing. You have no idea how much fun it is to sit there imagining stupid things that the characters in my novels can say, or taking revenge on some bureaucratic twit who's annoyed me by writing him or her up for a book. Even if it wasn't published, I'd still be writing this stuff. The only difference, when you have a publisher, is that you also have a deadline, and have to knuckle down and get the book finished. But that kind of stress is nothing compared to having to do a job where your boss is moaning at you all day. I used to have one of those, so I know exactly how lucky I am.'

Where do you go when you want to escape Paris?

'A coral reef. I never go anywhere without my mask and snorkel. Well, that's a lie – I went to Lithuania last February without a snorkel. But you see what I mean. I like to go anywhere with clean sea, colourful fish and cold beer and preferably no dictator or poverty, of course. I can't go to those paradise islands where tourists lounge about, gazing out past the barbed wire fence at all the colourful poor people.'

Knowing the kind of character Stephen is, I'm sure he must have a few funny incidents out of his travels. I ask him to recall some.

'One that made me laugh, but not my travelling companions, who were French, so they were able to understand exactly what was going on. It was all about the way we Brits speak French. We have trouble saying the French 'r' sound – the throaty 'RRRRR'. This isn't usually a problem, except when you say a word like 'coeur' (heart) that ends in r, because if you don't pronounce it properly, you say 'queue' which means a tail or a very rude word for a willy. I was travelling with some French people when we got into some minor trouble with the police. It was so minor that we were going to be let off, if we promised to do one simple thing. I wanted to be sure about this, so I asked the policeman, in French: "So you will let us off, oui? Do you put your hand on your heart and promise?" Except that I said "queue" instead of "coeur". My French friends nearly fainted; the policeman went white, then red, and scuttled off, apparently assuming that this was some traditional English threat to the manhood of treacherous public servants. The perils of learning a language...'

How much travelling have you done for promotional work?

'Loads – that's the second best thing about being a writer (the first being the moment when you first get the book in your hands and see, feel and smell your work in 3D). No, it's the third best thing, because the second is seeing someone you don't know reading one of your books. It's a great compliment. I've done readings in San Francisco, Sydney, Kracow, Mauritius, Antibes, Dublin, Auckland, Prague, New York and Lithuania, as well as slightly less glamorous places such as public libraries in Hertfordshire (which generally do great sandwiches, by the way). The best one has to be Australia. My publisher said she was trying to get a book festival to co-sponsor my visit, because it's an expensive trip, so, jokingly, I asked if it was possible to find a festival of books and snorkelling. She came back saying she'd wangled me an invitation to the Brisbane book festival, which sends its long-distance visitors to Fraser Island, a 100 miles-long (160 km) dune off the Queensland coast, to recuperate for three days before the festival begins. So books and snorkelling it was, though to be honest, the thrill I get when giving a talk to an audience of a hundred or so people in a marquee in Brisbane about a book that everyone told you wasn't worth publishing, even beats the snorkelling.'

I ask Stephen what itinerary he would recommend for someone coming to Paris for 48 hours.

'If you're coming to Paris for only two days, your choice of what to do depends entirely on the weather. If it's raining, of course, you might want to shut yourself away in the Louvre, which has everything you need to fill two days, and if you manage to avoid the guards and kip down on a bench, you won't even need a hotel. But let's be optimistic. Paris (like its citizens) is at its best when the sun is smiling. So you should spend as much time as possible outdoors.

Prime wandering places for me are the top part of the Marais, the medieval streets northwest of the Place des Vosges (which is quite nice itself, of course). It may not be very French but, when the sun is out, I love to go for a sandwich in the courtyard of the Institut Suédois. Those canny Swedes have taken over one of the most beautiful *hôtels particuliers* (city mansions) in the Marais and now use it to make open sandwiches and put on often rather saucy art exhibitions.

There is a great garden out the back, too; a haven of peace in the centre of the city. At the opposite end of the history scale, I love walking up the Villette canal basin from Stalingrad (the least romantically named Métro station in Paris). After spending years as a crack addicts' hangout, it has become trendy, and the Right (sunny) Bank of the canal basin is now the place to stroll, jog and, on balmy evenings, hold a pétanque picnic. The old men's boules game has a new young fan base now, and lumps of lead can be seen flying about as soon as the picnic weather arrives.

There are bars on barges up there, and even a little opera boat; seriously trendy. Though we shouldn't forget that a large proportion of anyone's time in Paris should be spent lazing about on a café terrace watching the world go by. It's a classic, but for a good reason. Personally, I avoid the clichéd cafés like the Deux Magots and the Flore, and go to one just around the corner, the Bonaparte – not cheap but a nice south-facing sunny terrace, one of the most generous chèvres chauds (goat's cheese salads) in Paris. And the customers are mostly chic Parisians bitching about each other. What more could you ask for?'

THERE'S MORE TO LIFE THAN CRAGGY ISLAND

Ardal O'Hanlon

Ardal O'Hanlon, accomplished comedian and actor, was born in 1965 in Carrickmacross, an Irish market town famous for its world-renowned lace. After graduating in 1987 from Dublin City University with a degree in Communication Studies, he set up the alternative comedy club Comedy Cellar. While this venue was only small, his stand-up routines were a hit and he was soon filling venues elsewhere with a capacity for 2,000 people. In 1994, he won the Hackney Empire New Act of the Year competition.

Ardal is undoubtedly gifted and his talent was spotted by Graham Linehan, and Arthur Matthews, Irish writers, who went on to cast Ardal as Father Dougal Maguire in the Channel 4 comedy, *Father Ted*. More awards followed and, in 1995, Ardal won Top TV Comedy Newcomer Award for his portrayal of Dougal and was also nominated for a BAFTA Award for Best Comedy Performance in 1999 for the same role. As Father Dougal Maguire, he became a regular on television, and scenes with him driving around the block repeatedly in a milk cart, sitting in a rickety caravan in the middle of a field, or simply slouched in his threadbare armchair in the parochial house, will be remembered by many. Although Dougal Maguire is the role for which he is best known, it kick-started a career in television and film for him and he went on to land other successful roles, most notably as Thermoman, the naive superhero from another planet in the popular BBC sitcom *My Hero*, and as Eamon in ITV's *Big Bad World*. He has also hosted *The Stand Up Show* and has guest-starred in shows *Shooting Stars* and *100 Greatest TV Characters*. His film credits include playing a gentleman from East Chiswick in *Moll Flanders*, the role of Myles in *Wide Open Spaces* and the minor role of Mr Purcell in *The Butcher Boy*.

It was the RTÉ sporting travelogue he wrote and presented in 2006, *Leagues Apart*, that really showcased his interest in travel and meeting people from different cultures and traditions. It also showed a different side of his personality that helped free him from his association with the character of Dougal. This series took him to the great historical cities of Athens, Rotterdam, Rome, Krakow, Barcelona and Istanbul where he investigated some of the biggest and most passionate football rivalries.

In addition to his prowess as an actor and comedian, Ardal has also had success writing fiction. In 1998 his debut novel, *The Talk of the Town* (known in the USA as *Knick Knack Paddy Whack*), was published. A humorous look at youthful rage and rebellion through the eyes of its main character Patrick Scully and friends, it won critical acclaim.

THE INTERVIEW
Ardal recalled his earliest travel memories.
'My father had the hare-brained notion of getting a caravan in Lough Sillan, eight miles from where we lived. Sometimes we'd go there for the weekend. It was great training for the episode in *Father Ted* where he took that memorable holiday in that pokey little caravan. Yeah, that was all very familiar.

Before that we used to go for far flung parts of Ireland. We went to Kerry and to Donegal as kids. The highlight in the hotel was the chilled fruit juice and the doilies – very sophisticated.

The most vivid holidays were those that we took in France in the mid '70s. That was considered to be very exotic, coming from rural Ireland. We went on a camping trip. I remember an overnight train journey from Paris to Fréjus, looking out of the window and watching place names passing by. I just couldn't sleep. I remember that quite well.There were eight of us crammed into a carriage and later into a tent. Those trips to France. They were exotic and special.'

Are your holiday memories of happiness and excitement?

'Absolutely, it was for a week, or two once a year. My father worked very hard and he was always rushing, so, to get your Dad to yourself for a while during the summer was great. It always seemed sunny back then and there were no seatbelts in cars in those days. There were loads of us in the car too so it was very helter-skelter. There was always a lot of action with three brothers and two sisters. We were all of a similar age'

I ask about the sporting travelogue he presented, *Leagues Apart*.

'That was a labour of love. I was always interested in football as a kid and fascinated by its universal appeal and I had this notion that football was a window into the soul of a nation and that you could combine football with travelling and make an interesting programme. You know, football overlaps with so many aspects of culture; it was borne out by the experience. You go to places, particularly places like Italy, Greece and Turkey, where football is so interwoven with the politics and the culture of the country. You couldn't contemplate running for political office in any of those countries without being associated with football and possibly owning a football club.

It's always interesting to see how people align themselves along various tribal lines. We went to Holland, Spain, Portugal, Poland, Greece and Turkey. We found six exciting games and spoke to a lot of people from all walks of life, especially people involved in football and people who were cultural commentators; people who would try to shed some light as to why passion runs so high for people in these games.'

Any language difficulties?

'No problems there. Luckily for us, English is such a universal language and surprisingly enough, in places like Greece and Turkey, English is really good as there is a huge history of emigration with a lot of returning immigrants. Some have been at university in America or the UK. We had a translator on hand.'

What was the most memorable country?

'They were all very memorable. Istanbul was one of the most exciting. I hadn't been there before and I would have had more prejudices about Istanbul than I would about other places.'

What were you expecting to see?

'I was expecting it to be scary for a start, not just Istanbul, but football in Turkey. I always associated it with mania and violence. To my surprise, people couldn't have been nicer or friendlier. Passions certainly run high with a sort of giddiness rather than violence, but Istanbul as a city is a magical place. It is a mass of contradiction so it was an eye opener for me. It's quite secular and contemporary European on the one hand, yet conservative and Islamic on the other hand. Sometimes you see women who are obliged to wear a headscarf in public buildings wearing a stylish wig instead.'

Would you like to return there?

'I have. We went on holiday just after Christmas with the kids. It has layers and layers of history, comparable with Rome or Athens. It's got everything you could possibly want, in terms of food, commerce, art. It has a unique culture. As somebody who really loves to travel, you know, you are always looking for an experience, a culture shock. You want to be thrilled.'

Shifting to something topical, I ask if he has anything to say about the recession in Ireland and about how relaxed we are as a nation compared to the efficient Germans or Swiss.

'I would be reluctant to resort to national stereotyping. However, if your observations are based on real experiences then that's okay. For example, I've done quite a bit in Switzerland. It's clear that they are more organised over there. Seeing the Swiss in action I found it helpful when putting together my show; i.e. comparing them to us, explaining why we could never have a large hadron collider in Ireland (or even a small one) and so on. When speaking to a Swiss audience they love when you reference local events or popular perceptions – I mean the Swiss have banned minaret construction. It's a very Swiss thing to do, very wilful and stubborn. It's well for those who can turn down good construction work for a start. We couldn't afford to do that in Ireland. That's a subject worth exploring. Also you had Swiss protectors guarding a German Pope before the new one came on board. How can you not talk about that when you're in Geneva?'

Ardal has presented comedy sketches in many countries. Do you modify the material to suit each culture? Is humour universal?

'Yes, people like to laugh, there's no doubt about it, wherever you go. It's what makes us unique among the animal kingdom. I've always tried to make my stuff universal, out of laziness as much as anything else. I'm not going to spend my whole life trying to change the whole act every time I go somewhere else, but you also find that the stuff that appeals to me also appeals to other people; family, raising children, relationships. As long as anything you say is based on some kind of truth, it should work. Having said that, people like local references. You do as much homework as you can to crowbar as many references into the set because people like that. But they want to hear your point of view and hear about your experiences. If I go to America there's no point in me trying to ape an upbeat American comic. That would be dishonest.'

Do comedy sketch ideas come easy to you?

'It's a torturous process, like going down a mine and chipping away, until you find a little nugget of gold. It's very difficult and pressurised to come up with new material all the time. I didn't think this comedy business was going to be such a hard job. When I started out, I thought it was going to be great craic. But you get out of it what you put in to it, so you work hard at it, always trying to hit the nail on the head. Doing comedy is not just about pleasing the audience, it's about pleasing yourself. You want to be the best comic you can be. You need to articulate yourself as best as you possibly can. Having said that, quite a lot of the stuff I do is very silly. But it's usually based on some sort of reality.'

I turn him to the subject of travel. Did you see any strange customs or anything weird?

'Yes I did a little tour of China not so long ago and I took the family. We just made a big trip out of it and tagged on a bit of a holiday. I remember the first day when we left the hotel in Beijing; it was my first time in China and it was very exciting. I think one of the first things we saw was a man on an ordinary bicycle. It was a push bike and he had two wardrobes on the back. That was phenomenal. And after that we saw up to eight people on a scooter.'

How did the children see it?

'Thankfully they're good travellers and went along with the plan. When it comes to travelling I like to do as much as possible and try to complete the experience. In China they ate scorpions, donkey, jellyfish heads and whatever was going. We can't be too judgemental about that. You experience the culture, although I think the insects and things like that are possibly a bit of a tourist thing.'

Spitting is a widespread problem in Beiijing, where the elderly especially spit up phlem anywhere and everywhere. The authorities decided to stop this practise in time for the Olympics in 2008. They put up posters and issued fines as well as watching the public on close circuit cameras. They even sent out officers to catch people. Did you witness any spitting in Beijing?

'Ah yes. There was plenty of that. Not so much in Beijing, but in other places such as Xian. Even in restaurants. It's a different culture.'

How did people react to you in China?

'My children got a lot of attention. One of my daughters, who is ten and quite fair, found the level of attention she got overwhelming at first. She was surrounded in Tiananmen Square and the Forbidden City, where there would be coach parties and they would just swarm around her. They would literally push me out of the way. At first we were protective and we'd be trying to shield her because she'd be looking up with a worried face. They'd just crowd around her and touch her face and hair or ask to be photographed with her. It was bizarre. We'd be working out why people would be doing this. I think superstition is a big part of Chinese life.'

Did you research China before going?

'Only superficially, you know, guide books and that kind of thing. Since then we've read a fair bit. I really didn't know what to expect.'

Would you return with your children?

'I would. They loved it. It's exciting to be there. It's not exactly witnessing the fall of Saigon or anything like that. But it's witnessing a country in transition. The pace of life is breathtaking not to mention the scale of everything. The history is incredible and for all those reasons we would go back because we only scratched the surface. We saw the major attractions, the tremendous street life and so much more. We were there for about a month. We got around quite a bit but it's so vast and there's so much to do.'

What of hilarious travel experiences?

'It's hard to pick a single incident. It's not that funny, but I did a tour of New Zealand a few years ago. I slipped a disc the day before I was due home. I was in agony. I remember thinking I wouldn't make it. I was on so many painkillers, valium and all sorts. I was in a bit of a daze and on the way to the airport we stopped off at the hospital so I could get more painkilling injections. Then I was stretchered every-where and got a wheelchair at the connecting airport. I was looked after. It was a bizarre experience.'

Did working on *Father Ted* result in travel?

'Yes, travelling over and back to Ireland. The series dribbled out around the world and was dubbed into different languages. A friend of mine was in Mexico. He stepped out of the shower and saw *Father Ted* on TV dubbed in Spanish. We did a few little things in America. It was funny. There was a questions and answers ses-sion in a Manhattan theatre and there were about 40 people asking questions; one of them was rock star Moby. He turned out to be a big fan of *Father Ted* and was on his own asking nerdy questions. A year later he was playing a big rock concert at Slane Castle in Ireland. He was supporting U2 and asked me to come on stage with him and sing *My Lovely Horse*. That was a nice little surprise. You never know what's going to happen when you're travelling.'

Do you enjoy flying?

'As I get older, I like it less. I think that's unavoidable, even for apparently confident travellers. There must be this low-level anxiety every time you fly. There has to be because it seems to be so unnatural. I tend to shut down. My heart slows to a rate of about three beats per minute. I go into a quiet zone. If I'm with my kids I can't do that, but when I'm on my own, which I am quite a lot, I can completely shut down, bury myself in a book and give myself loads of time to turn into a bit of a zombie.'

How do you pass the time on a journey?

'Novels I suppose. It's a good chance to catch up, particularly on long-hauls. I don't really enjoy the movie-watching experience on a plane.'

If you could choose a travelling companion other than your wife and family, who would that be?

'I remember doing an interview with a well-known political figure in Poland. I can't remember his name. He was a leading light in the solidarity movement. I re-member a two-hour interview with him ostensibly about football's place in Polish culture. I was riveted and in tears at the end of it, getting an eyewitness account of that particular revolution in Poland. So I'd travel with him. Wherever you go, you meet great people.'

What about your future travel plans? Is there likely to be another travelogue?

'It's the kind of thing I'd love to do. I really enjoy it, not necessarily a football show, but some kind of travelogue. I was interested in doing a humour travelogue. It would be great. I should, shouldn't I? See where the humour is similar and where it's different. I'd love to go to one of the Middle Eastern cultures and see how important humour is to the way people live. It's such an important thing in life. I don't know if you can suppress it really. I'm sure there's an outlet for it, for a great new series.'

THE MAN WITH NINE LIVES

John Simpson

ohn Simpson has a stomach for a good story. Prime Minister Harold Wilson evidently thought so – he punched him in the stomach on one of his early assignments. The reason? John asked a question he didn't want to hear. Here is a man that that can sniff out disaster and is inevitably drawn to it. Whenever crisis has befallen a nation, John Simpson has been there to record it. This instinct has taken him to 20 countries and 36 war zones. During his career, spanning more than four decades, his path has crossed those of tyrants, spies, royalty, world leaders and, just as important, ordinary people who have touched his heart.

Born in 1944, John was brought up in London and Suffolk. He read English at Cambridge University and after graduating his BBC career began as a radio sub-editor. He worked in the BBC newsroom for a time, and then became political editor, before finding his niche as Foreign Affairs Correspondent.

In the late 1970s, he was based in South Africa when apartheid was widespread; he was at the coalface in 1979 during the Iranian Revolution against the Shah of Iran. He lived with the threat of being bombed by the Israelis while flying with Ayatollah Khomeini. Thirty years ago, religious leader Ayatollah Khomeini returned to Iran from exile and launched an Islamic revolution. John Simpson was with the Ayatollah on the flight to Tehran.

He was there to report when Iraq invaded Iran on 22 September 1980 and was bombed with poisonous gas. He dodged bullets at the Tiananmen Square massacre in China (4 June 1989), was in Germany for the fall of the Berlin Wall (9 November 1989), and in Romania when dictator Ceausescu fell from power (25 December 1989). He reported first hand on the fall of communism in Eastern Europe (1989) and was in South Africa for the joyous occasion of Nelson Mandela's release (11 February 1990). He was the BBC's key correspondent in Baghdad during the first Gulf War (2 August 1990), staying in the danger zone and refusing to leave, despite being ordered to by the BBC for his own safety. John also reported from Belgrade during the Kosovo crisis of 1999.

John's mission is to inform, exposing injustice in any situation as well as those responsible for it. This was especially evident when he spoke out about the Bushmen of Botswana. It really saddens John how the Bushmen are treated as primitive and wholly under-developed. He compares them to people in his own country; people with the same characteristics and emotions and says they are simply at a different level of development to the western world technically, but ahead in other areas. Back in the '90s President Festus Mogae of Botswana once asked in a public speech; 'How can you have a stone age creature continuing to exist in the age of the computer?'

John spoke out when government forced them off their land and re-housed them in camps. The government moved against the Bushmen in 1996. In 2002 troops were sent in to force them out. Many were taken away in army trucks. John describes them as, 'Harmless men and women who want to remain in their ancestral lands.'

Once after suffering a painful bite a Bushman squeezed the juice of a leaf onto the bite to cure him. On another occasion his wife Dee, her brother and sister had bother with their Land Rover in the desert. The Bushmen came to their assistance too.

John became a patron of a group called Health Unlimited which provides a clinic for the Bushmen, though regretfully he had to leave it as the BBC doesn't allow staff to be associated with charitable campaigns of this nature.

One of the most difficult assignments in his long career was reporting on the death of Princess Diana; (31 August 1997) he had known the Princess personally so it was hard to keep his objectivity intact. Shortly after (November 1997) he was bound for Hong Kong to report on the changeover from British to Chinese rule. His timing is impeccable and he never misses an opportunity.

In the course of his reporting career, John has suffered savage beating in Beirut and Afghanistan, was hit in the face by shrapnel in Northern Ireland, and suffered two broken ribs in Baghdad. He has seen colleagues lose their lives. He has been hunted by Robert Mugabe's forces in Zimbabwe. Osama Bin Laden had a wish to kill him and was prepared to pay but, thankfully, didn't succeed.

John's journalistic endeavours have not gone unrecognised. He scooped three BAFTAS and a Golden Nymph Award for his reporting of Ayatollah Khomeini's return to Iran (1979). In both 1991 and 2000, he received a CBE for Journalist of the Year. He received an Emmy Award for his coverage of the fall of Kabul on BBC's *News at Ten* and is a recipient of a Peabody Trust Award for his services to news reporting. He has had recognition for his books; *GQ* magazine awarding him Author of the Year in 2003, and in 2004 his audio book on the wars against Saddam was awarded Audio Book of the Year by Pan Macmillan.

THE INTERVIEW

John's schedule is hectic. He has just returned from Baghdad and was in Libya the previous week.

He says, 'I was a very un-travelled child. After the war (World War II) my father had very little money. I think the most I ever did was when I was twelve and that was to go to Yorkshire. Then when I was 17 I went to Morocco for a holiday. It was the first time I ever left the shores of Britain.'

I asked him how different travel is now compared to when he was starting out in journalism.

'It's not really that different. I mean you get on a plane in the same way; the flight times are a little bit quicker. The airports a little bit better but not very much so, in that sense I think everything is rather similar. The plane I went on to Morocco was a very similar jet to the ones that go nowadays. When I went to America first I went on a Boeing 707, which is not quite as comfortable as planes today but it's pretty much the same otherwise.'

I know John has witnessed horrific events during his travels. He's seen poverty, war, riots and tragedy and got caught up in it so many times. How does he keep so optimistic?

'Well, I know I've seen some horrible things. I've seen people behaving disgracefully but there are some people that behave rather well out there, probably not as many as behave badly, but enough to make you feel there is a saving remnant, so in a positive way it's not all bad. You know, there are decent types that basically make life worth living. I find that to be the case again and again, and people who do bad things may behave well under certain circumstances and if they had more opportunities. People are people. One of the things that people do is, surprisingly and inexplicably often behave rather decently, and I think that's what keeps me going really.'

I ask John to recall one of the most moving things that happened during the course of his travels.

He tells me of the story of a lady who gave him her last rose from her garden. 'Her husband had been murdered by Saddam's people and her daughters had been mistreated by the army. Her garden had been destroyed as well as her house but, somehow, she managed to keep the garden going in memory of her husband. She had set up a rose garden as a memorial which had been utterly destroyed. She painstakingly picked up the concrete and gradually got the garden back again.'

We speak about his return to Afghanistan after the fall of the Taliban. He was prepared to go to any lengths to get into the country, even if it meant dressing up as a Pathan woman. He went at a time when journalists weren't welcome and, if found, the consequences would have been dire. Death or torture could follow. The Taliban were under orders to arrest any journalists that came into their country. They were in very real danger. It was at a time in history where there was a strange emptiness in the streets. People were afraid and tension was in the air constantly. Many had fled from their homes, or stayed indoors for fear of attacks from the Americans.

He and his cameraman were smuggled into Nangarhar Province with the help of heavily armed smugglers who were carrying vegetables. I asked him whose idea it was to get into Afghanistan in such an unusual way.

'Definitely not mine,' he laughs. 'The Taliban had taken over. That was back in 1996. They chased out the Mujahideen and the Soviets and, for five years, they ran the country. I was determined to get into the country. I had previously spent a lot of time there and I thought, "Well, who are those people to stop us from getting through?" So, then we negotiated with various groups of people, including one who claimed they could get us into Afghanistan and almost to Kabul. They said, "There's only one way for you to get into Afghanistan and that is if you dress up as women and wear the burka," John laughs. The average women in Afghanistan are only about 5 ft (1.5 m) and Peter, my cameraman, and I were much more than that. We were driven across in our burkas. We were sitting in the back. We covered ourselves up and thankfully never needed to get out. If you wear a burka in Afghanistan you simply become invisible, so we just got through. Under the strict Taliban law, women had to wear head-to-toe veils.'

John recalls how humorous it was: the burka is meant to reach the ground, but it only reached his knees, so it was hard to hide his big feet. At border checks the men would look in but wouldn't pay any attention to the women.

I ask John about the more terrifying moments he encountered on his travels.

'Being chased and attacked by crowds. That was a terrifying experience. There was a crowd in Iran which nearly pulled us apart. It was absolutely nerve-wracking. Another scary moment was where I nearly lost my life in Beirut; I was captured and made to go through a mock execution. The whole ordeal was a nightmare. Then I really feared for my life when bombed by the Americans. I came out with a bit of shrapnel in my backside and hearing loss. Many more were killed sadly,' he says philosophically.

John recalled how the Kurdish translator on his BBC team lost his life. He had been accompanying a convoy of special forces and Kurdish fighters that came under attack from an American warplane. Unfortunately, he was in the wrong place at the wrong time. There were bodies all over the place, as John reported. He is not bitter and he hasn't become anti-American, but having seen so many innocent civilians killed unnecessarily is upsetting; the weapons were carelessly aimed. He's grateful that he has survived all the atrocities but, at times the injustice of it all makes him feel quite angry.

What place would you love to return to?

'The places that are difficult to return to. The place I really long to go back to is Iran, which is a country I've loved for years. I was last there in 2009. It's one of the most beautiful countries. The people are charming and well educated. I just absolutely love the place and I'm really looking forward to the day when they are able to have a proper degree of freedom.'

Can you recall good resulting from bad experiences?

'Yes, there have been lots of them. I think one of them that comes to mind was while in Northern Ireland. I went up to the Ardoyne area and there was a lady outside cradling a British soldier in her arms as he died. She was shot, sadly, but thankfully there are people in the world who are prepared to do the right thing even in the face of adversity. Life is very cheap, so it's good to see that there is still good out there.'

John encounters difficulties on nearly all of his trips away, but what carries him through the difficult times? Is it knowing he'll return to his family?

'Lots of things help. Funnily enough I don't think about my family too much because it might make me too homesick. I'm there to do a job and I just do it. I think my curiosity carries me through and keeps me going; longing to know what's going to happen next and knowing that it's good just to be there and to see it happen.'

I ask him about the funny incident with a statue of Saddam Hussein. Immediately John lets out a hearty laugh.

'I was in one of Saddam's palaces in Baghdad and I bought this statue from a kid; he just wanted the money. It didn't cost much really. I quite liked it. It was in a gold coloured resin. It was about 3 ft (90 cm) high and Saddam had his arm extended out in that rather irritating way he had. I needed to get him back in one piece so I had a coffin box made. A Baghdad carpenter made the coffin wide enough to hold the extended arm.' John took him to Kuwait International Airport in Farwaniyah for his journey home. He felt confident that he would get through the x-ray machine at the airport undetected. How wrong he was. John recounts how the coffin was suddenly smashed open and 'there was Sadam lying in all his glory', laughs John.

There was an angry shout from the Kuwaiti soldier who was handling security. In that moment John was under arrest. The sergeant shouted in an intimidating way into John's face accusing him of insulting the dignity of the state of Kuwait. In the meantime a large queue was building up behind him. Eventually a senior official was called in and made the decision that John and Saddam could leave but he would have to take Saddam onto the plane with him. The airport officials wrapped it in clear plastic and John had to queue with his new travelling companion and endure being a spectacle in the long queue. He happened to be flying with British Airways who were sympathetic to his cause. 'They gave Saddam a seat to himself and even offered him a meal', John laughs heartily again.

John affirms that he has no intentions of stopping this rather challenging life of travel.

'I'm still very active and full of energy. I'm not exactly a spring chicken, but I need to work to support my son. He's seven now and he's going to need educating for another 13 years or so. I intend to keep going because travelling is what I do. I'm working on a new BBC series this year.'

John Simpson has been there for the highs and the lows of world events and it must be difficult to choose one single moment that stood. However, he tells me a time that made a great impression on him was when Nelson Mandela was released from prison. It was a jubilant time. He had met with the former president many times and they share a mutual admiration for each other. Upon Nelson's release, John interviewed the prison officer that was assigned to him while he was in prison. Since then, John has visited the iconic South African at his residence in Johannesburg and Nelson Mandela has made no secret of endorsing John's work, saying, 'John Simpson is a very fine journalist.'

ACKNOWLEDGEMENTS

I had interviewed Maeve Binchy (1940–2011), much loved Irish author for this book on travel but sadly she passed away before we could complete it.

I'd like to say a huge thanks to each and every one who contributed to this book in all their various ways. Very special thanks to all who helped me, listened to me and came to my rescue when I felt like pulling out my hair.

Many contributors have now become firm friends and I'd like to thank them all for coming into my life. It's truly enriching.

Many thanks to Jonathan Dimbleby for welcoming me in his London home and also to his production assistant Stella Keeley. A special thanks to Gillian McDade, journalist, author and friend, for all of her wonderful support with edits and proofs and her wonderful family (not forgetting Amelie). I'd especially like to thank Marianne Du Toit who shared her journey as well as her many areas of expertise with me in the writing of this book and huge thanks to The Fairy Editor (Turlough) who waved his magic wand throughout, not forgetting Fiona McGrath for her expertise in editing. Many thanks to Pat Hannon, Dublin Institute of Technology, who helped with everything technical, also his wonderful family who were very supportive. Paul Wilson was a tower of information and help along with Bryn Thomas at Trailblazer Publishers. To Elspeth Bennet, who encouraged me to keep going when I confided in her about my project, a sincere thank you, and Alison Bishop my coffee pot pal who has been far too good to me throughout.Very special thanks to Geoff Hill, author, travel adventurer and friend for all his encouragement, telling me never to give up. Vanessa O'Loughlin who was a marvellous help with all aspects of this book and not forgetting Patricia O'Reilly, author and lecturer. I'm most grateful to Tom Kinsella, computer whizz who saved my life when my laptop crashed during the writing of this book and who gave technical support all the way. Thanks to Michael Palin, Nigel Meakin and Prominent Television for all your support, also Basil Pao. I very much appreciate Ken Doyle's unceasing support. He went the extra mile to help and thanks also to his lovely wife Anne. Also to Vida Brooks and Gretta McWalter, special friends who gave great support and prayers and not forgetting dear friend Niamh Brady and her special family who spurred me on with enormous encouragement. Not forgetting Connor whose companion-ship and love no doubt kept me sane.

Thanks also to my Publishers New Holland for giving me the opportunity to make my dream a reality. I'm keeping the best wine until last, with thanks to my Mum for putting up with me, keeping me laughing throughout the arduous task of writing a book. Writing this book has been a pleasure and at times a very en-joyable nightmare. I have made many friends along the way. Sincere gratitude to you who have bought this book; 25 per cent of my royalties from the sale will go to the BBC Children in Need appeal. I hope it will go some way towards helping and enriching lives. I have a feeling that this is the start of a wonderful journey.